U.S. LABOR MOVEMENT
AND LATIN AMERICA

CRITICAL STUDIES IN WORK & COMMUNITY
STANLEY ARONOWITZ, EDITOR

U.S.
LABOR MOVEMENT
AND
LATIN AMERICA

A History of
Workers' Response to Intervention

Vol. I 1846–1919

PHILIP S. FONER

CRITICAL STUDIES IN WORK & COMMUNITY SERIES

BERGIN & GARVEY PUBLISHERS, INC.

MASSACHUSETTS

First published in 1988 by
Bergin & Garvey Publishers, Inc.
670 Amherst Road
South Hadley, Massachusetts 01075

89   987654321

Manufactured in the United States of America.

Library of Congress Cataloging-in-Publication Data

Foner, Philip Sheldon, 1910-
    U.S. labor movement and Latin America: a history of workers'
response to intervention / Philip S, Foner.
      p.   cm. — (Critical studies in work & community series)
    Contents: v. 1. 1846–1919.
    Bibliography: p.
    Includes index.
    ISBN 0-89789-131-7 (alk. paper): $36.95
    1. Latin America—Foreign relations—United States. 2. United
States—Foreign relations—Latin America. 3. Trade-unions—United
States—Political activity. 4. Socialists—United States—Political
activity. 5. United States—Military policy. I. Title.
II. Title: US labor movement and Latin America. III. Series.
F1418.F676 1988   87-38184
322'.2'0973—dc19   CIP

To Fabio Grobart
Who first suggested the writing of this book

CONTENTS

PREFACE

This study chronicles the reaction of labor unions and Socialists in the United States to events in Latin America from the Mexican War of 1846 to the founding of the Pan-American Federation of Labor in 1918. It reveals that important elements in both movements opposed imperialism as practiced by their own government. At the same time, it discloses that in seeking closer ties with Latin American labor, sections of the U.S. labor movement, especially the American Federation of Labor under the leadership of its long-time president, Samuel Gompers, consciously sought to aid U.S. economic and political domination over the area.

Previous historical treatments of the U.S. labor movement and Latin America, a field unfortunately too often neglected in scholarship, have concentrated on events since the first World War[1] or on a particular country.[2] The present volume is the first extensive treatment of the relationship between the labor movements in the United States and in Latin America from its early development to the second decade of the twentieth century.[3] A major part of study deals with the Mexican Revolution of 1910—its background, the ousting of the entrenched Porfirio Díaz dictatorship from power and subsequent developments up to 1918, together with the important activities of U.S. trade unionists and Socialists to aid the Mexican Revolutionists and prevent U.S. intervention aimed at crushing the revolution. A second volume will bring the story of the U.S. labor movement and Latin America from the formation of the Pan-American Federation of Labor to the present.

A work of this nature would have been impossible to produce without the kind cooperation of many libraries, historical societies, and other institutions. I am deeply grateful to the staffs of the National Archives, the Tamiment Institute Library of

New York University, the State Historical Society of Wisconsin, the Library of Congress, the library of the American Federation of Labor, the Archivo Nacional, Havana, Cuba, and the libraries of the University of California, Los Angeles; University of Pennsylvania; Ball State University; University of Wisconsin, Madison; Princeton University; University of California, Berkeley (Bancroft Library); Georgetown University; University of Kentucky; American University; New Mexico University; State University of New York at Binghamton; Catholic University of America; Ohio State University; Duke University; University of Southern California; Columbia University; the Puerto Rican Studies Departments of the City University of New York and the State University of New York, Buffalo; and the University of Virginia. I wish to express my gratitude to Mr. Jules Chazin of Madison, Wisconsin for his assistance in securing valuable material from the State Historical Society of Wisconsin. I also wish to thank Enrique Suárez Gaona and Esther Schumacher of Mexico City for assistance in obtaining materials from the Archivo General de la Nación in Mexico City.

Philadelphia, Pennsylvania
September 1987

· I ·

THE WAR WITH MEXICO, 1846–1848

In Mexico City's Chapultepec Park, a diorama portrays the history of Mexico. A map dated 1819 is followed by one of 30 years later, showing Mexico with more than half its national territory missing. This land had once comprised an area larger than France and Germany combined and included the present states of Texas, California, New Mexico, Arizona, Nevada, Utah, and parts of Wyoming and Colorado. These had been Mexico's richest farming, cattle-grazing, and fruit-raising lands—lands that bore immense oil and natural gas deposits, as well as incalculable amounts of other natural resources. Fifty-five million dollars' worth of gold was extracted from California alone in the ten years after gold was discovered there in 1849. The 1849 map bears the inscription: "The result of robbery by the United States!"

The tragic chain of events underlying this inscription began on January 17, 1821, when Moses Austin, a United States merchant and mine owner, recieved permission from the Spanish commandant-general of the Eastern Interior Provinces of Mexico to settle 300 families in Texas. After Austin's death, his son, Stephen Fuller Austin, took over the grant, and in January 1822, he established the first legal settlement of North Americans in Texas. In 1829, Vincent Guerrero, president of the newly independent Mexico, proclaimed the abolition of slavery throughout that country. Local Texas officials immediately petitioned to have Texas exempted from the emancipation decree. Failing that, and faced with the necessity of freeing their slaves, the American declared their independence from Mexico on March 2, 1836. At the Battle of San Jacinto on April 21, 1836, Texas forces routed the Mexican army and captured its commanding general, Mexican President Antonio Lopez de Santa Anna.

1

On March 1, 1837, the United States Senate recognized the "independent political exsistence" of the Republic of Texas. Its position on slavery was set forth by Stephen F. Austin: "Texas must be a slave country. It is no longer a matter of doubt."

Mexico never recognized this independence but made no serious effort to reconquer Texas. It did, however, warn the United States that it would not accept its former territory's annexation by the North American republic. Since many Americans did not want to risk war with Mexico and others opposed extending the boundaries of slavery, the question of annexation was put off in 1836—but not abandoned.[1] Seven years later, in 1843, that question reemerged. In April 1844, the pro-Southern Tyler administration presented the Senate with a treaty for the annexation of Texas as a slave state. At workingmen's meetings in New York City, opposition was voiced to the annexation of Texas "without provision for the extinction of slavery within her borders. . . . To admit Texas as a slave territory into this Union would, in the opinion of this meeting, have a tendency to strengthen the institution of slavery."[2] In New England also, workingmen organized meetings to protest annexation. The *Manchester Operative* stated in August 1844:

> We have therefore held our peace in regard to the annexation of Texas, for the purpose of seeing whether our Nation would attempt so base an action. We call it base, because it would be giving men that live upon the blood of others, an opportunity of dipping their hands still deeper in the sins of slavery. . . . Have we not slaves enough now? Are not two-thirds of our population now in abject slavery? In the South we hear the clanking chains and heart rending pleadings of the sons of Africa that they may have freedom— while in the North the voice of our laboring classes ascends up to the heaven in earnest prayer, that they too may be free from the galling yoke of the aristocratic power. What a picture our country presents—then why add more of this corrupting evil to the early heart-sickening fact of slavery and bondage?[3]

Irish workers in large numbers demonstrated in New York, Boston, and Lowell against the annexation of Texas, showing that while they might not be prepared to join the Abolitionists, they were opposed to the extension of slavery—especially at the expense of Catholic Mexico.[4] Irish and black workers attended the Convention of the People of Massachusetts held in Boston's Faneuil Hall, January 29–30, 1845, to take action against the proposed annexation not only because it was unconstitutional, but because it would further spread slavery. In the summer of 1845, Boston's black community set up booths to obtain signatures for the "Anti-Slavery Peace Pledge." Signers were obliged "not to countenance or aid the United States Government in any war which may be occasioned by the annexation of Texas, or in any other war, foreign or domestic, designed to strengthen or perpetuate slavery."[5]

In the election of 1844, James K. Polk, a Tennessee slaveholder, was elected president on a democratic ticket with a platform calling for immediate annexation of Texas. Polk was determined to incite a war with Mexico so that the United States could expand its territory, not only by annexing the new Republic of Texas, but by seizing New Mexico, Arizona, and especially California. With this in mind, Polk sought to create a boundary conflict between Texas and Mexico so that when the United States annexed Texas it could also annex a war.[6] He encouraged Texas to claim that its territory extended as far south as the Río Grande. The fact that Mexico claimed that the southern boundary of Texas was the Nueces River, and that every map in existence at the time showed the territory between the Río Grande and the Nueces as belonging to Mexico, meant nothing to the President.

Therefore, in mid-June 1845, a month before Texas ratified its annexation and six months before it became a state, Polk and his secretary of war, William Marcy, ordered an army under General Zachary Taylor to take a position south of the Nueces River. At the same time, Polk called on Texas, Mississippi, Alabama, Georgia, Arkansas, Kentucky, Missouri, Illinois, Indiana, and Ohio, to provide 17,000 volunteers. His objective was to arm 50,000 men, half from the South and half from the North.[7]

Clearly, Polk hoped that Mexico would go to war with the United States over the annexation of Texas and the boundary issue. On August 23, Taylor received the following instructions: "Should Mexico assemble a large body of troops on the Río Grande, and cross it with a considerable force, such a movement must be regarded as an invasion of the United States and the commencement of hostilities."[8]

Texas was formally annexed in December 1845 by an act of Congress. But war with Mexico did not follow immediately. Having little military strength, compared to the United States, Mexico was ready to negotiate. But Polk did not want negotiations to succeed, and while talk of negotiations continued, the president continued to exploit the boundary question to bring about a clash along the Río Grande. U.S. troops continued to push into the disputed areas along the Río Grande, challenging Mexicans to fire on them so that Polk could stampede Congress into a declaration of war.[9]

The anticipated clash along the Río Grande came in the spring of 1846. On April 25, a detachment of Mexican troops crossed the Río Grande and ambushed two companies of American soldiers on the left bank of the river. In the ensuing skirmish, eleven Americans were killed, five wounded, and the remainder taken captive. Word of the attack reached the White House at about six o' clock in the evening of Sunday, May 9, 1846. The cabinet met that same night, and agreed that a war message should be presented to Congress the following day.

The next morning, President Polk sent Congress a special message announcing war with Mexico. Regretting that he had had to use the Sabbath to write a war message, Polk said his main reason for the message was the commencement of hostilites "by Mexico . . . which had invaded American territory and by whose acts had shed American blood upon American soil."[10]

The war message evoked considerable opposition in Congress. Polk called it a defensive war but Congressmen assailed it as one of aggression, forced upon by the President when he ordered an American army into the area between the Nueces and the Río Grande, which was clearly Mexican soil, and then took possession of it. Abraham Lincoln, a freshman congressman from Illinois, pressed for an inquiry as to whether the spot on which American and Mexican forces first clashed was not in fact Mexican territory. As for himself, Lincoln said, he was convinced that Polk had ordered American soldiers into a peaceful Mexican community in a deliberate effort to provoke war. Consequently, Polk's efforts to blame the conflict on Mexico amounted to "the half insane mumbling of a fever-dream" and the product of a "bewildered, and confounded, and miserably perplexed man," whose mind had been taxed beyond its power.[11]

The imposition of a virtual prohibition on debate rendered the opposition fruitless. In the house, debate on the war bill was limited to two hours, and in the Senate only one day was allowed for discussion. Operating under this stampede and with the cry of patriotism in the air, both houses of Congress approved the bill within two days by lopsided majorities: 114 to 14 in the House and 40 to 2 in the Senate. On May 15, 1846, Polk signed the bill authorizing him to enlist 50,000 more troops and appropriating $10 million for national defense. The war was then official.[12]

Throughout the South and West, the war was popular; of 69,540 volunteers who enlisted, at least 40,000 were from these areas, whereas the more populous and wealthy North furnished only 7,930. Northern opposition to the war was immediately expressed and continued to be voiced throughout the conflict in newspapers, churches, antislavery societies, workingmen's meetings and conventions, and literary works. Frederick Douglass, the former slave and black abolitionist leader, denounced the "disgraceful, cruel and iniquitous war" that doomed Mexico to be "victim of Anglo-Saxon cupidity and love of dominion." He deplored the innocent blood being shed in the cause of slavery and declared that the nation's only hope of national redemption lay in a united demand of press, public, and pulpit for the "instant recall of our forces from Mexico." James Russell Lowell, Ralph Waldo Emerson, William Ellery Channing, Wendell Phillips, Horace Greeley, Henry Thoreau, and Charles Sumner were among the others who expressed their opposition to the war with voice and pen. In his satirical *Bigelow Papers*, Lowell directed caustic gibes at the war hawks:

> They may talk of freedom's airy
> Till they're purple in the face,—
>   it's a grand great cemetery
>   For the bartrights of our race.

> They just want this Californy
> So's to lug a new slave states in
>   To abuse ye, an to scorn ye,
>   An' to plunder ye like sin.[13]

Blacks organized meetings in Philadelphia, New York, Boston, Cincinnati, and other Northern cities,[14] to enunciate Lowell's view that the war was fundamentally one for the expansion of slavery.* New York workingmen also espoused Lowell's view at a meeting called in May 1846 to oppose the war. The meeting branded

*Although historians today differ as to what were the war aims of the United States, the view popular among the historians of the late nineteenth and early twentieth centuries that it was primarily caused by a concerted drive by the Slave Power to acquire new territory for slavery, is rejected by a number of scholars today. (See Norman A. Graebner, "The Mexican War: A Study in Causation," *Pacific Historical Review* 22[1980]: 405–26, and Norman B. Tutoron, *The Mexican-American War: An Annotated Bibliography* [Boston: 1979].) This trend began with the publication in 1919 of the two-volume *The War With Mexico* by Justin H. Smith. The author, a linguist and man of letters, gave support to Polk's contention that the

the war a scheme of slaveowners and their allies who lived "in such luxurious idleness on the products of the workingmen" and demanded of President Polk that further hostilities be avoided by withdrawing American troops "to some undisputed land belonging to the United States." Speaking through their delegates at the 1846 convention of the New England Workingmen's Association, the organized worker's of New England took a similar stand. They denounced "the foul disgrace of extending the area of slavery through war," and pledged that they would "not take up arms to sustain the Southern slaveholder in robbing one-fifth of our countrymen of their labor."[15]

The *Voice of Industry*, the most widely read and influential paper of the 1840s, was a persistent opponent of the war with Mexico. The *Voice* began publication as a weekly in Fitchburg, Massachussetts, May 29, 1845, and was issued "by an association of workingmen" under the editorship of William S. Young. In November 1845, it was combined with two other labor papers, and moved to the textile mill city of Lowell. Here it was issued by a publishing committee of three, consisting of Young, Sarah G. Bagley, the "Female Department" published articles and poetry on a wide variety of subjects of interest to women. The department carried articles and poetry by men, but the bulk of the material was written by women factory workers.[16]

The *Voice of Industry* supported the ten-hour movement, land reform, anti-slavery, temperance, women's rights, abolition of capital punishment, Utopian Socialism, and opposed war in general and the Mexican War in particular. On May 15, 1846, three days after Congressional action authorizing President Polk to recruit 50,000 volunteers, the *Voice* declared angrily: "Mexico is in a fair way to get soundly thrashed simply because she will not lie still and quietly permit herself to be robbed of her rightful possessions. . . . Truly the fruit of the Texas iniquity begins to ripen." Three weeks later, the *Voice* asked American workers:

> Are you ready to stand out now and be known as the uncompromising opposers of war in general, and of that piece of hellish iniquity, the present Mexican war in particular? Are you ready to pledge yourselves, before your fellow men, and in the sight of God, in no way to countenance or encourage the atrocious war, into which the country has been plunged by a slave-holding olgarchy, for the extension and perpetration of Slavery, and to do all in your power to persuade others to persue [sic] the same course?[17]

On December 8, 1846, President Polk requested authorization for the raising of ten additional regiments, above the original 50,000 men authorized in May 1846,

war had been forced on the United States despite "all our efforts to avoid it." Slavery, according to Smith, had nothing to do with bringing on the war.

While few historians fully endorse Smith's view, especially its national and racial chauvinism, some, such as Seymour V. Connor and Odie B. Faulk, do in *North America Divided: The Mexican War, 1846–1848* (New York: 1979). In Robert W. Johannsen's *To the Halls of the Montezumas: The Mexican War in the American Imagination* (New York: 1985), there is no analysis of the causes of the war. It is treated throughout as a great people's war, and the opposition to it as being of no consequence whatsoever. Mexican historians do not agree.

to carry on the war. One of these regiments was to be raised in Massachussetts, and the *Voice of Industry* strongly advised workingmen against enlisting. The war, in its opinion, should be fought by the politicians, spectators, and capitalists profiting from it. "Stand back and give them a chance," it urged.[18]

In a piece written for the "Female Department" of the *Voice of Industry*, Henry Thoreau approved the labor paper's opposition to the Mexican War. He had only contempt for those who condemned the war yet refused to act against it. "There are thousands," he complained, "who are in *opinion* opposed to slavery and to the war, who yet, in effect, do nothing to put an end to them."[19]

Agreeing with Thoreau, William Wells Brown, the black abolitionist, urged all Negroes who were called into the armed services in the Mexican War "to fight against the United States." But no blacks served in the American armed forces in the war. Federal law barred Negroes from state militias, and while the U.S. Navy accepted a limited quota of blacks, the Army excluded them from after the War of 1812 until the Civil War. However, as we will see, a battalion of American soldiers was later formed which did what Brown called upon his people to do.[20]

Dissatisfaction among the American troops emerged while Taylor's officers and men began preparing to march to the Río Grande. Though they had been told that their General was seeking to "avoid any acts of aggression" against Mexican forces across the river "unless an actual state of war should exist," many in his ranks believed that the United States was pushing for war and that the territory they were about to occupy was rightfully Mexican. Lieutenant Ulysses S. Grant, while serving as one of Taylor's regimental commanders, wrote: "As to the right of this movement, I have said from the first that the United States are the aggressors. We have outraged the Mexican Government by an arrogance and presumption that deserve to be punished. For ten years we have been encroaching on Mexico and insulting her." Grant later wrote in his *Personal Memoirs*, published in 1885, that he "felt sorry he had enlisted,"[21] and thought the armed march into Mexico "unholy." A Pennsylvania Lieutenant recorded similar views: "How unjust! To march to the banks of the Río Grande is of itself an act of hostility." He was convinced that his government, behind a posture of solemn virtue, was bent on goading Mexico to assume the "odium of beginning the war."[22]

These dissenting views, however, were confined to diaries, memoirs, or letters home. But others expressed these feelings by crossing over to the Mexicans. Most of them were foreign-born workers, many of them recent immigrants—Irish, German, English, French, Polish. For many, the Army was a place of refuge from the economic hardships of civilian discrimination, and for none more so than the Irish. During this period many immigrants from Ireland were confronted by signs proclaiming "No Irish Need Apply" when they sought employment. But they found army life scarcely an improvement. Discipline was harsh; flogging was legal, and even such severe punishments as bucking and gagging was common. Contempt by junior officers and noncoms for foreigners, fed by nativist movements of the period, caused smoldering resentment among immigrants in the Army units. A Scottish soldier wrote bitterly of the "various degrading modes of punishment, often inflicted by young, headstrong and inconsiderate officers in their zeal for discipline of the service, for the most trivial of offenses," and complained that recent arrivals from Europe were the main targets of their viciousness.[23]

Aware of rising disaffection among Taylor's men, Mexicans appealed to them in proclamations, distributed by leaflet, to switch to the side of justice. They stressed the aggressive nature of American military action, and pointed out that the nations of Europe from which the recently-arrived immigrants had come, would view their role with the utmost indignation. They called upon these men "to abandon their unholy cause and become peaceful Mexican citizens." Soldiers who came across the lines were promised bounties and grants starting at 32 acres of land for a private.[24]

"Efforts are continually making [sic] to entice our men to desert," Taylor reported with concern on April 6, "and I regret, to say, have met with considerable success." Up to this time, about thirty men had gone over to the Mexican lines. First to switch to the Mexican side was Sergeant John Riley, Company K. U.S. Infantry. Riley had served as drillmaster for the cadet corps at West Point, and was said to be in line for a lieutenant's commission. But he was a good Catholic, and increasingly resented the attitude of his Captain who viewed foreigners, especially Catholics, as an "inferior" race. The fact that Mexico, made up overwhelmingly of Catholics, was being invaded by an army, many of whose officers and men were contemptuous of his co-religionists, convinced Riley to abandon the American side and join the Mexicans.[25]

The stream of men who first crossed over did not regard themselves as deserting to the enemy in time of war, for there was as yet, no recognized war. In the month before an actual declaration of war, the ranks of the initial group was augmented. But even after the U.S. declared war, men continued to move across to the Mexicans, not only foreign-born but even native Americans. Many were Catholics who sympathized and identified with the Mexicans, but there were non-Catholics as well who, like the Catholics, were appalled at the conduct of their comrades in occupied areas.[26]

As Frederick Merk points out in his *Manifest Destiny and Mission in American History*, many Americans felt only the utmost contempt for Mexicans, viewing them as a mixed race, unfit then, and probably for a long time to come, to be considered as equals to citizens of the United States. After all, more than half of the 8,000,000 Mexicans were Indians, and many were Negroes and mulattoes. To many in the invading army, who considered the only good Indian to be a dead Indian and a Negro at best only equal to three-fifths of a man, Mexicans were hardly members of the human race. When even the liberal *New York Evening Post* could proclaim editorially that "the Mexicans were Aboriginal Indians, and they must share the destiny of their race, extinction," Mexicans had good reason to fear an American occupation.[27]

This fear was soon justified. Mexican troops abandoned Matamoros on April 17, and General Taylor's forces marched into town the same day. The behavior of the American Troops shocked Lieutenant George Gordon Meade. "They have killed five or six innocent people walking in the street," he wrote, revealing more than a touch of his own his own racism, "for no other object than their own amusement; to be sure they are always drunk, and are in a measure irresponsible for their conduct. They rob and steal the cattle and in fact act more like a body of hostile Indians than of civilized whites." Murders of Mexicans in Matamoros by the American occupiers became common; rape even more so. Among the most guilty of terrorism and crime were the Texas Rangers made up, in many instances, "of desperados and ruffians and renegades from the States." As Lieutenant Grant reported, the Texans "seem to think it perfectly all right to impose upon the people and to murder them." The officers of American volunteers were no better than the men they commanded; Lieutenant Colonel Ethan Allen Hitchcock complained that the "officers made themselves a public scandal." After visiting Taylor's front on the Río Grande, General Winfield Scott wrote in alarm to Secretary of War Marcy:

> The volunteers have committed atrocities—horrors— in Mexico, sufficient to make Heaven weep and every American of Christian morals *blush* for his country. Murder, robbery, rape on mothers and daughters in the presence of tied up males of the families have been common all along the Río Grande. . . . As far as I can learn, not one of the felons has been punished, and very few rebuked—the officers generally being as much afraid of their men as the poor suffering Mexicans themselves are afraid of the miscreants. . . . Most atrocities are committed in the presence of acquiescingly trembling volunteer officers.[28]

As the murder, rape, looting and plunder of Mexicans mounted—behavior that was becoming typical of the invading army—the climate of disaffection intensified. The last straw for many Catholics in the invading army was the desecration of Mexican Churches. That was too much for men who had seen Catholic Churches, schools and convents sacked and burned by armed mobs in Boston and Philadelphia. The Mexicans' plight reminded them of their own lot in the States. "What!" read a leaflet entitled *From the Mexican Nation to Catholic Irishmen,* "Can you fight by the side of those who put fire to your temples in Boston and Philadelphia? Come over to us!. . . . May Mexicans and Irishmen, united by the sacred tie of religion and benevolence, form only one people." Seeing that the Mexicans needed help to protect themselves, a number of American Catholics decided to join the group that had already switched sides.[29]

Commissioned as a Lieutenant in the Mexican Army, John Riley gathered the defectors together and organized them into a battalion under General Santa Anna's command. Although not all of the 300 men were Irish or Roman Catholic—Riley chose the name San Patricio Battalion (Battalion of St. Patrick). The San Patricio Battalion, called by the Mexicans *Legion de Estranjeros* (Foreign Legion), was also called *Los Patricos* or *Colorados* (Red Company) because many of them had ruddy complexions, and some of them were red-headed. The battalion carried a banner inscribed on one side with a figure of St. Patrick and on the other with a harp and the arms of Mexico. The members came from every branch of the invading army: infantry, calvalry, and artillery. But Riley decided that it was as artillerymen that the San Patricios could make their best contribution to the Mexican cause. Equipped

by Santa Anna's order with heavy field pieces, Riley and the other veteran artillerymen among the San Patricios trained the rest into crack gun crews.[30]

The San Patricios first went into action for the Mexicans in the battle of Monterey
towards the end of September 1846. Taylor was confident that his army would have
little trouble cutting to pieces, "pretty much with bayonet," the five thousand
defenders. But the Mexicans fought stubbornly, and Riley and his men, manning
Mexican guns, helped keep the invaders at bay. At the end of five days of fighting,
the Mexicans yielded in order to bring a halt to the massacre and destruction of
the beautiful city. Under the terms of capitulation, the garrison marched away, the
San Patricios among them.[31]

The Battalion of St. Patrick gained new adherents from the invading army, men
who were shocked by the pillage Taylor's soldiers visited on Monterey. "Nine tenths
of the Americans here," complained one U.S. observer, "think it a meritorious act
to kill or rob a Mexican." Lieutenant Meade summed up the occupation, describing
the invading army as composed of "a set of Goths and Vandals, without discipline,
laying waste to the country wherever we go, making us a terror to innocent people."
Of a regiment from Kentucky, he wrote: "They plunder the poor inhabitants of
everything they can lay their hands on, and shoot them when they remonstrate,
and if one of their number happens to get into a drunken brawl and is killed, they
run over the country, killing all the poor innocent people they can find in their
way to avenge, as they say, the murder of their brother."[32]

Reinforced by men who could not tolerate such barbarous conduct and who were
disgusted by Taylor's unwillingness to take action to put an end to such behavior,
the San Patricios fought again at Buena Vista on February 22–23, 1847. Here
Riley's men, now expert gunners, helped the Mexican lancers and for a while assisted
in overcoming the superiority of the American troops who had better equipment,
especially artillery. After two days of fighting, Santa Anna withdrew his battle
weary troops. The San Patricio Battalion retreated with the Mexicans, dragging
their cannon with them and two bronze six-pounders captured from the invaders.[33]

The Battalion fought again at the Battle of Contreas, August 20, 1847. Here
their cannon aided the Mexican defenders until the American troops under General
Winfield Scott battered down the resistance and captured the town. Later that same
day, the San Patricios gunners fought gallantly at Churubusco, and their cannon,
smashing back assault after assault, almost stopped the invaders. Only after their
ammunition was gone were the San Patricios overcome. Many died in action; some
escaped, and about eighty-five who survived were taken prisoners.[34]

Churubusco was the Battalion of St. Patrick's last stand. Most of the two hundred
men who formed the battalion had been killed in the hard fighting. These men,
nearly all workers, had been under no illusion that they had joined the winning
side. They were fully aware of the tremendous odds the Mexican Army faced. But
they had offered their lives for the defense of what they felt was a just cause against
an unjust aggressor.[35]

Before the invading army resumed its march upon Chapultepec, Mexico's capital,
the final episode in the history of the San Patricios was enacted, and it proved to

be another tragic episode in an inglorious war. Seventy-two San Patricios were ordered to trial by court-martial by General Winfield Scott. The trials were held under two courts, one sitting at San Angel, the other at Tacubaya. The trials resulted in the condemning of all prisoners, except one, to death or to severe punishment. The sentences were reviewed by General Scott and several were commuted from death to whipping and branding. In all, fifty prisoners were hanged, while sixteen were sentenced "to recieve fifty lashes well laid on with a raw hide on his bare back; to forfeit all pay and allowances that are or may become due him; to be indelibly marked on the right hip, with the letter 'D,' two inches in length; to wear an iron yoke weighing eight pounds with three prongs, each one foot in length, around his neck; to be confined at hard labor, in charge of the guard during the time the Army remains in Mexico; and then to have his head shaved and be drummed out of the service."[36]

In spite of pleas from the Archbishop of Mexico and the British Ambassador, fifty of the prisoners were hanged in batches, several days apart, at San Angel, Mixcoac, and Tacubaya. The Mexican Government protested the savage punishment, angrily terming it "a cruel death or horrible torments, improper in a civilized age, for a people who aspire to the title of illustrious and humane."[37] Mexico's condemnation was drowned out by the American victory at Chapultepec.[38]

In January 1847, after three days of fighting at Monterey, the Mexican army capitulated to Zachary Taylor, commander of the army of the Río Grande, and an eight weeks' armistice was drawn up. But the relatively lenient terms of the treaty were unacceptable to President Polk, who ordered hostilities with the Mexicans resumed. And so the fighting continued untill September 1847 when, in the final battle for Mexico City, American troops took the heights of Chapultepec and entered the city. Mexico then surrendered.

The demand was voiced that the United States seize all of Mexico. On March 10, 1848, the Treaty of Guadalupe-Hidalgo was ratified by the United States Senate, officially ending the war with Mexico. Under it, the United States took half of Mexico. "Peace! Peace! Peace!" the American newspapers rejoiced. But the *Voice of Industry* (renamed the *New Era of Industry*) declared: "With what blushes of shame will not posterity read that history which records the unfading fact, that at the very time when all Europe was agitated with the birth-throes of the sentiments of liberty, equality and fraternity,[referring to the revolutions which swept Europe in 1848] the people of this Republic were waging a war for the extension of human slavery."[39] And Frederick Douglass wrote in his paper, *North Star*, that the celebrations were not for peace

> but *plunder*. They have succeeded in robbing Mexico of her territory, and we are rejoicing over their success under the hypocritical pretence of a regard for peace. . . . Our soul is sick of such hypocrisy. . . . That an end is put to wholesale murder in Mexico, is truly just cause for rejoicing; but we are not the people to rejoice, we ought rather blush and hang our heads for shame, and in the spirit of profound humility, crave pardon for our crimes at the hands of a God whose mercy endureth forever.[40]

President Polk saw no need either to blush or hang his head in shame. In his final message to Congress, he told the American people that due to "the benignant Providence of Almighty God . . . our beloved country presents a sublime moral spectacle to the world."[41]

By the end of July 1848 the last detachment of the invading army had boarded their transports in Vera Cruz for the voyage home. A few months later an incident of the Mexican War momentarily occupied space in the American press when a jury in Cinncinnati ruled against John Riley who had brought suit against the United States to recompense for damages received in his flogging and branding. The verdict was not only adverse to Riley, but it assessed costs upon him and referred to him as *"late of the Mexican Army."*[42]

The San Patricio Battalion has received some attention in studies devoted to the war with Mexico.[43] But the members are treated simply as "neer-do wells and deserters," and their action in joining the Mexicans has been attributed primarily to "drunkenness."[44] No mention is made of their opposition to the war, which they regarded as one of aggression, nor that the barbaric treatment of Mexican civilians was an important factor in their decision to risk their lives by aiding the victims of aggression.

But the Battalion of St. Patrick is not forgotten by the Mexican people. They are not entirely forgotten by the American people either. A one-act play dealing with the unjust sentences of the members of the San Patricio Battalion was produced in San Francisco in the summer of 1987. Entitled "A Flag to Fly," it was written by Chris Matthews. In the play, seven of the San Patricios, captured during the siege of Mexico City, are shown, wounded and shackled, in front of the gallows. They recount their origins and the reasons that led them to desert the Mexican Army. Annual tributes are still paid to these American workers at the plaque at Mexico City's San Jacinto Church, bearing such names as Hogan, O'Connor, Shehan and Flaherty. The inscription reads:

IN MEMORY OF THE HEROIC SAN PATRICIO BATTALION
MARTYRS WHO GAVE THEIR LIVES FOR MEXICO
DURING THE UNJUST AMERICAN INVASION OF 1847
WITH GRATITUDE OF MEXICO.[45]

· II ·

"CUBA LIBRE"
AND THE WAR WITH SPAIN

After the war between the United States and Mexico, the U.S. labor movement showed no interest in Latin America. A study of labor publications prior to 1895 reveals no concern with events occurring South of the border. Only *The People*, organ of the Socialist Labor Party, edited by Daniel De Leon, took an interest in Latin American affairs. Born in Curacao, De Leon settled in the United States in 1872. For five years (1883–1888), he taught a course in the history of Latin America at Columbia University, becoming the first lecturer in an American university to offer such a course. Both at Columbia University and in *The People*, which he began editing in 1890, De Leon "defended the Southern republics against colonial and neocolonial interference in their affairs. . . ."[1]

In 1895 a dispute over the boundaries of British Guiana and Great Britain brought the United States close to war. The United States offered to act as mediator, but Britain rejected the proposal. Actually, the United States wanted Britain out of America altogether so as to leave the area entirely to U.S. exploitation. In a note to Lord Salisbury, the British Foreign Minister, Richard Olney, Secretary of State under President Grover Cleveland, raised the Monroe Doctrine,* and called upon

---

*In a message to Congress on December 2, 1823, President James Monroe enunciated the doctrine that now bears his name. The message had three parts. First, the United States considered the Western Hemisphere closed to any future European colonization. Second, the United States would regard any attempt by European nations "to extend their system to any portion of this hemisphere as dangerous to our peace and safety." And third, the United States would abstain in involvement in European political affairs. James D. Richardson, *A Compilation of the Messages and Papers of the Presidents, 1789–1897* (Washington, D,C.: 1900) 2: 217–18; Dexter Perkins, *The Monroe Doctrine, 1823–1826* (Cambridge, Mass.: 1932), pp. 200–2.

Britain to quit America: "Three thousand miles of intervening ocean make any permanent political union between a European and an American state unnatural and inexpedient," Olney wrote. Then he uttered these provocative words:

> Today, the United States is practically sovereign on this continent, and its fiat is law upon the subjects to which it confines its interposition. Why? It is not because of the pure friendship or good will felt for it. . . . It is because, in addition to all the other grounds, its infinite resources combined with its isolated position render it master of the situation and practically invulnerable as against any or all other powers.[2]

In the main, the trade unions in the United States were silent on this effort by American capital to penetrate into Latin America behind the cloak of the Monroe Doctrine. Neither President Samuel Gompers of the American Federation of Labor nor the AFL as a whole opposed Cleveland's blatant effort to use the Monroe Doctrine in the dispute with Great Britain to assist this penetration. On such an issue, Delber Lee McKee points out, "one is greeted by the A.F. of L. with official silence."[3]

But there was anything but silence when it became clear that pro-war elements were trying to involve the United States in a war with Great Britain over the boundary issue. Gompers lashed out at the warmongers: "Labor is never for war. It is always for peace. It is on the side of liberty, justice and humanity. These three are always for peace. . . . Who would be compelled to bear the burden of war? The working people. They would pay the taxes, and their blood would flow like water. The interests of the working people of England and the United States are common. They are fighting the same enemy. They are battling to emancipate themselves from conditions common to both countries. The working people know no country. They are citizens of the world, and their religion is to do what is right, what is just, what is grand and glorious and valorous and chivalrous. The battle for the cause of labor, from times of remotest antiquity, has been for peace and good-will among men."[4]

War was regarded in labor circles as a time-honored method of despots to drown the complaints of their subjects. Strong indignation spread among workers when reports were published in the press quoting U.S. Senators as welcoming the war with Great Britain over the Venezuela boundary dispute on the ground that "it would thin the ranks of the unemployed and idle men in the country," which had been growing alarmingly since the onset of the Panic in 1893. "Just as we get rid of an infuriated dog by 'sicking him' at something else," cried the *American Federationist*, the AFL's official organ, edited by Gompers, so did the agents of capitalists hope to stave off the rising wrath of an aroused working class by provoking war. *The People* argued that the whole Venezuela affair was an attempt to draw attention away from domestic problems. The administration action was necessary as a result of "manifestations of unrest against the rule of Capital. . . . " Charging President Cleveland with having sold the country to the bankers, the organ of the Socialist Labor Party stated that the effort to create a war over the boundary dispute might be an attempt "to revive business" through war and "turn away" from the problems of "5,000,000 unemployed." It drew an analogy between Cleveland's efforts to invoke the Monroe Doctrine over a "little" boundary dispute in order to draw "us in war" and his use of Federal troops to break the Pullman Strike of 1894 under pretext of the "Interstate Commerce Law."[5]

In February 1897, at the suggestion of the United States, Britain and Venezuela negotiated a treaty turning the boundary dispute over to international arbitration. In 1899, a final settlement was made. *Century Magazine* attributed the peaceful solution of the Venezuela dispute in large measure to "the action of trades' unions on both sides of the Atlantic," and declared that organized labor "gives the present peace movement its substantial basis."[6]

In the same year as the Venezuela boundary dispute, 1895, the Cuban people under the leadership of José Martí took up arms in the Second War for Independence to secure their freedom from Spain.[7] Soon afterwards the U.S. labor press reported that meetings were being held "in all parts of the country to discuss the Cuban revolution," and that "in most cases labor organizations are taking the initiative, passing resolutions of sympathy for the insurgents."[8] Such resolutions were passed by the AFL, the Knights of Labor, and labor groups all over the country, and most of them recommended that the President of the United States recognize Cuban belligerency.[9]

The fact that the trade unions sympathized with the struggle of the Cuban people for their liberation did not mean that they called for war, or for imperialist domination of the island by the United States. On the contrary, the organizations and journals most outspoken in their support of the Cuban revolutionists were also most vigorous in their condemnation of imperialism. This did not mean that the labor organizations understood and opposed every aspect of imperialism. In the main, they were silent on such questions as the efforts of U.S. capital to penetrate Latin America behind the cloak of the Monroe Doctrine, nor did they as a rule see the organic connection between the growth of monopoly and finance capitalism, and imperialist expansion. For the most part, they spoke out only against the actual annexation of foreign territory.[10]

At the 1897 AFL convention, the issues of expansion, jingoism, and war came clearly to a head. The convention took a clear and decisive stand against territorial expansion by declaring its strong opposition to the annexation of Hawaii and asking the Senate to reject a treaty of annexation which President William McKinley had submitted to that body.* Among other reasons for labor's opposition was the fact that the Senate had voted down an amendment to the treaty of annexation that would have repealed the contract labor laws in Hawaii—an action which convinced many trade unionists that once Hawaii was annexed, the contract labor systems would spread to the United States.[11]

---

*McKinley submitted the treaty to the Senate on July 16, 1897. Opposition to the proposed treaty was voiced immediately by scores of city central labor bodies, the majority of the labor press, and large sections of the labor movement. For this opposition, see Philip S. Foner and Richard C. Winchester, eds., *The American Anti-Imperialist Movement: A Documentary History*, vol. 1 (New York: 1983), pp. 68–110.

On the questions of jingoism and war, a considerable division arose at the 1897 AFL convention. The reason is not difficult to discover. On the one hand, labor's passionate hatred of oppression and equally passionate desire for freedom led delegates to support a resolution which urged that Congress should "waste no more time in useless debates and diplomatic chicanery, but should take such immediate action as (might) tend to put an end to the indiscriminate murder of the common people of Cuba by the Spanish soldiery." Some delegates admitted that the policy advocated in the resolution might lead to a war with Spain, but then insisted that this might be necessary to remove the "disgrace to our civilization."

The majority of the delegates expressed their sympathy for the Cuban struggle for freedom, but argued effectively that by adopting the proposed resolution, the labor movement would only be adding fuel to the fire of jingoism which "would result in involving the United States in war with the great European powers." One delegate was amazed that "jingoism should find defenders on the floor of the American Federation of Labor"; another said that in a war with Spain, the workingmen would be the sufferers and the trade unions would be disrupted; another asserted that war would play into the hands of the enemies of the trade unions; still another pointed out that "if the Cuban had the independence the American speculator wanted wanted him to have, the Cuban would not be independent, because it would simply be a change from the Spanish speculator to the American."

In short, the majority of the delegates saw clearly the dangers involved in permitting their sympathy for Cuban freedom to be used by the imperialists. They voted to defeat the strong pro-Cuban resolution. The expression of sympathy for the Cuban people, adopted at the 1896 convention, was reaffirmed.[12] "The sympathy of our movement with Cuba is genuine, earnest and sincere," Gompers wrote. In a private letter to AFL secretary-treasurer Frank Morrison, Gompers summed up the Federation's position saying, "but this does not for a moment imply that we are committed to certain adventurers who are apparently suffering from Hysteria but who simply assume the role to attract attention to their unworthy selves." The AFL would not permit these jingoistic elements to convert sympathy for Cuba into support of a war against Spain.[13]

Opponents of the annexation of Hawaii, spearheaded by labor's effective campaign against ratification of treaty, forced abandonment of the imperialist drive to acquire the islands.[14] But it was only a temporary abandonment. The imperialists had already laid plans to revive the annexation move once the United States become involved in the war with Spain.

Cuba was the key to a grand vision of American imperialists, a vision which saw all the Caribbean, all of Central and South America falling some day to the United States. Cuba was the key because of its strategic location in the Caribbean and its potential as a source of trade and investment. "That rich island," wrote James G. Blaine, Secretary of State and a leading expansionist, on December 1, 1881, "the key to the Gulf of Mexico, and the field for most extended trade in the Western Hemisphere, is, though in the hands of Spain, a part of the American commercial system. . . . If ever ceasing to be Spanish, Cuba must necessarily become American and not fall under any other European domination."[15]

Beginning in 1890, Captain Alfred T. Mahan started his campaign for a navy adequate to support and justify "a vigorous foreign policy." Mahan argued that "whether they will or no, Americans must begin to look outward." An expanding foreign trade was vital to national prosperity. The growing production of the country necessitated control of foreign markets, which in turn made necessary a powerful navy, a strong merchant marine, and secure bases and coaling stations from which they could operate. Strategically and in terms of trade the Caribbean area was crucial; indeed, nothing less than American supremacy in the Caribbean would suffice.[16]

The emphasis on Caribbean bases naturally focused attention on Cuba. Not only would acquisition of the islands offer the United States a strong naval station, but it would provide a market for surplus production and an area for the investment of capital. "Cuba offers a most inviting field for American enterprise," wrote an economic adviser to big business. "There are extensive mines in Cuba now lying idle for want of capital," one newspaper commented, "and if the island were annexed to the United States, this field of production would be fully developed." "Cuba," declared the *Detroit Free Press*, "would make one of the finest states in the Union, and if American wealth, enterprise, and genius once invaded the superb island, it would become a veritable hive of industry in addition to being one of the most fertile gardens of the world. There is a strong party growing up in the island in favor of annexation in the United States. We should act at once to make this possible."[17]

Finance capital was dominant in the United States by the closing years of the nineteenth century. And, as economist Victor Perlo points out, "The conquest of the United States economy by finance capital led to the accumulation of a super-abundance of capital in a few hands. The law of capitalism is continuous acquisition. The monopolies had to find new fields for investment of their surplus capital. Failing this, their profits would decline in the resulting economic crisis."[18]

The depression which began in 1893 sharply pointed up the monopolies' need to find new outlets for surplus goods and excess capital outside the continental boundaries of the United States. Increased productivity of the workers had seriously widened the gap between what they produced and what they could purchase with their wages. The surplus goods piled up for lack of foreign markets, bursting the warehouses. With monopoly profits building up record-shattering reserves of capital, the super-returns on investments in colonial areas could not be ignored by the Morgans, the Rockefellers, and their fellow monopolists.[19]

At the convention of the New York State Bankers' Association in 1896, James H. Tripp, President of the First National Bank of Marathon, emphasized the fact that surplus capital was accumulating at a rapid pace: "Million of dollars are today lying idle, not yielding one cent of profit to the owner; millions more are being loaned at 1 and 2 percent, and prime mercantile paper, with occasional exceptions, has for a long time been taken in our great financial centers at 3 and 4 percent."[20] Clearly Wall Street had an urgent need for empire, a point emphasized by the Senate Committee on Foreign Relations in its report of March 16, 1898:

The unoccupied territory has been taken up, and while much remains to be done, the creative energy of the American people can no longer be confined within the borders of the Union. Production has so outrun consumption in both agricultural and manufactured products that foreign markets must be secured or stagnation will ensue.[21]

Henry Cabot Lodge (who with Theodore Roosevelt was the leading spokesperson for American imperialism) declared in 1896, "Free Cuba would mean an excellent opportunity for American capital invited there by signal exemptions. But we have a broader political interest in Cuba. . . . "That "broader interest" was Spain's other colonial possessions—Puerto Rico, Guam, and the Philippine Islands. And the Philippine Islands was a stepping stone to the enormous potential of the China trade.[22]

The goal of American imperialists was to convert sympathy with the revolutionary struggle of the Cuban people for freedom from Spanish despotism and misrule into support of war against Spain. In this conspiracy the imperialists had the full support of the jingo press, headed by William Randolph Hearst's *New York Journal* and Joseph Pulitzer's *New York World*, which unscrupulously played upon the American people's sympathy for the cause of Cuban independence to raise circulation figures, and did all they could to drive the United States into war.[23]

In January 1898, the jingo press stepped up its campaign for a war with Spain over Cuba. On February 15, 1898, the battleship *Maine* exploded in the harbor of Havana, and the death of 260 American enlisted men and officers fanned the flames of war. A naval court of inquiry investigated the cause of the explosion. In its report, it was scrupulously careful not to imply that Spain was responsible for the disaster, but the jingo press and the imperialists spokespersons in Congress ignored this fact, denounced Spain, and called for war.[24]

As the clamor for war against Spain increased, as the headlines in the press whooping it up for war became shriller Extra by Extra, leading trade unionists made a valiant effort to stem the tide. The International Association of Machinists mourned for the loss of life on the *Maine*, But the loss of workers' lives in industry was even more horrible and costly. When the *Maine* sank, "men raved and women wept," and the press called for vengeance. Yet the shooting down of workers in strikes, and the "carnival of carnage that takes place every day, month and year in the realm of industry, the thousands of useful lives that are annually sacrificed to the Moloch of greed, the blood tribute paid by labor to capitalism, brings forth no shout for vengeance and reparation, no tear, except from the family and friends of the victims."[25]

The Craftsman, official organ of the Connecticut AFL, also refused to join in the hysteria being whipped up over the *Maine* explosion. It charged that the tragic incident was being deliberately used by the monopolists and their agents to drive the nation into a war against Spain whose outcome would be the end of liberty at home. It warned:

The concentrated wealth . . . who control the government of the United States . . . are moving with alarming rapidity either to a military despotism, or to such a curtailment of the ballot that the common people will have practically nothing to say in the legislation of the nation. See how this *Maine* disaster has been used. . . . A gigantic . . . and cunningly-devised scheme is being worked ostensibly to place the United States in the front rank as a naval and military power. The real reason is that the capitalists will have the whole thing and, when any workingmen dare to ask for the living wage . . . they will be shot down like dogs in the street.[26]

Labor had enough evils to fight at home, the *Coast Seamen's Journal*, organ of the Sailors' Union of the Pacific, insisted. War was an "expensive proceeding that the working-class pays for and gains least from." While a war lasted "and for a long time afterward, the interests of the working-class are neglected and frequently ruined past redemption." If only labor would announce in no uncertain terms that it would not fight, there would be no war.[27]

The Railroad Brotherhoods echoed these sentiments. The *Railroad Trainmen's Journal* charged that the demand for war came from "certain moneyed gentlemen, familiarly known as the bulls and bears of Wall Street." The workers, organized and unorganized, had nothing to gain from war, and the government should keep clearly in mind the all-important fact that "they [workers] are *not* for war."[28]

A few unions did succumb to the pro-war fever, the most important being the United Mine Workers of America. At the union's ninth annual convention, the delegates adopted a resolution which announced, in reference to the *Maine* explosion, that "we hold ourselves in readiness to demand justice be done to all concerned, or we will defend the honor of our country by force."[29] But the predominant sentiment in labor circles was definitely anti-war. The *Journal* of the Boilermakers' Union voiced labor sentiments accurately when it declared early in April 1898: "There is no cause for war; and to plunge this country into war, unless war is declared against us, would be ignoring the history of this republic, and *imitating* the grabbing examples of the monarchies of Europe."[30]

Throughout March and the opening weeks of April 1898, several leading trade unionists kept hammering away at the theme that war would mean reaction at home, and would put a halt to labor's efforts to secure social and economic gains. "Calm thought and discussion on economic questions will, I regret to say, be forced to the background," Gompers wrote to social reformer Henry Demarest Lloyd on March 25, 1898. Three days later, he warned P.J. McGuire, head of the Carpenters' and Joiners' National Union, that, in the event of a war with Spain, "legislation in the interests of labor will be forced to the rear and deferred for a very indefinite period." Only a few days before McKinley sent his war message to Congress, Gompers declared publicly that "All the socialism and humanizing influences that have been at work for twenty-five years will have been in vain if war is declared."[31]

"A war will put all social improvements among us back ten years," wrote Bolton Hall, Treasurer of the American Longshoremen's Union in a widely circulated document entitled, "A peace Appeal to Labor."[32] "If there is a war, you will furnish the corpses and the taxes, and others will get the glory. Speculators will make money out of it—that is, out of you. Men will get high prices for inferior supplies, leaky boats, for shoddy clothes and pasteboard shoes,[33] and you will have to pay the bill, and the only satisfaction you will get is the privilege of hating your Spanish fellow-workmen, who are really your brothers and who have had as little to do with the wrongs of Cuba as you have."[34]

With one solitary exception, namely the *Jewish Daily Forward*, the socialist press offered consistent opposition to the mounting war fever. One example was *The People*, the official organ of the Socialist Labor Party. (The Socialist Labor Party, originally called the Workingmen's Party of the United States, took on its new name in 1877. The WPUS was established in July 1876 after the International Workingmen's Association, the First International was dissolved.) *The People*, edited by Daniel De Leon, charged that the issue of Cuban freedom was "but a pretext" and "The real object was *War*." The ruling class needed war, first, because the "promise of prosperity" could not be realized by American capitalism without a war; second, because war would "distract the attention of the workers from their real interests," and third, because war would enable American capitalists to gain economic control and in a number of instances, outright political control of large parts of the Caribbean, Central, and South America. The organs of Social Democracy of America*[35] saw eye-to-eye with De Leon on the war question. The drive for war, said *Appeal to Reason*, was simply "a favorite method of rulers for keeping the people from redressing domestic wrongs."[36] *The Coming Nation* characterized the entire pro-war campaign as a plot of big capitalists. "It has given them an excuse for increasing the army and navy; for issuing more bonds; it has taken our attention from destitution and hard times, and it has developed the sham patriotism of flagism upon which the Republicans depend so much."[37]

In exposing the character of the war and opposing it, the Socialists stressed the identity of interests of the American, Spanish, and Cuban working classes. "It is a terrible thing," wrote a west coast Socialist in the San Francisco *Voice of Labor*, "to think that the poor workers of this country should be sent to kill and wound the poor workers of Spain, merely because a few leaders may incite them to do so." "If war comes," declared the Minneapolis section of the Socialist Labor Party on April 10, 1898, a day before President McKinley sent his war message to Congress, "its burden will fall upon the workers in this country and in Spain. Its fruits will be enjoyed by the capitalists in both countries. Our Comrades, the Socialists of Spain, have denounced war. Let us join hands with them."[38]

The statements of labor leaders, the resolutions of trade unions, and the editorials in the labor and Socialist press opposing war carried little weight with an administration prepared to put into effect the plans of American monopolists. The *Wall*

---

*Social Democracy of America was organized in 1897, and was the result of a merger of various Socialist groups and the American Railway Union, or what was left of it after its defeat in the Pullman Strike of 1894. The outstanding figure in the Social Democracy was Eugene Victor Debs, who had been president of the American Railway Union. Debs became a Socialist while he was in prison for having violated an injunction issued by a federal court during the Pullman strike. The Social Democracy gained the affiliation of sections of the Socialist Labor Party who differed sharply with the theories and tactics of Daniel De Leon, leader of the SLP.

Street Journal reported on March 19, 1898, that "a great many people in Wall Street" were demanding action against Spain at once. Congress, meanwhile, was being deluged with petitions from powerful business groups urging it to support a policy of expansion.[39]

On April 9, 1898, Spain completely capitulated to each and every demand by the United States government to achieve a peaceful settlement of the Cuban question. But the political agents of the imperialists were not interested in a peaceful solution of the Cuban crisis. President McKinley had already prepared a war bill, and the Assistant Secretary of the Navy, Theodore Roosevelt, with the assistance of Senator Lodge, had already sent a telegram to Commodore George Dewey, ordering him to hold his squadron ready for "offensive operations in the Philippine Islands."[40]

On April 11, two days after he had received Spain's complete capitulation, President McKinley sent his war message to Congress. He devoted nine closely printed pages to arguments based on the assumption that Spain had not given in, and two short paragraphs to the fact that it had. In short, the President deliberately concealed the news that Spain had already conceded every one of the U.S. demands. War was declared on April 25.[41]

After the war began, the majority of the trade unions succumbed to the war fever. Most of the unions either came out in support of the war or remained silent. What were the reasons for this development?

Many of the American workers were misled by the demagogy of imperialism, and supported the war in the sincere but mistaken belief that is was a just war, a progressive and democratic one. In an article entitled, "Labor and the War," Joseph R. Buchanan, one of the keenest minds in the labor movement, discussed the question "How does labor feel about the war?" He noted that there were two tendencies at work in determining labor's attitude. On the one hand, the workers were traditionally more patriotic than "the business, professional or leisure classes" and more eager "to resent an insult to the flag [than] the employers." On the other hand, many workers, in deciding what position to adopt towards the war with Spain, had asked themselves: "Isn't this flag they are waving now and calling upon me to defend the same flag that the butchers of Homestead, Pullman, Brooklyn and Lattimer carried?[42] Are not the militiamen with whom and under whom I am asked to serve those self same butchers? Have I any interest in common with the fellows who make wars, conduct them and generally get richer out of them?"

Ordinarily, Buchanan continued, the workers would have decided that the answer to these questions was not to support the war. But overweighing these factors was labor's traditional hatred of monarchial despotism and support for the revolutionary struggles of oppressed people. Thus, while for bankers and industrialists, the war with Spain was solely a matter of the "bond and the dollar," for the workers it was a question of liberty for an oppressed people and an end to the "cruel domination of Spain over Cuba."[43]

In short, many workers did not at first see through the fog of propaganda that surrounded the war. They had been fooled by the American imperialists and the jingo press into believing that the war was a war for the freedom of Cuba from

would bring more business to American industry and thus provide more jobs and higher wages to American workers.[52] But the editorials in the majority of the labor papers and the resolutions adopted by numerous trade unions reveal clearly that the general sentiment of the labor movement was one of outspoken opposition to annexation. The *Pueblo Courier*, official organ of the Western Labor Union,[53] observed that Hawaiian annexation proved that "the war which started as one of relief for the starving Cubans has suddenly changed to one of conquest." The Chicago *Labor World* declared: "This has been a poor man's war—paid for by the poor man. The rich have profited by it, as they always do, and now they demand that we shall grab everything in sight, in order that they may profit all the more." Condemning the passage of the Hawaiian annexation treaty in the Senate, the *Journal of the Knights of Labor* asked: "Is this step the beginning of imperialism with which we have been so long threatened?"[54]

Events rapidly demonstrated that these fears were more than justified.

· III ·

THE "NEW AMERICAN EMPIRE"

On December 10, 1898, the Treaty of Peace against defeated Spain was executed. Cuba was to be held by the the United States until it was sufficiently pacified to allow the withdrawal of American troops and the government of the island was to be turned over to the Cuban people. Puerto Rico, Guam and the Philippine Islands were ceded to the United States. Eleven days later President McKinley proclaimed to the Philippines a policy of "benevolent assimilation," and, at the same time, urged General Harrison Gray Otis to subdue the Filipino people who had fought two-score rebellions against Spain, who had captured Manila for the U.S. forces, and were still fighting for independence. Otis was to gain control of important towns and cities as soon as possible.[1]

But the administration had no easy time putting across these peace terms. *The United States Investor* could say blithely: "It is demonstrable that by far the greatest proportion of the people of this country either openly favor the acquisition of outside territory at this time, or are so indifferent to the matter as not to care to impose any obstacle to such a movement."[2] But vast numbers of the American people, shocked by the peace terms, had awakened to the true implications of the war—that in place of Spanish oppression, U.S. imperialism was proposed. And the anti-imperialist sentiments of these Americans was being expressed in resolutions of trade unions, farmers' organizations, Negro people's associations, and of various clubs and leagues. In a leading place in the developing battle against a war of conquest and an imperialist peace treaty stood the U.S. labor movement.

It is true that there were unions which remained aloof from the struggle over imperialism, devoting their entire attention to immediate job problems. It is also true that a section of the labor movement supported imperialism, and became apologists for the policies of the McKinley administration. Unions whose members were beginning to obtain benefits from the robbery of the colonial masses openly proclaimed their endorsement of expansion. The Typographical Union hailed the annexation of Hawaii and the proposal to annex Puerto Rico, Guam, and the Philippines, and freely admitted that it did so because, with English being used as the language in the schools of these territories, printing would "flourish more than heretofore." The journals of the Railroad Brotherhoods reported joyfully every shipment of American-manufactured goods to Cuba, Hawaii, Puerto Rico, and the Philippines, and pointed out that this increased trade meant more jobs and more money for the railroad workers. There were even unions which, voicing the ideology of the ruling class, advanced the thesis that expansion would end the danger of another depression in the United States, since the newly acquired territories would provide a market for surplus manufactured goods.[3]

But the supporters of the imperialism in the labor movement were definitely in the minority. "Most of the discussion in labor circles took an anti-imperialist line," concludes John S. Appel in his study of labor's attitude towards imperialism.[4]

The argument that the mass of workers would benefit from imperialism was met head on by the trade unions. Imperialism, they said, led to wars which were fought by the workers but from which only the capitalists profited. "How much better off are the working-men of England through all its colonial possessions?" the Carpenters' Union asked pointedly. On the contrary, it was the trusts and monopolies which benefited while the workers paid all expenses. The Cigar Makers predicted that the costs of imperialism "will have to be borne by the people, while a favored few— trusts and monopolies—will receive all the profits."[5] The *National Labor Tribune*, organ of the Iron, Steel and Tin Workers, agreed that the Philippines "possess wonderfully rich resources. . . . The same can be said of this country, but if anybody were to ask you if you owned a coal mine, a sugar plantation, or railroad, you would have to say no . . . all these things are in the hands of the trusts controlled by a few."[6] As George McNeill, New England labor leader, put it:

> The present war against the Filipinos, if endorsed and continued by the people, will certainly strengthen the trusts in the work of debauching public sentiment and will react against universal suffrage and all free institutions. "Choose ye this day whom ye will serve, God or Mammon"—the trade unions or the trusts, the principles of the Declaration of Independence, or an imperial government.[7]

The American labor movement's vigorous and stirring opposition to imperialism was set forth clearly and decisively at the AFL convention in December 1898. By that time, President McKinley had already toured the country in his campaign to sell imperialism to the people. The President had ended every speech with the question: "Shall we haul down the flag?" At the AFL convention, Samuel Gompers eloquently gave the answer of the trade unions: "The flag of the country should never be used as the cloak to hide tyranny." Challenging those who charged that labor should not concern itself with such issues as imperialism, Gompers declared that if labor had supplied the foot-soldiers for the war, "who then but the representatives of labor have the better right to consider the very grave questions which have resulted from our war with Spain?"[8]

The delegates agreed overwhelmingly with Gompers, and the convention endorsed a manifesto against imperialism which urged "workingmen to awake to a full realization of the dangers that confront them, and call upon their representatives with no uncertain voice to save them from the dangers . . . of imperialism." The convention also adopted a resolution condemning the peace treaty and instructing the officers of the AFL "to use every honorable means to secure its defeat."[9]

The proceedings of the AFL convention were widely reported in the press, and even pro-imperialist papers agreed that the convention had clearly demonstrated that "Labor opposes imperialism."[10] From the scores of unions—including the Brewery Workers, the Cigar Makers, the Coast Seamen, the Carpenters, the Hatters, the Journeymen Plumbers, the Meat Cutters and the Butcher Workmen, the Machinists, the Patternmakers, the Woodworkers, and the Western Federation of Miners—came letters and telegrams to the AFL headquarters congratulating the organization for having spoken out so clearly against imperialism. A significant letter came also from Erving Winslow, Secretary of the American Anti-Imperialist League. "I want to congratulate you," he wrote to Gompers, " . . . for the admirable and ringing resolutions adopted by the Federation. We should be glad to act upon any suggestions from you for promoting the work among the unions."[11]

The American Anti-Imperialist League was born on June 15, 1898, at a meeting in Boston's Fanueil Hall, the site of numerous historical meetings in the fight against slavery. The assembled audience adopted protest resolutions against the war of conquest of Spain, and declared that it would be time enough to think of governing others "when we have shown that we can protect the rights of men within our own borders like the colored race of the South and the Indians of the West and that we can govern great cities like New York, Philadelphia, and Chicago." The meeting selected an anti-imperialist committee of correspondence to contact "persons and organizations throughout the country." Special attention was given to winning labor's support for the cause.[12]

The league received the cooperation of a number of labor leaders in its campaign. In November 1898, Gompers was elected a vice president of the League, and thereafter he participated actively in its work, speaking for the organization, assisting in the distribution of the League's circular letters to the unions, and furnishing it with the names and addresses of the secretaries of the principal labor unions in the country.[13]

In the months following the AFL convention, the leaders of the Federation and the Anti-Imperialist League worked closely together to bring labor's influence on Congress against the Treaty of Peace with Spain. During the session of Congress at which the Spanish peace treaty was considered—December 1898 through March 1899—31 petitions from trade unions were entered into the *Congressional Record* opposing the acquisition of the Philippines. In addition, thousands of individual trade unionists signed petitions drawn up jointly by the American Anti-Imperialist

League and the AFL, and sent them to the President and Congress. These petitions protested "against any extension of the sovereignty of the United States over the Philippine Islands, in any event; or other foreign territory, without the free consent of the people, thereof."[14]

When Gompers signed a Memorial to the Senate, petitioning that body to amend the peace treaty to exclude the annexation of the Philippines and Puerto Rico, the *Philadelphia Telegraph* accused him of "treasonable hostility to the Government of this nation," and called upon members of the Federation to repudiate his stand. Instead, trade unionists continued to send petitions to Congress supporting Gompers' position. So many petitions poured into the Senate, that Henry Cabot Lodge, the leader of the imperialists in the Senate, wrote to his fellow-imperialist, Theodore Roosevelt: "We are going to have trouble over the treaty."[15]

It was at this critical juncture that William Jennings Bryan, the supposed anti-imperialist, standard bearer of the Democratic Party, came to Washington and told shocked Democratic Senators they should vote for the treaty. His argument was that it would be easier to accept the Philippines and then urge that the United States make them independent. If the McKinley Administration failed to do this, he said, the blame would be on the Republicans, and the Democrats would have a new issue to use against the Republicans in the presidential election of 1900.[16]

Acting on Bryan's advice, a group of Democrats in the Senate, led by the Southern Democrats, lined up with the Republicans in support of the imperialist treaty, and it was passed by one vote. Lodge described the struggle for ratification as "the closest, hardest fight I have ever known."[17]

But when the war with Spain officially ended, Congress did not grant the Philippines independence. On February 7, 1899, U.S. troops fired on a group Filipino soldiers and killed 300 of them. The war for the conquest of the Philippines was on.[18]

While the treaty transferred the Philippines, Puerto Rico, and Cuba to the United States, it did not determine their future status. The Joint Resolution of Congress, adopted at the time the United States declared war against Spain, it will be recalled, had committed this country to Cuban independence, providing that the United States would withdraw from the island once it was pacified. And President McKinley had stated publicly that U.S. retention of the Philippines was a traditional stage on the way to Philippine independence. Would the United States carry out these pledges? And how soon?

The answer would depend on the strength of the anti-imperialist movement. "Robbers never give up their gains voluntarily, no matter under what guise obtained," declared the *National Labor Standard*, in calling upon Gompers to take the lead in mobilizing the workers into action so as to guarantee "that the expansion or imperialistic policy . . . will not be carried into effect."[19]

But, as with a number of others in the labor movement, Gompers' anti-imperialism was the product of a strange combination of influences, which weakened its effectiveness precisely at this crucial point in the struggle against U.S. imperialism. For one thing, a major reason for his opposition to colonial expansion was a fear of competition from goods produced in the newly acquired territories, and a free traffic in "cheap labor." Anti-labor employers, Gompers argued, could "import cheap labor and goods" because neither the tariff nor the anti-contract labor laws applied in such cases. The competition would lower wages and reduce jobs for American workers. In answer to a critic who wondered why Congress could not legislate against the influx of "undesirable cheap labor" immigrating from the conquered territories, Gompers wrote:

> You say that we have "put up a legislative barrier against the Chinese,"[20] and ask why we can not do the same as regards "the Philippines, Hawaii, Cuba and Puerto Rico." The answer is that the Chinese come from China, which is neither a State, Territory nor possession of the United States. Should we annex the places you name they would be part of our country, and the constitution of the United States forbids the interdiction of the free entry of men and their products between our States, Territories and Possessions. . . .
> I realize that we are not living in an altruistic age, and that commercialism requires expansion in trade; nor are we opposed to such expansion.[21]

A few months before, in an address to the members of the New York Central Labor Union, Gompers had endorsed the policy of annexation, provided the problem of mass migration of "cheap labor" could be solved. "The government," he exclaimed, "may annex any old thing as long as the laws relating to Labor are observed."[22] But he must have realized that this position did not sit well with the majority of American workers, for he quickly dropped it. One thing, however, he never abandoned—a racist attitude to the people of the new territories whom he called "half-breeds and semi-barbaric" population, "perhaps nearer the condition of savages and barbarians than those of any islands possessed by any other civilization on earth."[23]

The maintenance of empires, Gompers argued, would require large military forces, and these might be used against the workers and might result in international conflicts from which American workers would suffer through the loss of lives and of hard-earned domestic rights. But he made a sharp distinction between territorial expansion, bringing with it colonial domination of a subject people—which he opposed—and economic expansion, by which the United States would be able to control the markets of the world—which he approved. He urged that the advantages allegedly accruing from territorial annexation could, if necessary, be obtained through expanded exports to, and overseas investments in, the territories obtained from Spain. Without the burdens of colonial empire, new markets would be available abroad for the nation and new jobs would be created to meet the increased demands.[24]

Gompers first outlined these objectives in 1897 in opposing the annexation of Hawaii.[25] But he developed them in the period following the war with Spain when he began to insist vigorously that economic expansion was possible and desirable without all the burdens and dangers of colonialism. "The nation which dominates the markets of the world will surely control its destinies," the AFL leader proclaimed. "We do not oppose the development of our industry, the expansion of our commerce, nor the development of our power and influence which the United States may exert upon the destinies of the nations of the earth. But to attain this end is the acquirement of the Philippines Islands with their semi-savage population necessary? Surely not. Neither its gates nor those of any other country of the globe can long be closed against our constantly growing industrial supremacy." The "higher intelligence and standard of life of the [U.S.] workers will largely contribute to the highest pinnacle of industrial and commercial greatness."[26]

By this last remark, Gompers meant that an improved standard of living for workers in the United States would contribute to America's overseas triumphs. Thus he told Congress that without shorter hours and higher wages, America would fail to gain the economic empire that was rightfully hers. "Yes, it is true," Gompers emphatically remarked, "we are and will continue to be the greatest conquerors of the markets of the world: but it will not be done on the basis of cheap labor or long hours of labor."[27] Adolph Strasser, former president of the Cigarmakers' International Union and a founder of the AFL, expressed agreement with Gompers when he told the U.S. Industrial Commission in 1900: "Shorter hours means better machinery and better machinery means capturing the markets of the world, cheaper production, and higher wages."[28]

"Were there any doubt about Gompers' distinction between colonies and overseas economic empire," writes one student of American Labor and imperialism, "he ended it with his views concerning the navy."[29] While the AFL president attacked the use of force which territorial annexation required, and opposed increases in the army, he and other top AFL officials endorsed a larger navy. A navy meant protection for the growing commerce which would develop phenomenally with overseas economic expansion. "No American," Gompers declared, "will oppose a reasonable increase in the size of our navy.[30] The natural increase of our foreign trade makes this essential; but the increase must be for the protection of our own—not for the conquests of others."[31]

A larger navy, moreover, would provide jobs for boilermakers, iron, and steel workers, carpenters and joiners, metal workers, sailors and seamen, dock hands, coal miners, tailors, bricklayers and masons, shipwrights, and mill hands; in short, a large assortment of workers. The Boiler Makers and Iron Ship Builders' Union rejoiced when the *Oregon* completed its historic voyage around South America, and pointed out that it had been built by union men. They were so pleased, in fact, that they adorned the cover of their official journal with a picture of the *Oregon*.[32]

As another student of labor and imperialism points out, "Gompers' anti-imperialism peaked early. . . ."[33] After the United States Senate ratified the treaty with Spain in February 1899, leaders of the AFL, with Gompers in the vanguard, began to move away from collaboration with the American Anti-Imperialist League. When, in the election of 1900, national and local unions that still continued to oppose an imperialist policy urged the AFL to form an independent political party around the issue of imperialism, Gompers opposed the plan. "The establishment of a political party among the workingmen is the division of their forces," he told a group of AFL unions in Ohio which favored such a party. Under pressure from Gompers, they abandoned their plan. The *Cleveland Citizen* criticized Gompers, asking what value there was in his declaration against imperialism if he refused to supplement those opinions with organized political power to defeat imperialism.[34]

In February 1899, the editor of the *Journal of the Knights of Labor* voiced confidence that "national expansion" was just a craze which would soon pass over. "As a matter of fact," he added, the sentiments existed mainly in the newspapers and Congress. In an intercourse with all sorts of men we found little interest in the question one way or the other."[35] But as the editor witnessed the re-inauguration of President William McKinley on March 4, 1901, he announced with a heavy heart: "IM-PERIALISM AN ACCEPTED FACT." Then followed the comment: "There was inaugurated at Washington, D.C., amid the glare of 30,000 bayonets an Emperor and a President."[36]

A few union publications, especially the *National Labor Standard*, the *Coast Seamen's Journal*, and the *Journal of the Knights of Labor*, kept up the agitation against imperialism. They pointed out, as before the re-election of McKinley, that imperialism conflicted with social reform at home; that the imperialistic tendency was "inseparable from materialism" and if unchecked would "prove so fatal to liberty and true social progress on this continent as it has proved in Europe." And they denounced enlistment for service in the Philippines. "No honorable American will volunteer for service in the Philippine Islands," cried the *National Labor Standard*. "Honorable men won't engage in robbery and man killing."[37]

But these voices became fewer and less vocal as the AFL ceased its opposition to colonial seizures. Throughout 1901, the *American Federationist*, official organ of the AFL edited by Gompers, did not carry a single statement opposing the brutal policy of the United States towards the Filipinos. Nor did it voice opposition to American acquisition of the islands and the crushing of the Filipino independence movement.

The decline of labor opposition to U.S. Philippine policy had an interesting by product. In March 1900, the *Garment Worker* published an article by a labor member of Britain's Parliament in which he stated that the British trade unions opposed the war begun by their government in October 1899 against the Boers in South Africa. He added that this attitude would "no doubt find an echoing response in the hearts of American workingmen," since it was apparent that the British policy of subjugating the Boer struggle for independence was similar to that of the Americans in the Philippines.[38]

The British laborite must have been surprised to learn that, in the main, the American labor press and trade unions were silent on this question. There were exceptions, to be sure. The *Cleveland Citizen*, the pro-socialist organ of that city's central labor body, sarcastically criticized Great Britain: "God save the Queen, and all her carnivorous class who are responsible for another one of the world's tragedies."[39] While not condoning Great Britain's action against the Boers, the organ of the International Wordworkers' Union refused to support the Boers because they were racist oppressors of the blacks in South Africa:

> The Boers are not, nor have they ever been more than good for nothing, lazy, intolerant bigots, who believe that they have rights which people of other

countries should be denied. While we detest the avaricious greed of Great Britain in her alleged philanthropic effort at "benevolent assimilation"—that is the aim—and to secure justice for the uitlander of all nations, yet we have very little sympathy for a people so bigoted, so intolerant and so manifestly unfair as the Boers.[40]

For most AFL unions and for the Federation itself, having come to accept the United States conquest of the Philippines, opposition to the British war against the Boers would have created problems. Hence, when an attempt was made to get the 1901 AFL convention to endorse a resolution sympathizing with the Boers and denouncing the British for the war and for their brutal treatment of their enemies, the Committee on Resolutions did not recommend its adoption "because of the fact that our government is engaged in operations of a similar character to those of which this resolution complains."[41] Rather than couple condemnation of U.S. policy in the Philippines with an attack on the British against the Boers, the AFL adopted a general policy of neutrality. This was precisely the policy which the American government had taken towards the Boer War, influenced by its realization that to condemn the British would be to judge American action against the Filipinos as unjust.[42]

The position taken by the AFL's Committee on Resolution was not surprising, as the few labor papers still upholding an anti-imperialist position pointed out. In order to condemn Great Britain, the AFL would have had to denounce the American forces in the Philippines for resorting to as "cruel tactics as any despot had ever used." By administering the "water cure," the U.S. army had violated the ordinary principles of justice. But this was only part of the U.S. policy of extermination in the Philippines, cried the *National Labor Standard*.[43] When General "Jake" Smith took over the job of pacifying Samar, a Filipino stronghold, his first move was to order all civilians out of the interior. When they came straggling into coastal towns, they were all thrown into stockades—concentration camps—and they died like flies. "I want no prisoners," Smith told his men "I wish you to kill and burn; the more you burn and kill the better it will please me." All persons who had not surrendered and were capable of carrying arms were to be shot, and this included Filipino boys of ten years of age! Finally, Smith gave his infamous order that Samar be converted into a "howling wilderness." The order was carried out to the letter by his subordinate, Major Waller and within six months Samar "was quiet as a cemetery."[44]

When the news of these brutal outrages reached the United States, there was a wave of protest. But this protest did not include the majority of the unions associated with the AFL and the Railroad Brotherhoods. Referring to "The Philippine Horrors," the *Journal of the Knights of Labor* called on the leadership of the AFL and Brotherhoods to join the Knights in condemning the Philippine policy of the U.S. government, and thus maintain "the credit and good name of the American people."[45] The response was a thunderous silence! As Richard E. Welch, Jr. points out in his study, *Response to Imperialism: The United States and the Philippine-American War, 1899–1902,* it appeared by 1902 that it did not "greatly matter" to most groups in organized labor "whether the United States kept the [Philippine] islands so long as the Congressional barriers were maintained against Asiatic goods and immigrants."[46]

The same outlook was evident in the approach to the annexation of Hawaii. Once annexation was accomplished, the AFL concern shifted to worry over the contract labor system in the islands. The AFL convention in December 1899 limited the discussion of the Hawaiian question to nothing more than a resolution urging the abolition of the contract labor system.[47] The bill making Hawaii an integral part of the United States became effective on June 15, 1900. It fulfilled the AFL's highest hopes by abolishing contract labor and applying the national contract labor laws to the islands. The interests of the seamen were satisfied by the bill because it included the islands within the coastwise trade regulations, and all the West Coast unions were pleased by the provisions forbidding Hawaiian Chinese residents from entering any state of the United States.

From that point on, American policy in the Hawaiian islands was rarely criticized at AFL conventions. The *National Labor Standard*, anti-imperialist as ever, continued to oppose Hawaiian annexation, and pointed out that in the election of a delegate to Washington under new territorial government, the Home Rule Party, using the slogan "Hawaii for Hawaiians," not only elected the first delegate to Congress, but won a substantial majority in both houses of the Hawaiian legislature. All this, the *Standard* insisted, was proof that Hawaiians were not satisfied with their ties to the United States, and the American trade unions should support their position with resolutions and other action.[48]

But only one union responded, the shoe workers. For some time the *Boot and Shoe Worker*, the union's journal, had been creating a vision of a great market in Hawaii for shoes produced on the mainland, increasing jobs for shoe workers at high wages. But it was to be "run on the American system and under American management." Gone was "another dream of wealth acquired by selling manufactured goods to a semi-civilized people," it lamented. Instead, American capital was migrating to the colonies, and the prospects were for diminished work opportunities at home as American workers lost job opportunities because of goods produced by Hawaiian cheap labor.[49]

The answer, said the *Boot and Shoe Worker*, was to support Hawaiian independence, and then impose a stiff tariff on goods imported from newly established independent Hawaii. But neither the AFL nor any of its affiliates endorsed the idea, and it quickly died.[50]

The AFL response is not surprising. Gompers had made it clear that it was only imperialist annexation that the AFL opposed. When it became evident that acquisition of foreign markets, and not territory, was the primary aim of those involved in building the "New American Empire,"*—in short, when it became evident that

---

*According to the "new empire" scholarship (to use Walter Lefeber's term), leading U.S. businessmen and policy makers at the turn of the century were convinced that only foreign markets could absorb the "glut of goods pouring out of America's highly mechanized factories and farms." The acquisition of these markets, and not territory, was their primary goal. Ideologically and politically opposed to old-styled European colonialism, they sought influence

imperialist annexation was no longer the major aspect of American imperialism—
the AFL leaders quickly abandoned their earlier participation in the anti-imperialist
movement.[51]

With respect to the territories already annexed in the first flush following the
war with Spain, the AFL sought not to undo the conquests and restore independence
to the conquered lands. Rather, as Gompers later put it, the American labor
movement set itself the task of establishing "an organized labor movement within
the territories."[52] Organizers went to Puerto Rico, Hawaii, and the Philippines to
enlist the workers of these areas in the cause of higher living standards and the
defense of their craft interests.

The AFL was also spreading American institutions into the territorial possessions.
"There is no influence so potent for the Americanization of the island as our labor
movement," Gompers said in discussing Puerto Rico.[53] The "Americanization"
process included inculcating the workers of the territories with knowledge of English
and American history, and the principles of "pure and simple" trade unionism and
those of capitalist free enterprise. But there was a risk too. Ed Rosenberg, Secretary
of the San Francisco Labor Union, was commissioned to investigate the situation
in the Philippines and Hawaii, with respect to the spread of AFL-unionism in the
territories. His report was optimistic, but in a private letter to Gompers, May 22,
1904, Rosenberg warned that the growth of unionism in the Philippines posed the
danger of a great increase of "agitation for Philippine independence, which is very
strong among the better class of workers, and has to be taken into consideration
when organizing these people." Since the AFL supported retaining the Philippines,
Rosenberg noted, this created a problem. However, he was confident that it could
be solved by an educational campaign which would convince the Filipino workers
that the advantages of being part of the United States outweighed any promises of
what would come with independence. One such advantage would be admittance
to the AFL.

Gompers agreed. AFL unionism would spread "the gospel of Americanism," and
this would effectively overcome tendencies towards independence. The AFL thus
had a vast mission. "Our limits are no longer from Maine to California, from the
Lakes to the Gulf," Gompers announced exuberantly in 1905, "but we include the
whole of the United States, Canada, Hawaii, Cuba, Puerto Rico, Mexico, the
Philippines, and British Columbia."[54]

While the AFL mentioned the benefits for workers in the new possessions, who
were to be organized and assisted by the Federation, the major purpose of the
proposed program to spread AFL-style trade unionism was to serve the interests of

through economic penetration and control rather than the conquest of territory and colonization, although they were in no sense opposed to the use of force through the Navy and
Marines or even occupation of territory when these were necessary to achieve their goals.

The framework of this theory was first suggested by William Appleman Williams in *The
Tragedy of American Diplomacy* (New York: 1959), but the details were provided in Walter
Lefeber, *The New Empire: An Interpretation of American Expansion, 1860–1898* (Ithaca, N. Y.:
1963).

union labor in the United States. Once the workers in the new possessions were organized, their wants would increase and they would henceforth import from the United States the manufactured products required by those growing wants. Such demands would not only bring more jobs but higher wages to workers in the United States. Those terms were all part of the bargain between labor and capital. As Gerald Melvin Torkelson puts it: "Broadly speaking, the Federation would hereafter cease on its part to condemn the acquisition of Hawaii, Puerto Rico, and the Philippines. In return, government and industry would allow the Federation to carry on organizing activities in these areas to gain a law prohibiting Chinese immigration from them, and to have a voice in their labor policies, insofar as the federal government was involved."[55]

As an increasing number of scholars have pointed out, the AFL's abandonment of its earlier anti-imperialist tradition was also rooted in the unity that emerged at this time between Gompers and other leaders of the AFL (and Railroad Brotherhoods as well) with dominant figures of American monopoly capitalism.[56] This was seen most clearly in the National Civic Federation.

The NCF was created in 1900 and was designed to ameliorate conflict between employers and workers within the existing capitalist economy. In return for supporting class collaboration and anti-radicalism at home and imperialism abroad, the skilled workers affiliated with the AFL and the Railroad Brotherhoods obtained employer recognition of their organizations and larger material benefits.[57]

"Imperialism," writes V.I. Lenin in his classic study, *Imperialism, the Highest Stage of Capitalism,* "tends to create privileged ranks among the workers and to separate them from the broad mass of the proletariat."[58] Just as British imperialists were able to blunt the anti-imperialist sentiments of organized labor in England by corrupting the skilled workers, giving them a share in the spoils of imperialism, so American imperialists succeeded in achieving the same in the United States. Out of the surplus profits derived from imperialism, monopoly capitalism in the United States could afford to pay the highly skilled workers a bit more above the average wage in order to reconcile them to imperialism, to develop indirectly a sense of superiority within among this stratum of the working class, and destroy their solidarity with their fellow-workers and their consciousness of class. These concessions accelerated the development of theories and practices of class collaboration in the ranks of labor's leadership; they accelerated the corruption of the labor aristocracy; and they weakened the earlier militancy and class-consciousness of the labor movement. As American imperialism expanded and completely outstripped its imperialist rivals, this process proceeded apace.

But the earlier militancy and class-conscious spirit of the American labor movement did not disappear. Nor did the tradition of anti-imperialism. The Fourth of July, 1905, provided an example of both these trends in the labor movement.[59] The *Railroad Trainmen's Journal* used Independence Day as an opportunity to praise two statesmen of American imperialism—"Patriotic Statesman," it called each of them—Elihu Root and John Hay—as one succeeded the other in the Department of State. Root had done much to bring the United States into the position of a world power; Hay had an opportunity to assert that power in an even greater future. The trainmen's paper proclaimed that "the United States is a mighty country. It has commenced to cut a wide swath in international affairs. It issues demands like a real warrior nation and it gets recognition, too, when it does so. It has recently proven that a commercial nation will fight like a nation when it makes its mind to fight and in consequence there is respect entertained for it that is quite new."[60]

On that same Fourth of July, 1905, another labor journal—the *Miners' Magazine*, official organ of the Western Federation of Miners—took a different approach. The WFM was not only one of the first unions to protest the annexation of the Philippines, and one of the few to call for class-conscious action at the ballot-box against imperialism, but, unlike the vast majority of the AFL unions and all of the Railroad Brotherhoods, it never supported economic expansion while opposing territorial annexation. "The finding of foreign markets," it insisted, "will not benefit the producing class of the country; only the capitalist class."[61]

It is not surprising, therefore, that on Independence Day, 1905, the *Miners' Magazine* took the position that the working class had nothing to celebrate "unless slaves can celebrate their slavery." Only the capitalists had reason to rejoice:

> We see the American nation entering upon a career of conquest at the behest of the capitalist class who demand foreign markets and people to exploit, a policy that places the United States among the conquering nations of the world, and pledges us to the noble and philanthropic duty of carving out our "manifest destiny" of bringing the heathen to the feet of Jesus and John D. Rockefeller.[62]

The WFM was one of the leading socialist unions in the United States. But it took a position unlike that of the American socialist parties when it vigorously opposed imperialism and called for working class political action against territorial expansion and the capitalists' drive for foreign markets.[63]

At the Paris Congress of September 1900, the International Socialists had unanimously adopted a resolution calling upon the proletariat to fight in every possible way against colonial policies.[64] This action, although coming late in the day, gave American socialists the opportunity to embrace anti-imperialism. To an extent, they had already done so. In contrast to most trade unions, it will be recalled, American socialists of various schools maintained "a firm anti-imperialist attitude" to the war against Spain from its inception, and Eugene V. Debs had reason to be proud of the fact that Social Democrats had not been swept off their feet by the war craze.[65] This anti-imperialist position continued for a period after the war, and was reflected in support of the Filipinos' struggle for independence. "Remember, Workingmen! that these patriots are fighting for you as well as themselves," Charles Trench appealed in the *Social Democratic Herald*. Was there a single workingman, Trench asked, who doubted that the triumph of imperialism in the Philippines "will be attended with disastrous results to our working classes?"[66]

Nevertheless, American socialist organizations played no real role in the anti-imperialist movement. For one thing, neither the Socialist Labor Party nor the Social Democratic Party took any part in the American Anti-Imperialist League. In fact, commenting on the formation of the League's Chicago branch, the *Worker's Call*, organ of the SLP in that city, referred to the delegates as "strange birds" who, confronted with "the unavoidable results of the economic system which they still defend," gave forth a "foolish and useless note of alarm." The SLP saw the dispute between the imperialists and anti-imperialists as a struggle between small and large business groups, between half-bankrupt capitalists and trusts, "a dispute in which the Socialists had no stake."[67]

In the 1900 presidential election, the Socialists insisted that "from the point of view of the working class, expansion is not worth talking about."[68] Hence neither the SLP nor the SDP had a foreign policy platform.[69] "What is the paramount issue of the campaign?" asked the *Workers' Call* on behalf of the SLP. It answered: "McKinley says: Sound money, expansion and prosperity. Bryan says: Imperialism. The Socialist says, as workingmen that is is whether they shall continue to be wage slaves."[70] Eugene V. Debs, the SDP's candidate, virtually ignored the Philippines during the campaign, and insisted that such issues as "imperialism" and "expansion" "do not concern the working class."[71]

This attitude continued after the 1900 campaign. When Debs ran for president in 1904, this time as the candidate of the Socialist Party of America, he asserted that the issue of imperialism and anti-imperialism concerned only capitalists. "They [the workingmen] know by experience and observation that . . . imperialism and anti-imperialism . . . mean capitalist rule and wage slavery."[72]

Most socialists viewed the anti-imperialist crusade as merely a side show to the class struggle at home. While some socialists argued that workers must oppose imperialism because, by providing capitalism with a renewed lease on life, it retarded the revolution, many socialists advanced the argument that capitalism was a prerequisite for socialism, and that imperialism, for all its brutality, introduced capitalist production in backward areas, thus paving the way for the ultimate triumph of Socialism.[73] In the *International Socialist Review*, one member of the Party argued that opposition to imperialism would retard the spread of capitalist methods of production, and added: "It is capitalistic methods of production that produces a wage-working class of men and women . . . And it is these men and women who become the revolutionists that will one day arise to make the world a world of, for and by the workers themselves."[74]

After an examination of the platforms of the Socialist, Republican, and Democratic parties from 1900 to 1912, Wilfred H. Peterson concludes: "In comparison with the statements of the major parties, the Socialist platforms gave almost no attention to current issues of foreign policy." He finds the same indifference to foreign policy issues in Party convention debates, Party referenda, speeches of Party candidates, and, with occasional exceptions, nearly all Socialist publications.[75]

There was one major exception as we shall see—namely, the socialists' stand on the Mexican Revolution. But prior to this epochal event, the American Socialist movement, in the main, displayed indifference to the issue of U.S. imperialism.

During this same period, the chief leaders and affiliates of the AFL and Railroad Brotherhoods became champions and defenders of the "New American Empire."

We shall now see how these attitudes unfolded as we examine the U.S. labor movement and Latin America during the administrations of William McKinley, Theodore Roosevelt, William Howard Taft, and Woodrow Wilson.

· IV ·

THE U.S. OCCUPATION OF CUBA

S hortly after the outbreak of the war with Spain, an American newspaper editor predicted that victory for "Cuba libre" would benefit the United States more than Cuba, for "the Americans will make the money."[1] About the same time, the *New York World* predicted "a new invasion of Cuba" following the war. It would not be an invasion of soldiers and sailors, but of United States businessmen and investors. The *World* also predicted that "whatever may be decided as to the political future of Cuba, its industrial and commercial future will be directed by American enterprise and stimulated with American capital."[2] In his book, *Our Island Empire,* published in 1899, Charles Morris wrote: "To the United States, among the chief advantages of the liberation of Cuba will be commercial ones." Cuba offered rich fields for investment and greatly expanded markets.[3]

These predictions came true. Even before the Spanish flag was taken down in Cuba, U.S. business interests set out to make their influence felt. Merchants, real estate agents, stock speculators, reckless adventurers, and promoters of all kinds of get-rich schemes flocked to Cuba by the thousands.[4] Most of the American businessmen, financiers, and speculators who came to Cuba early in the Occupation were seeking franchises and contracts. The War Department had franchises, grants, and all kinds of concessions at its disposal, and the men at the head of the Department, business-minded Secretary of War Russell A. Alger, was inclined to issue them with a free hand. (In the Philippines, the U.S. military government began to issue licenses to American firms in September 1898.) In Cuba, this policy had the support of most of the military commanders, especially General Leonard Wood who openly encouraged the invasion of American capitalists.[5]

By the second week of February 1899, barely six weeks after the formal beginning of the Occupation, the process of dispensing franchises, railway grants, street car-line concessions, electric light monopolies and similar privileges in Cuba to American financial syndicates and individual capitalists was about to begin in earnest. The War Department had created a new board for this purpose, and the group was set to leave for Cuba to look over the situation and then grant applications for concessions.[6] (Puerto Rico was also to be surveyed for the purpose of granting applications by American investors for concessions in that island.)

When this scheme to divide up Cuba's resources came to the attention of Senator J.B. Foraker of Ohio, he decided to act. He introduced an amendment to the current army appropriation bill in the Senate; the first section forbade the U.S. from granting "franchises and concessions of any kind whatever" in Cuba, during the American Occupation. The second part of his amendment declared that, "the pacification of the island of Cuba having been accomplished," the President was authorized to withdraw the army and "leave the government and control of the island to its people."[7] The second part was eliminated by the Senate Committee for Appropriations so that the Senate considered only the section relating to franchises or other concessions. The Foraker Amendment, passed by the Senate by a vote of 47 to 11, stated that, "No property franchises, or concessions of any kind whatever, shall be granted by the United States, or by any other military or other authority whatever in the Island of Cuba during the occupation thereof by the United States."[8]

Even with the Foraker Amendment, at least $30,000,000 in American capital was invested in Cuba during the military occupation.[9] A major focus of that investment was the sugar industry. In 1901, a syndicate headed by United Fruit Company's president, Andrew W. Preston, bought 1,900,000 acres on Nyre Bay at a cost of $400,000. While United Fruit company was planting bananas elsewhere in the Caribbean, in Cuba it was raising sugar cane.[10] The Francisco Sugar Company was founded when the McCahan sugar refining interests of Philadelphia joined the Rionda family in 1901 to develop the 80,000 acre estate called Francisco on the Southern coast of Cuba. Toward the end of 1901, an American company backed by railroad financier Stuyvesant Fish bought the sugar mill Cienfuegos and combined it with the Gramercy refinery in Louisiana.[11]

Henry D. Havemeyer, president of the American Sugar Refinery Company, known as the Sugar Trust, was already the owner of a sugar mill in Trinidad, and had interests in the sugar factories at Cappawa and Santa Cruz. The Sugar Trust also had an interest in the McCahan refineries which, controlled the Francisco Sugar Company. Moreover, the Sugar Trust was already the principal purchaser of Cuban raw sugar since little of it was now refined on the island.[12]

It is impossible to determine the place of American capital in the sugar industry in Cuba by the end of the occupation. But complete American dominance of the Cuban sugar industry was on the way to becoming a reality, and the American tobacco trust was not far behind. Formerly a Spanish monopoly, the tobacco industry came under the domination of the U.S. tobacco monopoly during the Occupation. In 1899 the Havana Commercial Company, organized in New York City, bought up twelve cigar factories and one cigarette factory in Havana. This company then took over the leaf-importing business of F. García Brothers and Company, bought a number of tobacco plantations, and by December 1900, had advanced up to $1,300,000 to Cuban planters. Its success and huge profits stimulated the Tobacco Trust in the United States—the American Tobacco Company—to invade the Cuban cigar business through its cigar affiliate, the American Cigar Company. The Tobacco Trust gained control of Henry Clay and Block Co. LTD., and then absorbed the Havana Commercial Company in May 1902. At this point 90 percent of the export trade in Havana cigars was concentrated in the hands of the American Cigar Company. This comprised nearly one half of the entire manufacture of cigars and cigarettes in Cuba.[13]

In addition, by the end of the Occupation at least 80 percent of the export of Cuba's minerals (nickel, manganese, iron ore) was in American hands, the greatest part under control of the Bethlehem Steel Company.[14]

Viewing the economic penetration of Cuba during the Occupation, American historian James Clark Redpath commented in summer 1899 that "the idea that we are in Cuba on a philanthropic and humane mission has gone to join the other misplaced, absurd and hypocritical pretexts which history has flung with a lavish hand into limbo near the moon."[15] Years later, a Foreign Policy Association study pointed out that in winning political freedom from Spain, "Cuba lost control over its economic resources."[16]

When the news was made public in the United States that the Cuban people were being denied the right to govern themselves and forced to endure military occupation by the U.S. Army, a number of labor voices rose in protest. In an address to the Chicago Peace Jubilee, October 18, 1898, Samuel Gompers demanded that "freedom and independence to which she is entitled, be immediately given to Cuba." "What has become of our paens of praise for the brave Cubans?" the AFL president asked. "Was our charge against Spain in her refusal to give the people of that island independence baseless? . . . Is it not strange that now, for the first time, we hear that the Cubans are unfit for self-government, that whether they protest against it or not, they must be dominated by us, annexed by us or become a dependency of ours?" Gompers explained this development as clear evidence of the emergence of American imperialism:

> There are some Americans—our money makers—whose only God is the almighty dollar, whose only human or divine trinity is dividend, interest and profit. They have come to the conclusion that if poor, suffering Cuba can be handed over to the tender mercies, their deity and their deviltry can hold full sway. To these gentlemen, when there is a question between liberty and profit, present or prospective, liberty is thrown to the dogs as a wornout and threadbare thing of the past![17]

For once *The People*, organ of the Socialist Labor Party, edited by Daniel De Leon, agreed with Gompers (whom it usually attacked as a "labor lieutenant of the capitalists"). It urged the American people to rise up in protest against the Administration's Cuban policy, under which "we merely displace the Spanish Captain

General for the American one, and the [American] volunteers will be called upon to 'preserve peace' much the same way as the Spanish troops have 'preserved peace.' "[18]

Unfortunately, while *The People* continued to attack the Administration's Cuban policy, Gompers remained silent after his initial outburst of indignation. So, too, did the American Federation of Labor and the Railroad Brotherhoods. Neither of the two organizations called for a speedy end to the military occupation. The *Railroad Trainman* conceded that eventually the United States would have to withdraw from Cuba, but warned that "the United States cannot leave Cuba until a stable government has been organized and that is something that cannot be brought about in a day."[19]

In fact, a number of trade unions in the United States set out cynically to profit from the occupation of Cuba. The occupation would foster widespread use of the English language on the island, the Typographical Union predicted, and create a demand for printers which would be supplied from its ranks. The Woodworkers' Union reported a heavy demand for walnut used in the making of guns for the occupation forces, and declared that as long as the Occupation continued, the lumber industry would continue to employ its members. *The Carpenter,* organ of the Brotherhood of Carpenters and Joiners, extolled the fact that so long as the United States occupied Cuba, American contractors and American workmen would do the work there.[20] The Glassworkers' Union reported a growing demand for bottles to meet the need of the occupation army for beer, ale and other beverages, all of which meant more work for members of that union.[21] The Bricklayers' and Masons' Union was confident that its members would find great opportunities in the construction of barracks and other buildings for the use of the U.S. forces in Cuba.[22]

All of these unions agreed that there should not be an early end to the Occupation. *The Carpenter* argued that only with the investment of American capital could Cuba become a viable society, and this development could not occur on an extensive scale until a stable government was assured. It might take even an entire generation, the Brotherhood's organ said: "There will not, in this generation, be any such satisfactory government in Cuba, unless it is that of the United States."[23] The *United Mine Workers' Journal* agreed. The army of occupation had to remain "for some time." Order had to be maintained.[24]

While American labor was not in the same league as American capitalists when it came to profiting from military occupation of Cuba, the *Typographical Journal* boasted in its issue of May 1899 that "if the occupation of the island by the United States had done no good to anything else, it certainly has immensely benefited the printing business."[25] But, as we shall see, the Occupation held out a real threat to labor in the United States.

The 1899 census revealed that the labor force in Cuba was 678,000 out of a total population of 1,572,797, or 43 percent. Of this number, those in agriculture, mining, and fisheries totaled 336,271: 330,271 in agriculture, 5,000 in mining, and 1,000 in fisheries. The urban working class population of 342,301 was divided into the following categories: domestic and personal services, 151,912; manufacturing and mechanical industries, 97,703; trade and transportation, 81,918; and professional services, 8,768. In order of numerical importance, main urban occupations were: clothing trades, tobacco trades, building trades, transportation, metal workers, foods and liquors, leather workers, printing trades, brick masons and potters, and woodworkers. The clothing trade was still largely cottage industry. Actually, the tobacco workers were the dominant force in urban labor.[26]

One other point about the Cuban labor force revealed by the 1899 census is worth noting: the ratio of black to white workers.

	Urban	Rural
White	196,647	198,230
Negro	117,750	106,967

While the agricultural economy was no longer based mainly on the labor of the black Cubans, blacks still occupied an important place in it as well as in the labor force.[27]

Unemployment was widespread when the Cuban-Spanish-American War* came to an end. Only a handful of industries functioned in the cities. Unemployment, however, dropped during the early months of the Occupation, partly because of the numbers employed in sanitation and public works, and partly because of the slow but steady recovery of the economy in the island.[28] While employment improved, conditions of work did not. "There are many shops in which workers labored from dawn until ten or twelve at night, [with only 30 or 40 minutes permitted for meals, and] with only one day off every two weeks." Workers often slept where they worked, in ill-ventilated barracks completely lacking in sanitary facilities. Wages were "barely enough to furnish food to keep the workers in a state of being able to work." Apprentices were kept working for months, even years, without receiving any pay at all.[29]

In rural areas, conditions were even worse. Living conditions for field laborers and mill workers on the sugar plantations were deplorable. Wages were often paid in scrip, redeemable only at stores operated by employers. The working day was still from sunup to sundown. Unemployment was the lot of farm workers for several months of the year, for after the sugar harvest there was little work available.[30]

Spain left nothing that could be characterized as social legislation dealing with conditions of work, and the U.S. military government did not concern itself with this problem. "There have been no laws enacted for Cuba, either by the Spanish or by the military government relating specifically to labor, "Victor S. Clark observed in 1902, in a bulletin published by the U.S. Department of Labor.[31] Hence the employers had a free hand in exploiting workers, and they did so, confident that they would meet with little resistance. The vast majority of the workers' organi-

---

*Professor Samuel Flagg Bemis deserves credit for changing the name of the war from Spanish-American War to Spanish-Cuban-American War in the 1959 edition of his *Short History of American Diplomacy* and for acknowledging the contributions of Cuban historians in causing this change. The correct name for military events in Cuba from 1895 to August 1898 in Spanish-Cuban-American War (*La Guerra Hispano-Cubano-Americana*).

zations had been suppressed by the Spanish authorities during the war. Only three trade unions—all belonging to the tobacco industry—survived the persecution and they were in weakened straits.[32] Indeed, so feeble was the status of the labor movement at the beginning of the Occupation, that American capitalists planning to invest in Cuban industry were assured that there was "little organization, little class spirit among her working people."[33]

Gradually, the labor organizations which had been forced to suspend activity during the war reappeared, and a number came into existence for the first time.[34] If anything, there were now too many individual unions and insufficient centralization of organization. The cigar rollers of Havana, for example, were not in a single organization; there existed as many societies as there were shops, each working by itself.[35]

Two new organizations emerged during this period: the *Partido Socialista Cubano* (Cuban Socialist Party) and the *Liga General de Trabajadores Cubanos* (General League of Cuban Workers). The Cuban Socialist Party, founded by Diego Vicente Tejera, a poet and intellectual with influence among workers, announced its birth in a manifesto addressed "To the People of Cuba." Distributed throughout Havana on March 29, 1899, the manifesto called for "a radical transformation of the entire society" through the establishment of socialism. Meanwhile, however, until socialism was achieved, there were injustices which had to be eliminated from Cuban society. There was a crying need for the passage of laws which would "remove from the neck of the unhappy proletariat the iron hand of the exploiter which is choking him": laws for protection of women and children, the achievement of a peaceful old age for those who worked in the shops and factories, indemnification for families whose breadwinners were worn down by sickness and death, and for the reduction of the hours of labor so that the worker "should not only have sufficient time to care for and enjoy his family, but also for recreation and cultivation of his mind so that he can enjoy society and life. In a word we must exalt the humble ones, raising them in dignity and well being to the level of the privileged ones of today."[36]

Although the Cuban Socialist Party—the first Socialist party in Cuban history— had a brief existence, its very existence was an indication of the growth of socialist thought in Cuba.[37] Moreover, its founder, Diego Vicente Tejera, was chosen honorary president of the General League of Cuban Workers in recognition of his contributions to Cuban labor.

On September 1, 1899, at a meeting in Havana, the General League of Cuban Workers was formed with Enrique Messonier as president and Pedro A. Navarro as secretary. Its birth coincided with events of a far-reaching nature which were beginning to take shape in Cuba. Since August 27, the masons of Havana had been on strike for higher wages and an eight-hour day. On September 7, General Juan Luis Rivera, civil governor of Havana, made an effort to settle the strike, but got nowhere with the employers in the building trades. The latter had received public assurances from General Rafael de Cárdenas, chief of police, that the forces under his command were ready to protect *rompehuelgas* (strikebreakers). The employers, then, were in no mood to grant the strikers' demands, especially the eight-hour day. Meanwhile, the masons' battle was winning wide support in working-class circles; indeed, in late August, Major Tasker H. Bliss, Collector of Customs for Cuba under the Occupation, wrote worriedly to General Adman R. Chaffee, Chief of Staff in Havana, that "other trades may join in this strike out of sympathy." Bliss feared that laborers and lightermen "who practically have the entire commerce of this Port at their mercy," would join the strike, and he recommended abolition of the lighterage system and the construction of landing piers "which will enable every vessel to discharge immediately upon the wharves."[38]

On September 16, representatives of the principal labor organizations in Havana met to discuss a general strike to help the masons. Speakers emphasized that the masons' demand for an eight hour-day was clearly justified, and that a victory for these workers would pave the way for a shorter working day for all Cuban workers. A meeting was scheduled at the *Circulo de Trabajadores* (Workers' Circle), to which the presidents of all unions were invited. The purpose was to plan a general strike.

At this meeting, on September 19, representatives of all labor organizations in Havana voted unanimously to call a general strike to begin the following morning at 6 A.M. A resolution ordering the general strike in sympathy with the masons referred to the action as made necessary by "the constant contempt for their rights displayed by the arrogant bosses, and the indifference of the authorities to the abuse of a class which constitutes a most important part of the Cuban population, but realizes only hunger and misery." Two days later, the reasons were more fully set forth in a printed manifesto circulated throughout Havana and pasted to the walls of many buildings.[39] It began with the bold statement:

A country lacking workers is no good to anyone. The capitalists and the rich landowners need the workers, and they owe them a decent life. But this is not the case in Cuba, and as such a state of things cannot continue, we have determined to promote the struggle between the worker and capitalist. For the workers of Cuba will no longer tolerate remaining in total subjection.

Then followed a demand for the eight-hour day and a historical analysis of the movement for it, especially the struggle in the United States in the 1880s, climaxed in the Haymarket Affair of 1886.[40] The demand for an eight-hour day, the manifesto continued, was not a new idea even in Cuba. Those who wished to change the existing situation were urged to attend a mass meeting on September 24, at the Little Square Balboa. The manifesto closed: "Workers! Come to the meeting on which depends the life or death of the workers of Cuba."[41]

Between 4,000 and 8,000 workers gathered in the Little Square of Balboa on September 24, in response to the manifesto, making it the largest meeting held in Havana for many years. A bevy of trade union leaders addressed the gathering, urging an effective general strike in support of the masons. Finally, a committee was elected to direct the general strike—Francisco de Armas, César García Simón Camacho, Serafín del Buston, José González Pintado, Juan Aller—and a declaration was adopted, without a single dissent, affirming the determination of the workers "to go out immediately on a general strike."[42]

When news of the action taken at the meeting reached General Ludlow, he immediately set out to break the strike. Up to now, the U.S. military authorities had anxiously watched the developing struggle, but had refrained from interfering directly, believing the plans for a general strike would quickly collapse. But the tremendous gathering at the Little Square of Balboa, and the militant stand in favor of a general strike unanimously adopted by the thousands at the meeting, caused them to abandon the wait-and-see attitude. In the early hours of September 25, General Ludlow notified the Mayor of Havana that forces were joining to carry through a general strike, that "seditious and disorderly language" had been used in the public meeting at the Balboa Square, and "seditious publications" had been distributed throughout the city. In view of these circumstances, Ludlow ordered the Mayor to arrest eleven trade union leaders and detain them until "the formulation of the proper charges against them." Mayor Perfecto Lacoste immediately jumped to do the American general's bidding, and at his order, the police proceeded to arrest all eleven of the men listed by Ludlow.[43]

The jailing of the strike leaders did not succeed in stopping the workers from joining the general strike. Nor did the fact that Havana was placed under siege, with U.S. troops occupying the railroad stations and the docks while police moved through the city attacking and breaking up workers' gatherings and preventing meetings at various workers' clubs. Economic activity in the city came to a halt; even the theaters were empty.[44]

Forty-five tobacco shops voted on September 26 to join the movement, and the printers went on record as ready to walk out "as faithful soldiers of the proletariat." Obviously, more arrests were necessary. At the request of General Ludlow, C.V. Casiero, Adjutant General, notified Mayor Lacoste immediately to arrest the leaders of the Bakers' union. Perhaps then Havana would get bread. At the same time, General Ludlow himself ordered the civil governor of the province to prohibit "political meetings, processions or demonstrations of any type which have as their object to support the strike."[45] And Ludlow ordered all newspapers immediately to publish a proclamation which he had written, addressed "To the People of Havana."

It was an amazing document. It began with an explanation of the reasons for the proclamation, which made it appear that the general strike was the work of a handful of "irresponsible and seditious individuals" rather than the expression of the will of thousands of Cuban workers. Ludlow then went on to remind the Cubans that the United States had "guaranteed to establish in the island of Cuba a firm and orderly government," and that it did not intend to allow a few "irresponsible and seditious individuals" to prevent it from carrying out its obligation. He then proceeded to contradict his interpretation of who was behind the general strike by noting that "the workers of Havana" were involved in the strike, but attributed this to the fact that they were "seduced" into becoming involved. Then followed a blunt warning that if these workers continued to carry through the general strike, they would be responsible for making "the exercise of liberty and the enjoyment of the rights of man recede for an indefinite period." In other words, the Occupation would be indefinitely extended unless the general strike was immediately terminated! Ludlow issued still another warning:

> No man can be compelled to work against his will. But if he can work yet will not, he is only a vagrant and a burden, and he must take responsibility for his own acts and the needless and innumerable sufferings which he imposes upon his kindred, as well as upon the public.[46]

Translated into specific language, this meant that while the United States authorities could not compel any man to work, it would do so just the same.

Ludlow's proclamation appeared in the Havana press on September 27. The same day, his threats became a reality as mounted police and units of the Rural Guard moved through the streets attacking workers.[47] A demonstration headed by a worker carrying a white flag with the number 8 printed in the center was attacked, the demonstrators beaten, and 150 of them arrested.[48] That same afternoon, crowds of workers gathered before the police headquarters to protest police brutality towards the strikers and demand the release of hundreds of strikers, men and women, who were in jail.[49]

Many strikers were driven back to work by the combined forces of the police, Rural Guard and U.S. Army. On October 3, General Ludlow announced that the general strike had been broken, and sent congratulations to Mayor Lacoste, expressing appreciation of his cooperation and that of his police force in breaking the general strike. "The disappearance of the danger," Ludlow wrote, "is due principally to the tact and firmness with which you have conducted the matter and to the discretion and vigilance of the police under the capable direction of General Rafael Cárdenas."[50] The "discretion and vigilance" of the police had consisted of trampling down the rights of the workers, attacking them whenever they gathered, breaking up their meetings, and arresting and imprisoning hundreds of strikers.

A number of anti-imperialists in the United States pointed to the breaking of the strike in Cuba as evidence of what militarism held in store for workers everywhere if American power became dominant.[51] Many trade unions in the United States agreed, and adopted resolutions condemning General Ludlow for breaking the strike. A mass meeting of trade unionists in Chicago demanded his immediate recall from Cuba. In his report to the U.S. government, Ludlow cited these protests against his strikebreaking policy as proof that the Cuban strikers had received "expert guidance from abroad." The greatest denunciation, he noted, came from "a labor organization in Chicago, showing how close was the connection between the two localities." He boasted that he had broken the general strike which he described as having been precipitated by "certain professional agitators" aided by subversive elements in the United States.[52]

The labor and socialist press in the United States was filled with denunciations of Ludlow's role. *The Carpenter*, organ of the Brotherhood of Carpenters and Joiners, protested that Ludlow's policy "struck at the fundamental rights of labor." The *Coast Seamen's Journal*, voice of the Sailors' Union of the Pacific, denounced Ludlow for having "deprived the Cuban workers of one of the basic principles for which they fought against Spain." The *Labor Advocate* of Oshkosh, Wisconsin asked, "Are not the workmen of Cuba free agents and can they not work when they will and be idle at their pleasure?" "Now, then, what in Hail Colombia is it Ludlow's business to stick his nose where it is not wanted."[53]

The People, official organ of the Socialist Labor Party, was even more vehement. It called Ludlow "a military tool of the capitalists" for having taken upon himself "to terrorize the Cuban workingmen into submission . . . to protect the American and incidentally, the few Cuban capitalists in their right to squeeze the life out of their wage slaves." Ludlow had, however, accomplished one good thing: by his action, he had, "brought out the true class character of the war [against Spain] and . . . made clear to the uninitiated what the socialists have maintained all along, that it was a war waged in order to bring strange people within the speedy grasp of the American capitalists."[54]

The Knights of Labor held President McKinley and his Administration responsible for the Ludlow policy. The President had not disavowed it nor had he reprimanded the General, although he was urged to do so by "prominent labor leaders." For that reason, the convention of the Knights of Labor, held in Boston, November 1899, resolved that workingmen should use their votes to defeat McKinley in the election of 1900.[55]

At the convention of the American Federation of Labor, held in Detroit, December 1899, the delegates applauded President Gompers for lashing out at the U.S. military authorities who had broken the strike in Cuba. Gompers declared in his presidential report to the convention that the Cuban workers had full justification for having sought "to secure some of the advantages resultant from modern civilization; that is, a reduction in the hours of daily toil," and they had "exercised their natural and legal right to cease work" when their request was denied by employers. He then condemned Ludlow's proclamation, describing it as "containing the most offensive and unjustifiable attacks and abuse of the workers who sought an amelioration in their conditions, and relief from burdensome toil." Ludlow, Gompers told the delegates, had even threatened to arrest the strike leaders if the workers did not immediately return to their jobs, and as a result, the general strike was broken. Gompers warned American workers not to make the mistake of thinking that events in Cuba did not concern them. "It is not difficult to imagine that it is but a step from military rule applied to Cuba to the territory constituting the present United States. We have already seen . . . the attempt made in the Coeur d'Alene district of Idaho and elsewhere."[56] Every American worker knew what the reference to Idaho meant. In the spring of 1899, federal troops had been called in to break a strike of the Western Federation of Miners at Coeur d'Alene.[57]

Gompers soon learned that he had underestimated General Ludlow's strikebreaking activity in Cuba. In February 1900, following an accident caused by a collision with a trolley car, Gompers went to Havana to recuperate. He decided to use the opportunity to investigate labor conditions, the labor movement, the rule of the military, and the full part General Ludlow had played in breaking the general strike. He soon discovered that he had been mistaken when he told the AFL convention that Ludlow had only threatened the leaders of the general strike with arrest. "I learned," he wrote in the *American Federationist* from Havana, "that they were not only 'threatened,' but really were arrested, and this too without any shadow of a cause or excuse. I have it upon the most reliable authority that there was no disorder, connected with the Havana 8-hour strike; that the employers who would have been compelled to yield to the just demands of the men successfully induced General Ludlow to arrest 'the leaders' of the strike."

Gompers reported that Pedro Roca, president of the Estivadores (Longshoremen's Union), was seized at his home by an armed guard, brought before General Ludlow and threatened with indefinite imprisonment unless he called off the strike. Roca argued that he had no authority to do so, but agreed to visit the imprisoned strike leaders and urge them to call off the strike. Under guard, Roca was taken to the jail where he consulted with the imprisoned men, and told them that unless they issued a manifesto recommending to the workers of Havana that they call the strike off, they would remain in prison "during the Governor's pleasure."[58]

Gompers also had interviews with Governor-General Leonard Wood and other American authorities for the purpose of protesting General Ludlow's actions. Later, he reported to the AFL convention: "Without at all attempting to take or attribute credit to ourselves or to anyone, it can be stated that within a few weeks General Ludlow was removed from his command as governor general of Havana."[59] Ludlow's office was abolished on May 1, 1900, and the General was later transferred to the Philippines. But his removal from Havana was due more to Wood's desire to get rid of Ludlow than to Gompers' influence, or to the part Ludlow played in the general strike. Hermann Hagedorn, Wood's biographer, notes that Ludlow acted independently and "followed Wood's lead with reluctance when he followed it at all."[60] Wood was not one to tolerate such conduct.

Gompers addressed several meetings of workers while he was in Havana, urging the need for organization along the lines of the AFL. He also reported that he had been instrumental in settling a strike of 14,000 cigar makers. The workers had walked out four weeks before Gompers' arrival on the island because of the refusal of their employers to promote Cuban cigar makers to positions of superintendents or foremen, filling these places with Spaniards. According to Gompers, he obtained an agreement from Gustavo Bock, representing the employers, that in the future there would be no discrimination against Cubans in employment as workers, apprentices or foremen. Thereupon, Gompers wrote, the cigar makers voted to end their strike and return to work.[61]

No Cuban historian of the labor movement in his country refers to this activity on Gompers' part.[62] Indeed, Rito Estaban, referring to Gompers' visit to Havana, writes: "Mr. Gompers . . . in conformity with his reactionary position, collaborated with North American imperialism, abandoning his duty, which should have been to aid in the liberation and complete independence of the Cuban people."[63] While Estaban ignored the fact that Gompers had spoken up in favor of an early end to the occupation of Cuba and the achievement of self-government by its people, he may have been referring to Gompers' statement from Havana: "There can be no doubt but that General Wood is regarded with favor in Cuba. It is believed that he is sympathetically inclined toward Cuban independence."[64] If there is one thing every Cuban patriot knew, it was that Wood was not regarded "with favor" by the friends of independence and that he was not "sympathetically" inclined towards Cuban self-government.[65]

Gompers' reputation really sank in Cuba when it was learned that he played an important part, together with the International Cigar Makers' Union (an AFL affiliate) and the cigar manufacturers of Tampa, Florida, in wrecking *La Sociedad de Torcedores de Tampa y Sus Cercanias.* Popularly known as *La Resistencia,* this trade union was formed by the cigar workers of Tampa who were mainly Cubans. When cigar workers in Havana sought to prevent scabs from leaving Cuba to break the strike called by *La Resistencia,* General Wood—the man Gompers so highly praised— jailed 150 of them.[66]

Wood also took action to break strikes in Cuba itself. When the stevedores, warehouse laborers, and sugar handlers at Cárdenas struck early in January 1901 for more wages and shorter hours, Wood sent two cavalry troops and justified this action with the announcement: "Unreasonable demands should not be acceded to. Acts of this kind are serious menaces to the commercial prosperity of the country. Every effort should be made to suppress demonstrations of this nature." To the commander of the cavalry troops, Wood wired: "Make every effort to bring outside workers and to resume business." Business was resumed with scabs, and the strike was broken.[67]

Wood's strikebreaking activities did not go unnoticed in the United States. *The People* denounced Wood for "following in the footsteps of Ludlow and the officials of Puerto Rico who imprisoned the labor agitators," as we shall describe in the next chapter.[68] The *National Labor Standard,* in an article entitled "Despotism in Cuba," accused Wood of acting to guarantee the profits of American and Cuban capitalists. This attack on the Cuban workers had to be denounced. "He [Wood] should be repudiated and his deposition and recall demanded. Therefore, the American Federation of Labor, the State Federations and all the local trade unions and reform associations throughout the United States should take prompt action against the infamous action of an infamous despot.[69]

Unfortunately, the AFL and its leadership remained silent. Gompers had been outspoken condemning Ludlow's policy as a strikebreaker, but he said nothing at all about the fact that Wood was pursuing the same policy. Indeed, following his return from Havana and for the duration of the American occupation, Gompers never mentioned Cuba again; neither in the *American Federationist,* which he edited, nor in his presidential address to the 1901 AFL convention did he refer to events on the island or American policy toward Cuba.[70] Perhaps, having assured the American workers that Wood was a friend of the Cuban labor movement, he was not anxious to eat his words in public. More likely, his return from Havana coincided with Gompers (and other AFL leaders) becoming closely associated with the National Civic Federation. Associating with Mark Hanna and with representatives of the House of Morgan, Gompers lost interest in combatting American imperialism, which was being promoted by the industrialists, financiers, and political leaders active in the National Civic Federation.[71]

Meanwhile, Wood's strikebreaking activities continued. When the laborers loading coal in tugs at Matanzas went on strike in February 1901 for higher wages and shorter hours,[72] Wood notified Colonel Noyes that the strikers were halting "military work, and nothing must be allowed to interfere with it." Colonel Noyes hired strikebreakers and boasted to Wood: "I have arrested the chief of the strikers for interfering with our laborers (the strikebreakers) this morning. Have notified the laborers union that I will release him if they promise no more interference." The union agreed; the strikebreakers continued to do the work of the strikers, and the strike ended in defeat.[73]

Beginning in February 1901, a series of strikes broke out among the workers constructing the Central Railway of the Cuban Company. The American workers received higher wages than the Cubans, and were paid in American money while the Cubans were paid in Spanish currency. When the Cubans protested, the company reported that it "cannot pay the Cuban Laborers the same wages as to the Americans because the former do not render the same work as the latter." At first when the Cuban and Spanish laborers walked out, the Americans continued working. But on March 10, at Santa Clara, Cuban, Spanish, and American laborers went on strike together, demanding payment for all workers of $1.00 per day in American money. On March 13, at General Wood's order the Rural Guard arrested 51 "Spanish, Cuban and American strikers."[74] These strikers spent several weeks in prison, but work stoppages continued. In July 1901, a call was issued from Ciego-de Avila in Sancti Spiritus for a general strike on the entire line. This time, in addition to payment of $1.00 a day in American money, the demand was for an eight-hour day instead of ten. At the request of R.G. Ward, manager of construction for the Cuban Company, the three men who had signed the call—José Rodríguez Lopez, Ramón Puertas, and Juan Rodríguez Martinez—were denounced by the American military authorities as "bandits," arrested by the Rural Guard, and imprisoned on the charge of mutiny. Ward demanded the most severe punishment for "[José] Rodríguez and his associates," warning that otherwise "we will have serious difficulties in this vicinity." His warning was heeded. Rodríguez, the chief leader of the railroad construction workers, was sentenced to eight years of penal servitude.[75]

All the strikebreaking actions during the Wood administration described above were public knowledge. But it was not known that as soon as Wood assumed office as Governor General, he had the "Sección Secreta" (Secret Section) of the Havana Police Department compile lists of "leaders of agitation" among workers and "leaders of the disturbing elements." These lists were kept for use in case it was necessary to move swiftly to cripple a strike. It is interesting to note that the men on these lists were also described as "bitterest to the Government of the Intervention."[76] When one considers the way strikers were dealt with during the Occupation, it is hardly surprising that militant Cuban labor leaders should have been bitter. José Rivero Muñiz concludes his study of the Cuban labor movement during the Occupation on the following note: "The state of misery of the majority of the proletariat at the end of the Occupation was depicted by the way in which it lived, dressed and fed itself. Working class families were housed in miserable dwellings and ate miserable food. The children were half nude, and many workers had no more to put on than their trousers and shirts. Their shoes were of the worst quality. The women were often clothed in sacks."[77]

Still the years of the Occupation had proved one thing: Cuban workers did not accept exploitation without protest. As the socialist *Daily People* put it: "The capitalists who thought that owing to centuries of Spanish rule the spirit of Cuban labor had been entirely broken, are much disappointed to find that the workers kick against the greater exploitation now imposed on them."[78]

The American military government did not withdraw from Cuba until the Cubans under duress accepted the Platt Amendment in June 1901. Formulated by Secretary of War Elihu Root, the amendment's provisions included clause 7 which read: "That the government of Cuba consents that the United States may exercise the right to intervene for the preservation of Cuban independence, the maintenance of a government adequate for the protection of life, property, and individual liberty. . . ."[79]

Leonard Wood, who had played a large part as Elihu Root's agent in forcing the Platt Amendment on the island, wrote on Oct. 28, 1901 in a letter to President Theodore Roosevelt: "There is, of course, no independence left Cuba under the Platt Amendment."[80] "This is not the Republic we fought for," Máximo Gómez, the great Dominican fighter for Cuban independence from Spain and commander-in-chief of the Cuban Liberating Army, almost wept in 1902. "It is not the absolute independence we dreamed about, but there is no gain in discussing it now. . . . What we must study with profound attention is the manner to save what remains of the redemptive Revolution."[81] Unfortunately, not too much remained, as we shall see.

With some notable exceptions, the Platt Amendment was either supported in the American labor press or totally ignored. In the former category the view of the *Railway Conductor* is most interesting. The labor paper conceded that the Platt Amendment "virtually provides an American protectorate," and was like "the farmer who fed his chicks with one kernel of corn to which was attached a string, so that the kernel while fed might still be considered as being in the farmer's possession." Yet the *Railway Conductor* believed it would be a mistake to leave Cuba an independent nation without any organic connection with the United States. For that would mean the United States would be abandoning the full advantages of possessing this island with "Its commercial value and its value as a strategic point in the time of war. . . . " Hence it suggested that the island be given statehood, as was proposed by Senator Morgan of Alabama, and which the *Railway Conductor* deemed an honorable suggestion."[82]

To the *National Labor Standard* the Platt Amendment symbolized a new and more subtle approach to imperialism. The *Standard* called attention to a speech by the leading Senate spokesperson for imperialism, Albert J. Beveridge of Indiana, in which he hailed the protectorate as "the most important development of national power since the constitution was adopted." Beveridge, noted the *National Labor*

Standard, had "let the cat out of the bag about what we may expect when we attain our full growth of imperialism." Eventually this policy would include "the grasping of Mexico and the other South American republics and possibly the whole of China and many other countries that the other great powers of the world may allow us to have." Hence, under the Platt Amendment, while Cuba now occupied a place in the American empire different from that of an outright colony like Puerto Rico, it was just as certainly a part of the "New American Empire."[83]

On May 20, 1902, the military government ceased and the Cuban republic commenced. But in less than five years the United States was back in Cuba. In the election of 1905, conservative President Tómas Estrada Palma, the U.S. candidate for that office, was accused of resorting to bribery, intimidation, and violence in assuring his re-election. When an uprising against his government started, Estrada Palma secretly urged Frank Steinhart, the American consul general in Havana, to ask President Roosevelt to dispatch two vessels immediately as Cuban government forces were unable to quell the rebellion. On September 8, 1906, Steinhart telegraphed Estrada Palma's request to the State Department at Washington.[84]

On September 28, Estrada Palma and his entire cabinet resigned. On the following day, William Howard Taft, Roosevelt's Secretary of War who had been sent to Cuba to prevent a successful rebellion, issued (with Roosevelt's approval) a proclamation of intervention, established a provisional government, and proclaimed himself provisional governor of Cuba. All this was justified by the Platt Amendment.[85]

On October 1, 1906, in an address before the opening exercises of the National University in Havana, Taft praised President Tómas Estrada Palma's administration because he had realized "the necessity" for bringing U.S. capital to Cuba and convincing capitalists outside the island of the conservative character of the Cuban government "in order that foreign capitalists might depend upon the security without which capital cannot come." This policy, so necessary for Cuba, had been interrupted by the rebellion against Estrada Palma. But it would be continued under U.S. occupation.[86]

It was continued, but not by Taft, for the Secretary of War did not stay long in Cuba. His position as provisional governor was filled by Charles A. Magoon, who has been ambassador to Panama, another U.S. semi-colony. Magoon's reign as Provisional Governor of Cuba lasted from October 13, 1906 to January 28, 1909.[87]

It was during the second military occupation of Cuba by the United States that Samuel Gompers made his second visit to the island. He came in January 1907 when, "suffering severely from neuralgia," he was advised by his physician to visit Cuba "and receive the benefit of the warm, sunshiny weather." Gompers used the opportunity to study the condition of labor under the second intervention by the United States. He reported privately that "the condition of the workmen of Havana had by no means improved. In fact, from the information which was conveyed to me, I had every reason to believe that notwithstanding [the fact that] the cost of living had increased tremendously, wages had remained stationary and had in several instances decreased."[88]

Publicly, however, Gompers said nothing, nor did the AFL. In fact, Gompers' only public comment was to express regret that his friend Estrada Palma had had to resign the presidency.[89]

But *The Worker*, official organ of the Socialist Party of America, published in New York City, did not remain silent. Under the new military occupation of Cuba, it predicted:

> Capital will rule in Cuba, as it already rules in the United States, but perhaps in Cuba with more crude brutality—until capitalism itself in Cuba has created and educated a revolutionary working class which will be able to join forces with the working class of this and all other lands in the long but ultimately victorious struggle for the emancipation of all the world from all class rule.[90]

In August 1908, the *International Socialist Review* reported that the Socialist Party of Cuba had been organized "a little over a year ago by Sr. Manuel Condoya, who was a leader of the cigarmakers in the recent strike."[91] This referred to the famous "Money Strike" (*Huelga de la Moneda*) of the cigarmakers, which lasted from February 22 to July 15, 1907, and ended in a victory for the strikers. The battle erupted over efforts of cigarworkers to end the practice of paying them in Spanish currency, and to pay them instead in the U.S. currency which would have meant a ten percent wage increase. Not only did the cigar factories, led by Henry Clay and Bock Company (the Trust), refuse this demand, but they locked out the workers.

For five months the strikers' ranks remained solid, and they received wide support from other workers who contributed part of their wages to the cigarmakers' strike fund. Support came also from the cigarworkers (and other workers) of Tampa, Florida, many of them originally from Cuba. In a letter to the leaders of the strike in Cuba, the committee in charge of mobilizing support for the Cuban strikers in Ybor City, Tampa, wrote on July 6, 1907:

Dear Comrades:

On July 3, we received a letter from you, and the receipt for the money order we sent last week, in the sum of 2,380 pesos (dollars). We are very grateful that our work has earned the approval of the committees.

We just went through a very bad week, for in addition to a number of firms closing down, almost all of the rest stopped production for one, two, or three days, with the excuse of the Fourth of July holiday, and that they had fulfilled their weekly production.

On Tuesday we held a meeting of the committee at which we studied the difficulty of the situation and how to save it. All agreed that they would impose from that same moment an active propaganda to make all the comrades understand the necessity of helping to continue the collection. On the following day, the day of the national holiday, a demonstration would take place, sponsored by this society, throughout Ybor City, Ellinger, and West Tampa, and that meetings would be held in those places.

For this occasion, several comrades prepared numerous placards and, moreover, the musical comrades lent the orchestra of Comrade Felipe Vazquez.

Well ahead of the agreed hour for the beginning of the demonstration, the surrounding streets of the Society of the Torch were crowded with comrades. Also several comrades rented cars, for which they paid out of their own pockets, and also brought kites and fly-wheels, pinwheels, which were distributed throughout the demonstration.

We began the march under the burning sun, meeting up with each other, and receiving on every hand, obvious signs of sympathy toward our cause.

Several meetings were held at which the necessity of saving the collection was emphasized, and at the end of the meeting, it was decided to send a telegram giving a description of the meeting (which you received).

On Sunday, the 5th, we held another meeting in West Tampa, which was well attended. In addition, during the whole week, we sent committees and manifestos to different shops, that were dedicated to the increase of the collection. The shop El Sidelo and the one of Leopoldo Powell met this week to hand over their collection to the committee in order to increase the amount that was going to be sent to you.

The letter closed: "Our work has not been useless in spite of the shut-down of the houses, and in spite of the loss of several days. The collection of this week has been one of the best in this locality, reaching the sum of 3,079 pesos (dollars) from which we send today by money order, 3,070 pesos(dollars), and in addition, we sent you another money order of 300 (dollars), which because it was a holiday on Thursday, we could not send until today. I assure you that by Tuesday, we will be able to send you at least 250 stef (dollars) and maybe also something on Thursday. As you see, the spirit of solidarity continues. The solidarity of the workers of Tampa will never abandon your cause. We hope for your approval of our actions."[92]

The strike ended in victory for the workers. Provisional Governor Magoon has been praised by several historians for standing by the workers during the strike and aiding them in winning their demand.[93] On the other hand, Cuban historians, if they mention Magoon's role at all, tend to minimize its significance, attributing it to his desire to make U.S. currency the standard for payment of wages in Cuba.[94] In his study, *The Politics of Intervention: The Military Occupation of Cuba*, Allan Reed Millett does point to Magoon's role in the strike, but he argues that he was motivated by two factors in siding with the strikers. First, he was anxious to avoid a repetition of the Ludlow strikebreaking activity in order to create a more favorable attitude toward the United States among Cuban workers, and second, he understood that the strikers could not be forced to call off the strike by intimidation, and that the support they were receiving from other workers, including those in Tampa, enabled them to hold out.[95]

Magoon's letters to the Secretary of War in the United States indicate that he was anxious to dissuade the Cuban workers from the belief that resistance to their demands was "the work of the American Government itself." He also believed that the demand of the cigarworkers to be paid in American currency was not only of value to the workers but would be of importance for the U.S. corporations seeking to invest in Cuba. "It is undoubtedly unnecessary," he wrote, "to present arguments to establish the proposition that a stable currency is essential to the full development of the country's trade and commerce. . . . Any country afflicted with an unstable currency ought to take steps to secure a stable currency. The only question is whether the country should take steps to secure a stable currency immediately, or to accomplish the desired change gradually."[96]

It seems that Governor Magoon was finally able to convince the Henry Clay and Bock Company (the Cigar Trust) and the independent cigar companies that their own economic future would be enhanced by a stable currency. In addition, the strikers were fixed in their determination to hold fast until they won their demand. It is not surprising then that on July 14, 1907 J.N. Staples, Jr. director of Henry Clay and Bock Company, wrote to Magoon:

> We fully appreciate the wisdom of the Governor's opinion, which we accept as a guide to the future stability of the monetary standard, the total benefits of which, it is pointed out, more than offset the total disadvantages of the change.
>
> We shall, therefore, open our cigar factories in Havana, Bejunal, Guanajay, Santiago de las Vegas, and Hoyo Colorado on Tuesday next, and shall pay wages in American money, to all the cigar makers employed therein, including as well those of the factory at the San Antonio de los Banos. . . .
>
> All employees of this company on February 22nd last, whose idleness was caused by the suspension of operations, may apply for their positions, and will be reinstated as soon as it is possible to provide work for them in approaching normal conditions.[97]

On July 21, 1907, 15,000 workers paraded through the streets of Havana celebrating the great victory of the cigarmakers.[98] In its August 1908 article on the Socialist Party of Cuba, the *International Socialist Review* noted that largely as as result of the long strike and the victory of the Cuban cigarworkers, the Socialist Party of Cuba had increased "from a small band of eight [8] . . . to about four thousand members." The party established *El Socialista* which it issued twice a week, and which, according to the *Review*, conducted most of its work "along educational lines."[99]

Millett points out that while Magoon may have been more friendly to Cuban labor during the cigarworkers' strike than Ludlow or Wood had been during labor struggles on the island during their administration, "the Provisional Government (during the Second Intervention) did nothing to alter permanently the basic conditions under which the Cubans worked, earned, bought and sold."[100] *El Socialista* had made the same point during the intervention, and in addition, charged that Magoon was implanting a system of corruption more blatant than the Cuban politicians had succeeded in doing during the first four years of so-called Republic. Public funds were finding their way into private pockets, and the penetration of U.S. capital in and domination of Cuba's economy was accelerating. The *botella* (sinecures) was being institutionalized—and jobs were being handed out to political or personal friends who collected salaries for doing little or no work. Boondoggling, bribery, nepotism, and outright robbery of public funds, *El Socialista* charged, were becoming hallmarks of the "Republic of Cuba under the Provisional Administration of the United States," the official name of the Military Occupation.

Among Magoon's questionable dealings, reported *El Socialista*, was beneficent handout to the Roman Catholic church, a necessary ally of American imperialism. Using Cuban funds, he gave the Church $1,387,083.75 as indemnification for property taken by the Spanish government during the 19th century. Spain, from 1861 on, had already paid the Church more than the value of the property, the equivalent of twenty million dollars. For this and other transactions, Magoon was awarded with the Order of Saint Gregory the Great by Pope Pius X.

By the time the military intervention was ended, a government apparatus had been created which Allan Reed Millett points out, "was a far handier tool for waste and oppression," and a permanent army established that served both the interests of American imperialism and unscrupulous Cuban politicians after the United States withdrew.

Looking at what had occurred in Cuba since 1902, *El Socialista* recalled the prophecy made by Juan Gualberto Gómez, the militant black opponent of the Platt Amendment. Cuba, Gomez had predicted, would have nothing better than "a shaky, miserable government, obliged to seek the good graces of the United States instead of serving and defending the interests of Cuba."

Gómez's prophecy, *El Socialista* concluded sadly, had been fulfilled.[101]

In 1901 the AFL engaged Santiago Iglesias Pantín, formerly of Spain and Cuba, as "General Organizer for Cuba and Puerto Rico." As we shall see in the next chapter, Iglesias spent nearly all of his time as an organizer for the AFL in Puerto Rico, and it was not until 1910 that he was asked to take any step to fulfill the first part of his commission. In that year Iglesias was instructed by the AFL Executive Council "to begin, if possible, an intelligent campaign to organize Cuban workers on behalf of the international labor organizations in accordance with the principles and practices of the national and international unions affiliated with the American Federation of Labor."

Iglesias thereupon corresponded with labor leaders in Cuba, informing them of his mission, pointing out that he had "spent 17 years in Havana and there I took the first steps in my present field of labor, but it is now several years since I have had no connection with your people and I would like to know something more." He was particularly anxious to learn if his effort to create a Cuban labor *Federation Libre* in Puerto Rico, would meet "with enthusiasm or indifference."

Iglesias never undertook his organizing mission. Cuban labor leaders dissuaded him from making the effort. As Iglesias explained to Frank Morrison, AFL Secretary, the Cuban labor leaders believed that Cuban workers were not too sympathetic to the "principles and practices" of many unions affiliated with the AFL because (1) they were not convinced that blacks would be permitted to join most of these unions;[102] (2) they had been alienated by the failure of the AFL and its president, Samuel Gompers, to support the struggles of Cuban workers to achieve real independence and a better standard of living; and (3) they had learned from the experience of Puerto Rican workers that affiliation with the AFL had not improved conditions for most workers on the island and had, instead, made them more and more dependent on U.S. political and economic control. Morrison forwarded the entire correspondence to the AFL Executive Council with the observation that "it gives a pretty good idea of the situation in Cuba and makes it clear that it would not be worth pursuing the matter any further."[103]

Let us now turn to the experience of the Puerto Rican workers that influenced the decision of the Cuban leaders.

· V ·

U.S. RULE IN PUERTO RICO

I n his book *Denial of Empire: The United States and Its Dependencies* (1962), Whitney Perkins writes: "When the United States went to war with Spain in Cuba, it could not consistently permit Spanish rule to rule unchallenged in nearby Puerto Rico."*[1] So Puerto Rico was conquered by U.S. military forces under the command of General Nelson Miles. Puerto Ricans were not permitted to govern their own island; instead, under the Treaty of Paris signed on December 10, 1898, Puerto Rico became part of the United States, and has remained a colonial possession of the United States since that year.

The typical justification for the annexation of Puerto Rico was that there never was a national independence movement on the island; that unlike the people of Cuba and the Philippines, Puerto Ricans did not participate in the fighting against Spain, and that the people of the island not only welcomed American soldiers but wanted Puerto Rico to become part of the United States.

Actually, the yearning for independence existed in Puerto Rico under Spanish colonial domination as it did in Cuba and the Philippines. Conspiracies to separate Puerto Rico from Spain and establish an independent nation occured in 1823, 1824,

---

*The proper Spanish name is Puerto Rico ("Rich Port"), but from the time of its conquest of the island in 1898 the United States used an incorrect, Americanized "Porto Rico." On April 21, 1900, the *New York Times* reported that it had "yielded to governmental compulsion, and now uses the spelling 'Porto Rico' when it has occasion to refer to our new possession. We are still firmly convinced that the form 'Puerto Rico' is, or rather was, the better of the two, but official action of such a definite and conclusive kind has been taken on the subject by Congress that continued resistance to the change would be useless, and therefore highly unwise." The spelling was finally corrected by an act of Congress in 1932.

and 1835, none of which succeeded. The 1835 conspiracy involved 1,500 civilians. It was followed three years later by another conspiracy which failed.[2]

The spiritual and organizational leader of the independence forces in the 1860s was Dr. Ramón Emeterio Betances. Betances, who earned a medical degree from the University Paris, devoted his life to the fight for independence and the abolition of slavery. Because of his political activities he was exiled to Spain in 1867. However, he managed to escape the colonial authorities and fled to St. Thomas and later to Santo Domingo, where he organized the greatest movement for independence in Puerto Rico: the uprising on September 23, 1868, known as *El Grito de Lares* (the Cry of Lares).[3]

Led by Manuel Rojas, the revolutionary army—400 strong— marched to Lares and took the town without meeting resistance.[4] The revolutionaries immediately established a provisional government and declared Puerto Rico a free and sovereign state. They decreed the abolition of slavery and an end to the infamous *libreta* or pass system, introduced in 1849, whereby anyone over the age of 15 who did not own some form of capital or belong to a profession was required to register with a local judge, who would then issue him a passbook which effectively bound him to his employer. Under this system, the worker's freedom of movement was severely limited, and his failure to obtain work was in effect penalized as a criminal offense. The system also made blacklisting of militant workers easy.[5] Little wonder that workers piled up hundreds of passbooks in the center of Laras Plaza and burned them.

Lares ended in defeat. But shortly after the uprising, the Spanish government did away with the passbook system, and still later, slavery was abolished. Spain, however, retained its rule over Puerto Rico.

El Grito de Laras was neither the first, nor the last, attempt by the Puerto Rican people to secure their independence from Spain. Uprisings occurred in 1873, 1874, 1875, and 1897. Meanwhile, a number of Puerto Ricans were active in the Cuban Revolutionary Party, founded by José Martí, the Cuban "Apostle," whose aim was the achievement of independence for both Cuba and Puerto Rico.[6]

The invasion of American troops in 1898 was welcomed at first by the independence forces, confident that the United States had come to bring independence to the island. A number of Puerto Ricans offered their services to General Miles, and a group aided the forces of Colonial Hullings. Betances, however, warned that "if the long-sought independence were not assured at once, Puerto Rico would remain forever an American colony."[7]

To prevent such a tragic outcome was the main aim of Eugenio Maria de Hostos, the great Puerto Rican sociologist, educator, political analyst, and juridical writer. Hostos was in Chile when the war broke out between the United States and Spain. He immediately left for the United States where, on August 2, 1898, at a meeting of the Puerto Rican section of the Cuban Revolutionary Party, he urged the unity of Puerto Ricans in facing the United States and seeking the best solution for the island's political future. With the dissolution at this meeting of the Puerto Rican section of the Cuban Revolutionary Party, Hostos created the Liga de Patriotas

Puertorriqueños with the same members as the dissolved group; they in turn elected him as president. Its publication *Estatatos* (Statutes) was begun, which circulated among the Spanish-speaking population of New York.[8]

Before the United States annexed Puerto Rico in 1898, Hostos had been a great admirer of the North American republic, viewing it, with its democratic principles, as redeeming the Caribbean from the despotic rule of Spain. But when the war was over and he saw the United States taking Spain's place in his country—coming not as a liberator, but as a colonial master—he wrote in fury:

> Puerto Rico has been annexed by an act of force. . . . The annexationist policy, the imposition of a foreign sovereignty over a people without their asking for it and even without consulting them was never conceived by the Puerto Ricans for a single moment. They imagined the purpose of the United States to be, first, a military blow at Spain; second, use the opportunity for putting an end to Spain's mismanagement in the Antilles, creating in our island a free and independent government.[9]

"We have to insist everyday," Hostos argued, "that Puerto Rico has been robbed of its own, of its national liberty, of its national dignity, of its national independence." On October 23, 1898, the Liga de Patriotas Puertorriqueños was established in Puerto Rico, itself, and requested a plebiscite in which the people could voice their desire for the independence of the island. However, as Hostos soon observed: "I Know that Puerto Ricans are scandalized when someone demands from the Americans the independence of their country."[10] Such Puerto Ricans joined forces with the United States in opposing independence. Realizing that the League he had founded could not achieve its goal, Hostos abandoned Puerto Rico, and joined his followers in Santo Domingo, where he died.

While he was in the United States, Hostos found little support for Puerto Rican independence even among the anti-imperialists who were concentrating their major attention on the Philippines.[11] Moreover, the American labor movement appeared to be indifferent to the annexation of Puerto Rico. At the AFL convention at Kansas City in the fall of 1898, no more was said than "Puerto Rico invaded as a war measure, with its semi-nude people, has been conquered and taken as a possession."[12]

A few trade unions did speak out for Puerto Rican independence. But they did not rely on the usual anti-imperialist argument, namely, the right of all people who desired independence to achieve it, for they accepted the thesis circulated by the U.S. imperialists that no Puerto Ricans aspired to independence. The Cigarmakers' International Union frankly said it opposed annexation of the island because it feared the effects of "cheap labor" on the jobs and wage standards of the mainland cigarmakers.[13] The Knights of Labor took the position that even though there did not appear to be evidence of a Puerto Rican desire for independence, American possession was proving to be so terrible for the islanders that they would be better off on their own. The *Journal of the Knights of Labor* pointed to the fact that the U.S.-Puerto Rican currency exchange rate had been changed; instead of being $1 for one peso, the rate was now 60 U.S. cents for one Puerto Rican peso. This change led to incalculable hardships for the poor, because their wages were cut to suit the new rate but the prices of food were not lowered. A laborer who had received 50 centavos in Puerto Rican coin now received 30 cents in U. S. money; however, rice—which had formerly cost him four centavos—now cost him four cents (when it was actually worth two and two-fifths U.S. cents under the new rate), as if the peso and the dollar were still equivalent.[14]

Another labor advocate of independence for Puerto Rico, the *National Labor Standard*, charged that the island's plight was due to the policy of the McKinley Administration towards Puerto Rico, a policy formulated by the interests of the Sugar and Tobacco trusts, rather than the needs of the islanders. This would continue to be the case, said the *Standard* so long as the island remained under U.S. domination. For it was the trusts, not the Puerto Ricans, that financed the politicians who formulated policies.[15]

In the main, however, American labor took the position that Puerto Rico was a permanent possession of the United States. For that very reason, the United States was morally obliged to extend all of the liberties and rights of American citizens to the Puerto Ricans as soon as possible. These rights included the right to organize into trade unions and to strike for higher wages, shorter hours, and better working conditions.

The American trade unions were forced to adopt this position whether they liked it or not. If only in self-defense, the unions had to take an interest in Puerto Rican workers, first, because if wages remained abysmally low in the island and its goods could be shipped tariff-free to the mainland, this would spell loss of work for men in the United States. Second, if Puerto Rican workers could not enjoy the right to organize and strike under the American flag, it would not be long before these rights would be jeopardized on the mainland. However, as we shall see, U.S. labor's interest in Puerto Rican labor was not consistent and varied from time to time.

For their part, Puerto Rican workers looked to the United States for aid of various kinds. They developed their own organizations and political parties, but felt the need for organic unity with American unions in the same fields, which could offer advice and both political and monetary help.

The need was indeed a desperate one!

The first Puerto Rican Census Report of the U.S. Department of Commerce and the War Department revealed the following figures for 1899: 62.9 percent of the employed persons on the island were occupied in agriculture; 28.8 percent in trade, transportation, communication, public service, professional services and domestic and personal service; and the remaining 8.4 percent in manufacturing and mechanical industries.[16]

In 1899 field workers earned from 35 cents to 50 cents a day; skilled field workers, from 60 to 75 cents a day. On the other hand, craftsmen in towns earned from $1.00 to $1.50 for eleven hours of work, but unskilled workers received 3 cents an hour, and had to work from sunup to sundown.[17] By way of comparison, labor in the U.S. earned at this time from 12 to 14 dollars a week. Moreover, as we have seen, Puerto Rican workers sustained a great loss in purchasing power in the currency shift from the peso to the American dollar.[18] Then again, while U.S. workers bought in local markets the goods that were often produced locally, Puerto Ricans paid for imported goods and so paid more.[19]

Even at these low wages the most that a Puerto Rican worker could expect in 1899 was about six months of steady work. In addition, plantation workers were paid in scrip—paper called "vales"—that were only valid at a company store where stale codfish and other staples were sold at triple the price of any other store.

Reporting for the U.S. Treasury Department in 1898, Commissioner Henry K. Carroll found poverty so widespread among the working class of Puerto Rico that most lived in shacks where "almost no furniture is visible," the vast majority were "small and thin and generally anaemic" since "more nourishing food can be said to be the universal need." Only 150,000 of the 900,000 inhabitants wore shoes regularly, and 50,000 irregularly, "leaving 700,000 belonging to the barefoot class."[20]

This terrible condition was made worse on August 8, 1899 by one of the most devastating hurricanes that ever hit the island. Thousands were left homeless and starving. To meet a disaster of such proportions Congress appropriated $200,000— to feed 950,000 stricken people—until a new crop of bananas and other foods could be grown.[21] "Twenty cents to feed a human being for six months," exclaim historians Bailey and Justine Diffie. "The attitude of American people toward Puerto Rican interests was clearly defined."[22] The *Journal of the Knights of Labor* featured a report from the island describing that "in a number of districts the people are actually starving," and that "utterly heartsick, the people gather at the wharves, gaze out on the water and beg ship owners to take them anywhere." Many were leaving for Hawaii, Cuba, Santo Domingo, other islands, and Ecuador. "If this be the fruits of American sovereignty," thundered the official organ of the Knights of Labor, "it does not appear that people have gained much by a change of political masters. They could not have been in worse plight under Spanish rule."[23]

On August 12, 1898, fighting stopped on the island and General Miles established a U.S. military government which continued until the Foraker Act, providing a form of civil government for Puerto Rico, was passed on April 12, 1900. The Act excluded the Puerto Ricans from citizenship in the country under whose flag they were now forced to live, and left them with very little voice in government. It provided for two houses which would constitute a "legislative assembly." One was a "house of delegates" to be elected by the qualified voters of Puerto Rico (property-holders). The other was an executive council composed of 11 members and the Governor. All 12 members were to be appointed by the President of the United States and only five of them had to be Puerto Ricans. As for the others, they merely had to reside in Puerto Rico during their term of office. Six members of the presidentially appointed executive council also functioned as heads of executive departments, and until 1914, all six men appointed to those dual posts were non-Puerto Ricans.

We can understand why so little power was left in the hands of the Puerto Ricans when we realize that the real author of the Foraker Act was Elihu Root, who, as we have seen, was also the author of the Platt Amendment.[24] In 1899, then Secretary of War Root expressed his view of Puerto Ricans when he wrote:

> Before the people of Porto Rico can be fully entrusted with self-government they must first learn the lesson of self-control and respect for the principles of constitutional government, which requires acceptance of its peaceful decisions. This lesson will necessarily be slowly learned. Under the "strong and guiding hand" of the United States, the Porto Ricans might yet prove to be entitled to become "a self-governing people."[25]

However, by the time that the Puerto Ricans could become "a self-governing people" in the new American empire, they would find their economic resources gobbled up by American capitalists. For under the Root-authorized Foraker Act, the non-elected executive council had the sole power to make "all grants of franchises, rights and privileges or concessions, of a public or quasi-public nature. . . ."[26] As Earl King Senff points out in "Puerto Rico under American rule": "When the Foraker Act was passed it was clearly the 'green light' for some Americans, who interpreted the passage of this bill as opportunity for American industrial and economic expansion in Puerto Rico. In a short time, American capital began to find its way into Puerto Rico through investments, the purchase of land, and various business channels."[27]

Indeed, the U.S. Consul General in San Juan reported that immediately after passage of the Foraker Act, his office was deluged with thousands of letters from businessmen on the mainland, asking about establishing factories in Puerto Rico and expressing their desire to "teach the people there, who have been accustomed to labor at very low wages, to labor in the factories that we shall establish." A major reason for this interest was that the businessmen had heard of the island people that "they are not a class of people acquainted with strikes. . . ."[28] Governor William H. Hunt publicized this statement, and warned the Puerto Rican workers that they had better be submissive, for "capitalists are cautious and seldom invest unless they know that the citizens of the land are quiet, obedient to the law, and in sympathy with development. Unrest, discontent, agitation, turbulence gain nothing, but they do postpone the growth which capital will insure."[29]

There was a good reason for Governor Hunt's warning. Puerto Rican workers were proving that reports of their docility were false!

On February 28, 1899, the *New York Herald* published an Associated Press dispatch from San Juan, reporting that 500 laborers working on the highways from Ponce to Adjuntas, had gone on strike on February 26. They marched into the town of Adjuntas with placards reading: "We, the workers, demand five cents an hour." The workers elected a committee that went to the highway contractors to discuss a raise from three to five cents an hour for a ten-hour day. The *New York Herald* headlined the dispatch: "First Great Strike in Porto Rico."

Actually there had been some strikes in Puerto Rico before, but they were sporadic and difficult to maintain in the face of the Spanish colonial version of the "conspiracy doctrine," which held it a crime to attempt collectively to raise the "price" of labor.

Labor activity during the Spanish regime was mainly concentrated in local associations and mutual-aid societies. Not until 1897 did a movement begin that was to create the first national union. Ramón Romero, a printer, with José Ferrer y Ferrer (another printer) and Fernando Gómez Acosta (a carpenter), founded the weekly *Ensayo Obrero* in which they openly stated the need to transform society, and, as a prerequisite to this transformation, to found a union of all the workers.

The slogan of the labor weekly, *Ensayo Obrero*, was "No Fatherland But the Workshop, No Religion But Work," revealing how much these early labor leaders were imbued with the ideas (mainly anarchist) of European workers of the period.[30] It was this group that Santiago Iglesias Pantín joined on his arrival in San Juan. Born in Coruña, Spain in 1872, Iglesias had been a labor activist in Cuba for a decade before going into exile in Puerto Rico.* Strikes had taken place before 1896, and groups of urban handicraftsmen—printers, tinsmiths, carpenters, cigar makers, painters, shoemakers, and others—had secretly been reading anarcho-syndicalist and other radical ideas, brought in from Europe long before 1896. Copies of publications of Puerto Rican artisan groups dating as far back as 1873 have been discovered by students of the labor movement.[31]

In any event, soon after Iglesias' arrival in Puerto Rico, the more militant artisans of San Juan began to organize. Study circles were founded, and, in May 1897, as we have seen, the radical labor weekly *Ensayo Obrero* was issued. On June 1, 1897, the foundation was laid for the establishment of a regional federation of workers. However, the authorities began to crack down, and the Church warned the workers to turn deaf ears to those who spoke of labor's rights, and to remember that "the owner is at one and the same time the king, the priest, the Emperor, and the pastor of the laboring man."[32]

An order for the detention of Santiago Iglesias went out on March 26, 1898, and when he attempted to flee the island, he was captured and imprisoned outside San Juan by the Spanish authorities. He was released by the Spaniards after seven months, on October 5, 1898, when U.S. army units approached San Juan from the other side of the island.[33]

Having returned to San Juan with the U.S. military contingent, Iglesias launched *Porvenir Social* (Social Future) with a group of colleagues on October 23, 1898, less than a week after the beginning of the 28-month military occupation by the United

---

*Angel Quintero Rivera, a critic of the "great-man view" of labor history, criticizes the tendency of writers on Puerto Rican working class history who assert that "the labor movement began in Puerto Rico because Santiago Iglesias Pantín arrived on the island; that the movement took a trade-unionist position because of his relations with North American unions." (*Workers' Struggle in Puerto Rico,* 1976, p. 19.) Other Puerto Rican scholars are critical of the fact that many writers on the history of the island also emphasize that not until the United States took possession of the island could a labor movement develop. See, for example, Turnbull White, *Puerto Rico and Its People* (New York: 1938), p. 73, for the view that only under American rule could a labor movement flourish in Puerto Rico. In an interview in *Noticias de Trabajo,* July-August 1967, Puerto Rican historian Lido Cruz Monclova tells of having found references to more than forty strikes before 1896 by "coachmen, furniture makers, bargemen, laundry workers, printers," among others.

States. That same week the *Federación Regional los Trabajadores de Puerto Rico* was established, and the founders swore to continue struggling "until the complete emancipation of the proletariat is achieved."[34]

Internal conflict over the degree of association with political parties led Iglesias and his followers to leave the *Federación Regional* and found the *Federación Libre de Los Trabajadores de Puerto Rico* (Free Federation of Puerto Rican Workers), which had representatives of unions of construction workers, carpenters, painters, seamen, longshoremen, construction helpers, iron workers, food and drink workers, printers, tobacco workers, and general workers. Two rooms at 10 San Sebastian Street in San Juan served as headquarters for the Federation's organ, *Povenir Social*.[35]

May Day was celebrated for the first time in Puerto Rico on May 1, 1899. It was organized by the Federation Regional, and was mainly the work of the Regional Federation Social Study group, which acted as a sort of disciplined ideological vanguard of the first federation of Puerto Rican workers. The celebration took place in the Municipal Theatre in San Juan, and among the speakers were Santiago Iglesias, Estanislao Sherman, and José Rivera. That same evening a cultural celebration took place in front of the headquarters of the Regional Federation.[36]

On August 27, 1899, *The People*, official organ of the Socialist Labor Party, published in New York, carried on its front page the text of a letter addressed to Henry Kuhn, SLP National Secretary, signed by Santiago Iglesias and 300 members of the Socialist Labor Party of Puerto Rico for three sections: Arecibo, Río Pedra, and Bayamón.[37] The letter explained that the signers were applying for membership in the SLP, and that they represented unions of carpenters, cigarmakers, masons and bricklayers, compositors, painters, blacksmiths and sailors and seamen, stevedores, cooks, laundrymen, and miscellaneous trades. "We wish to say," the letter concluded, "that our propaganda is very active. We hold frequent meetings and they result in favor of our ideas. The workingmen are being rapidly converted, and they join the Socialist Labor Party in good faith."[38]

The applications for admission were granted, and the three Puerto Rican sections of the SLP were officially charted. However, the SLP reported at its convention in June 1900 that it never received further word from the sections even though "report blanks and letters were sent. . . ."[39] The reason seems to be that Iglesias and other SLP leaders in Puerto Rico had decided to join the anti-De Leon faction of the SLP in the U.S., and they ceased all contacts with *The People* and the New York group controlled by De Leon.[40] When Iglesias and Eduardo Conde were sent to New York by the SLP of Puerto Rico, they did not visit the office of *The People* or contact De Leon. Instead, they met with Julius Gerber, Henry Slobodin, and Morris Hillquit, leaders of the anti-De Leon faction in the SLP.[41]

Iglesias and Conde had come to New York to seek support for Puerto Rican workers, and they publicized the fact that "the working class of the island had been reduced by reason of war, the hurricane and the action of this U.S. government since the storm, to a condition of extreme destitution." Indeed, 600,000 to 1,000,000 inhabitants were absolute paupers, and riots were inevitable unless something was done quickly to improve their conditions. Iglesias urged American labor to demand that the United States government make radical changes in its administrations of Puerto Rico when the military occupation ended. Specifically, three ordinances adopted during the military occupation should be annulled:

(1) That which fixed the wages on public works at "25 cents per day for eight hours work"
(2) That which restricted the voting privileges to literate property holders
(3) The levy of a $1.00 poll tax[42]

Nothing was said about independence for Puerto Rico.

Encouraged by the anti-De Leon socialists, Iglesias and Conde went on to Rochester, New York where they attended the convention of the Bricklayers and Masons and appealed for aid for Puerto Rican workers and for the admission of the bricklayers and masons in the island as members of the international union.[43] The two emissaries gained the support of the *National Labor Standard* and the *Bricklayer and Mason.* The *Standard* described the American administration in Puerto Rico as "pure and simple capitalistic spoliation," and urged the trade unions on the mainland to stop avoiding the Puerto Rican labor movement and begin helping it solve their pressing problems, if not in the interest of the Puerto Ricans, at least in their own interests. The *Bricklayer and Mason* agreed, and supported the appeal of the Puerto Ricans: "Since these countries have become ours, their workingmen are ours, and are entitled to the fraternal consideration of the trade unions."[44]

Unfortunately, Iglesias and Conde returned to Puerto Rico empty-handed. Not even a touching appeal from Iglesias indicating how joyful the bricklayers and masons in Puerto Rico were when they heard there was a chance they might be accepted into the international union, produced results. It would seem that fear of initiating a body of black Puerto Rican craftsmen was too much for the Bricklayers' and Masons' Union. While the union did not bar blacks constitutionally or in its ritual, it treated them as second-class union members and was not at all anxious to increase their numbers.[45]

Unable to obtain solid support from trade unions on the mainland, the Puerto Rican labor movement decided to act on its own. On July 8, 1900, determined to demand wages that had their value in purchasing power, the *Federación Libre* presented employers with wage scales which would accomplish this objective. In addition, it demanded adoption of the eight-hour day. The demands were promptly rejected; indeed, the employers refused even to meet with the Federation's arbitration committee. Thereupon the first general strike in Puerto Rico history began.[46]

It took great courage for the workers to go out on a general strike. In April 1900, U.S. troops had been used to suppress a dock strike when strikers and their sympathizers fought against the importation of strike-breakers from St. Thomas and St. Kitts. The municipal police stood by, "as spectators," while a company of U.S. infantry arrested the strike leaders, and, operating under martial law, broke the strike.[47] But this did not deter the Puerto Rican workers when they decided to go out in general strike to end the miserable wage system in operation under U.S. occupation.

Immediately, U.S. military authorities arrested Iglesias and over a hundred officers of the different unions and threw them into prison. The imprisoned unionists appealed to various labor groups in the United States to intercede for them at Washington. In his appeal, Iglesias insisted that the Puerto Rican labor movement was being persecuted with the same arguments and techniques as those used against American workers. The American occupation authorities had openly accused the labor movement of Puerto Rico of consisting of "revolutionists" and "anarchists," just as the open-shop enemies of labor were doing on the mainland. They even accused the Puerto Rican workers of disrespect for the American flag.[48] In other words, the economic activities of the Puerto Rican workingmen were made to appear treasonable. If employers on the island got away with this, with the aid of the military authorities, they would next go after the unions on the mainland and accuse them, too, of treason. All the more reason, therefore, why the American trade unions should help the Puerto Rican workers in their hour of peril and tribulation.[49]

This appeal brought only a limited response. The *Typographical Journal* publicized the plight of the strikers in Puerto Rico, and urged the "organized workmen of this country . . . to appeal to the administration at Washington to obtain the release of Porto Rican labor officials and relief from further persecution." But only the New York Central Federated Union appears to have acted, voting to send contributions to the strikers and to urge President McKinley to intercede on behalf of the imprisoned unionists. Otherwise labor on the mainland appeared to be indifferent.[50]

The general strike ended in what the *Bricklayer and Mason* called "an honorable arrangement."[51] But it hardly seemed that to Puerto Rican workers. There were moderate wage increases, but a number of trade union leaders were kept in jail and the others subject to re-arrest. All were to be tried on the charge of having violated the old conspiracy law of the Spanish colonial period, which made it a crime to conspire to raise the price of labor—a law still in full force under the U.S. occupation.[52]

Blacklisted, set upon by anti-labor goon squads, unable to find work in his craft as a carpenter, Santiago Iglesias left Puerto Rico and moved temporarily to New York City. He went to work as a carpenter in Brooklyn, joined the Brotherhood of Carpenters and Joiners, and attended night classes at Cooper Union where he learned English. In his spare time he addressed some sympathetic union meetings calling for workers in the United States to assist the efforts of Puerto Ricans to improve their living standards.[53] Meanwhile, Iglesias continued his relations with anti-De Leon SLP'ers, and was advised by them to contact the AFL in Louisville where it was in convention.

Late in 1900, in a letter (translated from the Spanish by a Socialist friend), Iglesias appealed to the AFL convention on behalf of the workers of Puerto Rico who were being "kicked and cuffed and imprisoned without any cause whatsoever." The workers did not mind being under American law, he assured the AFL, but they did want "just and equal treatment." Specifically, Iglesias asked for AFL help along two lines:

(1) Pressure on public authorities to extend to Puerto Rico a fuller measure of freedom of assembly, freedom of speech, and freedom of the press

(2) An AFL commission that would go to Puerto Rico to investigate conditions on the island and help organize the workers[54]

A special convention committee on Puerto Rico studied the request, and recommended to the delegates the establishment of a special Puerto Rican fund to be obtained through a penny-per-capita levy on the entire membership. But so much money was needed for organizing at home that opposition greeted this proposal. After considerable debate, the convention authorized the expenditure of $3,000 to facilitate an organizational effort on the island. The convention also pledged its assistance in securing the right of fair trial, as well as freedom of assembly, speech, and press for the workers of Puerto Rico. While no action was taken on the question of sending a commission to the island, the decision of the convention at least indicated interest in the plight and problems of Puerto Rican workers.[55]

After the convention, a correspondence began between Samuel Gompers and Santiago Iglesias. Gompers asked Iglesias: "Are you a worker?" and "Are you a member of a union in your trade, that is, if such a union exists?"[56] (Clearly, the AFL president knew very little of the labor situation in Puerto Rico.) Learning that Iglesias was not only a trade unionist, but a socialist as well, Gompers decided to invite him to AFL headquarters in Washington for a series of briefings. During the discussions, Gompers did not ask Iglesias to abandon connections with the socialist political movement—such a step, he knew, would have been fatal to Iglesias' influence among Puerto Rican workers—but he made it clear to the Puerto Rican that the trade union movement in the United States believed in and practiced "pure and simple" trade unionism, and rejected socialist practices. Iglesias was quick to learn that if he wanted AFL support, he, too should play down his socialist ideas and move toward "pure and simple" trade unionism.[57] "Thereafter," writes William G. Whittaker, "Santiago Iglesias would be Gompers' confidential advisor on Caribbean affairs."[58]

In 1901, the AFL took steps to organize Puerto Rican workers. First, it arranged for the translation of union material into Spanish. Then, in September, the Executive Council engaged Iglesias to return to Puerto Rico as a representative of the American Federation of Labor, with the title of "General Organizer for Cuba and Puerto Rico." The AFL gave him the $3,000 (a considerable sum in those days) as authorized at its convention and issued a charter to be presented when the unions complied with AFL regulations.[59] In a letter to Iglesias, October 1, 1901, Gompers instructed him "to organize new unions and attach them to the national and international unions of their respective trades."[60]

Iglesias returned to Washington in early October for further briefings at AFL headquarters. On October 14, Gompers took him to the White House for an interview with President Theodore Roosevelt. The AFL president informed Roosevelt of Iglesias' projected mission, and assured him that the Federation's representative would work purely along trade union lines, and not engage in political activity, especially agitation for independence. At Gompers' suggestion, Roosevelt dictated a letter to Governor William H. Hunt in San Juan introducing Iglesias and asking that he not be molested by insular officials so long as he conformed with the laws of Puerto Rico and the United States.[61]

That same day Gompers himself sent a personal letter to Governor Hunt in which he introduced Iglesias as "the representative of the American Federation of Labor in Porto Rico . . . whose mission is to endeavor to organize the working people of the island in trade unions, and to have them affiliated to the American trade union movement under the auspices of the American Federation of Labor," As with Roosevelt, Gompers emphasized Iglesias' trade union role, pointing out:

> It may be well to say that the mission is no way political or partisan. Inasmuch as the Porto Rican people are now so closely allied with us, have interest and mission in common, it is believed that an effort should be made to organize the wage earners of the island, upon the rational and progressive basis of trade unions, the same as have been formed and are conducted in the United States.[62]

In a private letter to Iglesias, Gompers warned him to remain strictly within the bounds of what "You and I understand your mission to be." Iglesias was entrusted with a charter for the *Federación Libre*, "to be presented to the organization provided you are fully satisfied that the same is organized in compliance with the laws and policy of the American Federation of Labor."[63] To make sure that Iglesias did not stray from this specific mission, he was instructed to report to AFL headquarters not less than once a week—and in English. Clearly Gompers was doing everything he could to prevent Iglesias from yielding to the militant, nationalistic, socialist forces among Puerto Rican workers.

On November 11, 1901, Gompers again visited President Roosevelt in the White House, this time bringing with him a cable he had received from Iglesias. It read: "Was arrested when stepped ashore. No warrant was shown. Ignored [ignorant] charges. Remain in jail." Roosevelt cabled Governor Hunt in San Juan for an explanation while Gompers cabled Iglesias.[64]

It turned out that the arrest stemmed from the previous arrest during the general strike in the summer of 1900 when Iglesias, Eduardo Conde, and six others had been arrested and charged with conspiracy to raise the price of labor. On several occasions the trial had been postponed while the arrested labor leaders were blacklisted and remained unemployed. Finally, as we have seen, Iglesias was then arrested on his return to San Juan and charged with failure to appear in court and involvement in the conspiracy to raise the price of labor.[65]

Bail was posted at $2,000 in cash, a sum much too great for Iglesias to obtain locally. When he appealed to Hunt, the governor turned the matter over to the insular Attorney General James Harlan, recommending that the amount of bail be reduced. The Governor then left for Washington for consultation and a rest.[66]

While in jail, Iglesias gained the support of the influential *San Juan News* (a daily paper published in English and Spanish, which had a circulation greater than that of its seven competitors combined). The reason for this confirms once again the compromises that Iglesias would make, given the conditions that he faced. At first the *News* denounced Iglesias as "an agitator whose teachings were incendiary, resulting frequently in riots and bloodshed," and then advised the labor leader on how to conduct himself:

> It is a dangerous thing to have such a large number of ignorant laborers, under the tutorship of a man like Iglesias. If the labor leader should reform his methods, and council order, instead of disorder, he could be a great service, both to his country and his laborers.[67]

Interviewed in prison by a reporter for the *News*, Iglesias assured the paper that his mission had "nothing at all to do with politics and that he is peaceably inclined."[68] He followed this up with a letter to the *News*, published the next day, in which Iglesias declared that "my mission was always one of peace, of love and fraternity; never, at no time, one of riot and criminal deeds." He then emphasized: "My mission is most eminently American, for the organization of the working people, for their education, and for their liberty. . . . To unite them to the American Federation of Labor."[69]

Editorially, the *News* praised the "conservative and rational tone" of Iglesias' letter, urged him to use his influence "for the uplifting, enlightening and education of the laboring class," and appealed that he no longer be imprisoned upon "any trumped up charge." For the moment, the *News* called for reduction of the bail which, it declared, "seems excessive, especially if the contempt of court was unintentional."[70]

Although bail was reduced to $500 cash, it was still too much for Iglesias to raise, and an appeal was made to AFL headquarters. Even though Gompers was annoyed that Iglesias had not told him about having left the island before his trial, and felt that his arrest for breaking his parole was justified, he wanted to challenge the conspiracy law which was the basis for the original charge against him. He therefore appealed to the AFL Executive Council, reminding that body that Iglesias "went to Porto Rico as a representative of the American Federation of Labor and it seems to me that we are duty bound to make arrangements for bail for him pending his trial. . . ."[71]

The money was raised, and dispatched to Sidney S. McKee, city editor of the *San Juan News*, who "acted as Gompers' agent. . . ."[72] Iglesias was released on bail. He immediately began addressing meetings of unions, urging them to affiliate with the AFL and emphasizing that they should do so "with the object of mutually protecting ourselves and to improve our conditions and acquire gradually, the immense progress of the American organizations."[73]

On December 6, 1901, at a meeting attended by over 400 workers, the *Federación Libre* voted to affiliate with the AFL, and Iglesias presented the body with its charter. He urged the Federation and its affiliated unions to uphold the "pure and simple trade unionism" of the AFL, and Leo S. Rowe, chairman of the Puerto Rican Code Commission, who was then in San Juan, noted the "surprisingly conservative spirit" manifested by Iglesias and other labor leaders who worked closely with him.[74]

But neither the capitalists nor the authorities were impressed. On December 12, 1901, the District Court of San Juan found Iglesias and his colleagues guilty of conspiracy to raise the price of labor. Iglesias was sentenced to serve three years, four months and eight days in prison while his colleagues were sentenced to lesser terms in jail. The *Federación Libre* was ordered dissolved.[75]

In the United States, the events in Puerto Rico had been noted, and commented upon. Even before Iglesias had been arrested, the unity convention which founded the Socialist Party of America in July 1901,* protested the "shameful and disgraceful manner" in which "the organized workingmen or Porto Rico and especially the Socialists," were persecuted by the "political and military tools" of the Republican administration and American capitalists. Organized labor was urged "to assist our struggling workers of Porto Rico and to call a halt to the brutalities and crimes committed . . . against the wage workers of the island." The AFL in particular, was called upon "to assist in the trades union organization of the working people of the Island of Porto Rico, for the organization of labor will be their only salvation."[76]

The AFL was in convention at Scranton, Pennsylvania when news of Iglesias' conviction broke. The delegates, "indignant" and protesting vigorously, instructed Gompers and the Executive Council to use every means at their disposal to secure a reversal in the Iglesias case and the repeal of the conspiracy statutes.[77] Protests from central labor councils of New York and Washington followed, and the Columbia Typographical Union (District of Columbia) denounced the conspiracy code as "a relic of Spanish tyranny."[78] E.A.M. Lawson, the union's president, presented a personal protest to President Roosevelt during an interview at the White House. Even the conservative *New York Evening Post* agreed with this estimate:

If we have annexed a lot of barbarous medieval statutes, which deprive men of liberty for the exercise of natural rights to improve their condition—men who are under our flag and entitled to claim the advantages of our civilization—those statutes must be stamped out like yellow fever or any other tropical plague.[79]

Iglesias was released under bail with permission to go to Washington, where he met with Gompers and President Roosevelt. After hearing the facts in the case, the Chief Executive wrote a letter to Governor Hunt in Puerto Rico urging repeal of the old Spanish law. In his own letter to Hunt, Gompers urged him to pardon Iglesias and to call a special session of the General Assembly to revise the law code and the judicial system of Puerto Rico.[80]

Hunt did not pardon Iglesias, but he did recommend to the legislature that the code be changed to legalize all organizations of labor formed to regulate wages, hours of work, and conditions of employment, and not have them regarded as

*For the formation of the Socialist Party of America, see Foner, *History of the Labor Movement in the United States*, 2: 388–406. All of the SLP sections in Puerto Rico affiliated with the Socialist Party of America, as did Santiago Iglesias himself. Iglesias, *Luchas Emancipadores* 1: 488–92.

conspiracies in restraint of trade. "There is no room for lawlessness in Porto Rico," he insisted, "but the right to organize to secure better wages by peaceable measures is perfectly lawful and consistent with good government." He noted that "ambition to better one's condition is intensely American and oftentimes only gratified through organized effort, and where the purpose of an organization is merely to increase the profit of labor or dignify its worth, through peaceful ways, a law which is susceptible of a construction forbidding the execution of such a purpose is unworthy of an American government and should be abrogated."[81]

On March 1, 1902, the Puerto Rican legislature repealed the Spanish laws and authorized trade assemblies or unions to organize for the purpose of increasing wages and improving working conditions. However, it was unlawful, the Statute stated, for such associations to employ force or violence in attempting to obtain their objectives.[82]

On April 9, 1902, James S. Harlan, Attorney General of Puerto Rico, expressed the opinion that labor societies were not unlawful and that the concerted acts of workers, going back to 1842 in the case of Commonwealth *v.* Hunt, could not be considered conspiracies.* Harlan stated further that according to the revised laws of Puerto Rico (1902), workers now had the right to assemble in an association, but that such a right did not set aside the principle that violence should be repressed on all occasions.[83] On the basis of these revised codes, on April 15, 1902, the Supreme Court of Puerto Rico overturned the sentence of the lower court, and Iglesias and his colleagues were granted their freedom. The *Federación Libre* was permitted to function legally.[84]

The next day, delegations of unions affiliated with the *Federación Libre*, each preceded by a band and carrying banners, paraded through the streets of San Juan. The celebration ended with joyful mass meeting at the Federation's offices.[85]

But it soon emerged that there was not as much to celebrate as had been expected. To be sure, with the repeal of the Spanish conspiracy law, labor in Puerto Rico now had the right to organize and strike to attain its objectives. Employers, however, did not sit idly by and accept these developments. They reacted by organizing goon squads known as "Las Tubas" or "the mob."[86] Sponsored by the large land owners of the old regime and the new capitalists from the United States, the organization had the specific purpose of nullifying the new status of labor.[87] "Reign of Terror. Public Authorities Sanction Attacks on Trade Unionists and Socialists by Capitalists' Hired Thugs," was the headline in *The Worker,* the socialist weekly published in New York. The paper carried a dispatch from Puerto Rico reporting that "a band of outlaws, organized under the name of Las Tubas, is being used to terrorize the trade unionists and Socialists and to compel them to disband their organizations." What the employers had not been able to accomplish by the conspiracy doctrine, once the law was repealed, they achieved by sheer terror![88]

---

*In the case of Commonwealth *v.* Hunt, Chief Justice Shaw of Massachusetts delivered an opinion in which for the first time the right of workingmen to organize and bargain collectively was judicially recognized. See Foner, *History of the Labor Movement in the United States,* 1: 162–65.

Puerto Rican labor appealed to local governments for relief from physical attacks made on militant workers; but then accused the police, the courts of justice, even high officials in government of supporting the terror.[89] Appeals to the Governor were dismissed, and when the complaints mounted, he merely ordered the police to be vigilant in maintaining order, and left execution of such orders to them. Since police wages were extremely low, employers had little difficulty in bribing them to ignore "the mob." Puerto Rican labor thus could not depend upon the police, the courts, or the legislature for justice, since all were dominated by either the old Spanish or the new American capitalist order, and often by both.[90]

By the beginning of 1904, the reign of terror unleashed by the former Spanish landowners and the new mainland capitalists had reached such heights that Gompers was urged to visit the island and see the results for himself. In February, Gompers made his first trip to Puerto Rico, visiting nearly every city and important town. He published two reports in the *American Federationist* recounting what he had found on the island. The results of American rule were shocking, Gompers reported. He had seen men working in the sugar refineries 15 and 16 hours a day for 30 or 50 cents, women working in coffee houses 10 and 12 hours for 15 to 20 cents; myriad of workless men; the small dark rooms of their homes often housing eight or more persons, without facilities to let in air or light except through the open door; workmen paid in tokens that had to be redeemed at company stores, where prices were 20 to 30 per cent higher than in the open market for inferior goods, resulting in indebtedness and peonage.

Gompers mentioned the terror against workers, inspired by the employers, and other difficulties in the way of improving living standards. He concluded: "I have seen more ragged men and women and children in Porto Rico than I have seen in my whole life; I have seen more squalor, more degradation, and more poverty, hunger and misery stamped upon the faces of men and women and children in Porto Rico than I have ever seen in my whole life, and I pray and hope I may never see the like again."[91]

In the spring of 1905, determined to improve their abominable conditions, the agricultural laborers working on the sugar plantations of the Southern provinces appealed to the *Federación Libre* for assistance. The Federation agreed to help, and demands were presented to the planters for seventy-five cents for a nine-hour day and the abolition of child labor. When most of the planters refused to acknowledge the demands or to submit them to arbitration, 14,000 workers went out on strike. Santiago Iglesias explained the strike as the result of "the horrible misery they (the sugar workers) suffer, the very small salary they earn; the exhausting work they are compelled to do under a burning sun and torrential rains, and in the obscure and cold night. The life of the country laborer in Porto Rico is anything but human."[92]

But this was just the way the planters, most of them American corporations, wanted things to be. The Puerto Rico Sugar Company, which owned five plantations and employed 1,200 laborers, hired Charles Hartzell, former U.S. Secretary of the island, as its attorney for the strike. When Hartzell applied to his friend Justice Charles F. MacKenna of the U.S. District Court for Porto Rico for an injunction to halt the strike, Justice MacKenna promptly complied. He issued a sweeping injunction prohibiting strikers from meeting and ordering them back to work. The strikers refused to comply, and they were attacked by police, arrested, and a number were seriously wounded.[93]

In a dispatch to the *Washington Star*, reporter A.C. Haeselbarth hailed the judge's action as dooming the strike to defeat, and as "the most severe blow yet dealt to Santiago Iglesias, labor leader and personal representative of Samuel Gompers in Porto Rico." It was, moreover, a signal "that the American flag must be respected." The *Star's* reporter assured the people of the United States that "if left alone the Porto Rican laborer is a faithful, inoffensive workman satisfied with his pay which wages meet all his requirements." However, he was being aroused to anger by "Iglesias and his fellow-agitators." Still, the real culprit was the President of the AFL, for "since the visit of Samuel Gompers to Porto Rico last spring labor circles have been kept in a state of agitation."[94]

Gompers immediately responded with a bitter attack on Haeselbarth's "mendacious, willful and malicious perversions of the truth." Pointing out that Iglesias was not his personal representative but "organizer and representative of the American Federation of Labor in the island," he noted that the *Star's* reporter had failed to reveal that the plantation owners in Puerto Rico were "none other than our American sugar trust." Gompers then described the terrible conditions that he had found among the sugar workers, most of them working on American-owned plantations "from thirteen to sixteen hours a day for wages ranging from 40 to 50 cents a day." Was it surprising, then, that they struck? As Gompers said:

> If the Porto Rican laborer is so "satisfied with his pay, which wages meet all his requirements," how is it then that 14,000 of them have gone on strike, enduring even greater privations in order that they may effect some improvement in their condition and to demonstrate to the world the unmitigated misrepresentations which Mr. Haeselbarth and a few of the coterie with whom he trains have tried to make the American people believe?[95]

Simultaneously, Gompers dispatched a letter to the island's new governor, Beekman Winthrop, describing the treatment of the sugar strikers as causing one "to imagine that the occurrences took place in Russia, rather than in a country over which the flag of the United States floats, and to which the guarantees of the Constitution of our country extend. Even under the rule of the czar of Russia, where nearly all assemblages are unlawful, those participating are warned to retire and permitted to retire and permitted before the gendarmery or soldiery are permitted to make any assault or to disperse the assemblage. This, according to the complaints made and the evidence before me, was not even observed by the police at Ponce."

Gompers enclosed a statement by H.P. Leake, a lawyer in Ponce, who described witnessing from his window on April 16, 1905 the police as they fire their Colt revolvers into the crowd of unarmed men and women strikers. "The thing that impressed me the most," Leake wrote angrily, "was the terror which forced the people to run against a stone wall with an iron fence on it and break that wall and fence down in getting out of the plaza, and the fact that they struggled with each other in getting through the gates." The police did nothing to assist the wounded men and women, but went about arresting strikers.[96]

Gompers then asked the new governor to consider whether this was the way "to instill American ideas and American ideals . . . into the hearts and minds of the people of Porto Rico." He closed, "I urge that you may once and for all make it clearly understood that neither the greed of corporations nor sordid notices of a few shall hamper the development or stand in the way of the progress and uplifting of the working people, so unfortunately situated as they are in the island."[97]

Despite this appeal, police brutality and arrests continued, and before the strike was over, 30 workers were seriously wounded. But the strikers held firm, and in the end won a nine-hour day and an increase in wages of 20 to 30 percent.[98]

In his report from San Juan, published in the *American Federationist*, Santiago Iglesias wrote: "The visit of President Gompers greatly increased the interests in organization, and the unions which are affiliating with the A.F. of L. are free of all political associations."[99] This was in keeping with the message Gompers had delivered in every speech he made while on the island. To socialists and non-socialists alike, he emphasized "pure and simple unionism," cooperation with the United States' occupation of the island, "and abjuring socialist and revolutionary propaganda."[100]

The AFL aim, Gompers also emphasized, was to "spread the gospel of Americanism among the people of the Island." He made it clear what he meant when he learned that during the Fourth of July parade in San Juan, which was reviewed by Governor Winthrop, a banner was planted in front of the reviewing stand which read: "Give us work, and hunger and anemia will cease." Gompers informed Iglesias that the message was unjustified, dangerous, and in bad taste. Later in the year, he urged Iglesias not oppose the establishment of the U.S. naval station in San Juan. It would be advantageous, he insisted, to the United States to have such a base on its own territory.[101]

In an address to the National Civic Federation, Gompers told the assembled capitalists that the AFL was interested in playing its part in the new American empire by combatting radical influences among the workers of these possessions. But it could only do so if the workers saw some gains from American occupation of their lands. He pointed with pride to the fact that "it was at the instance of the American Federation of Labor, with the cooperation of Governor-General Hunt that the conspiracy law was repealed." Had this not been achieved, Gompers insisted, radicalism would have emerged triumphant in the Puerto Rican labor movement.[102]

By 1907, May Day—with its revolutionary connotations—was no longer observed by the Puerto Rican labor movement and had been officially replaced by "Labor Day." Gompers counted this as one of the triumphs of AFL policies in Puerto Rico, clear proof of the Americanization process that the AFL and its representatives had been carrying out on the island.[103]

What Gompers had seen in his visit to the island in 1904 was, his biographer notes, "not a testimonial to the benefits of United States rule."[104] Still, in his farewell address in San Juan, he pleaded with the Puerto Ricans for patience with the island's colonial status: "I want you to bear in mind that the people of the United States are a just and generous people, I want you to understand that the Government of the United States is founded upon the everlasting principles of justice and fair dealing among men. . . . The time will soon come when you will no longer be regarded as stepchildren, but that you will be recognized as members with full rights in the family of the great American Republic."[105]

After his return from the island, Gompers declared that the time had come for the United States to admit Puerto Rico to "full fellowship in the family of the American republic" with a complete share of home rule. However, he was not willing to go even as far as Puerto Ricans who were content to work within the framework of colonialism. At the 1904 AFL convention, Santiago Iglesias and Esteban Padillo, representing the *Federación Libre,* asked the AFL to sponsor a bill granting Dominion status to Puerto Rico similar to that of Canada within the British Empire. They also petitioned the convention to work for an amendment to the Foraker Act which would convert the Executive Council of Puerto Rico into an elective upper house instead of an appointive one, and to have appointive offices filled with Puerto Ricans. But instead of approving these specific demands of its own representatives in Puerto Rico, the AFL merely adopted a general resolution favoring greater freedom for the island under American rule.[106] Again Gompers urged patience. But many Puerto Rican workers were in no mood for patience. There was a growing feeling, moreover, that Santiago Iglesias capitulated to Gompers' approach too readily, and that in general he was pursuing a policy which was more suited to the outlook of the AFL on the new American empire than to the needs of the Puerto Rican workers. Indeed, Gompers received protests from trade unionists on the island charging that Iglesias "does as he pleases and acts always as a czar and never as an organizer," and that while he continually praised the benefits of AFL unionism, little had actually been accomplished in improving conditions for the Puerto Rican workers:

> From the time when the island was seized by the United States during the Spanish war down to the present day [November 1910], the Puerto Rican workingmen have been more severely oppressed than they were under Spanish rule. The Spanish landlords and other capitalists were greedy and cruel, of course, but they were also lazy and careless. The American capitalists, who now have the upper hand, equal them in rapacity and far surpass them in energy.[107]

Gompers ignored these complaints, and conditions continued to deteriorate. On February 2, 1913, the Executive Council of the *Federación Libre* warned in a public statement that while "the labor organizations of the American Federation of Labor . . . desire and uphold American institutions in the country," the sad state of the working class in Puerto Rico was causing the "enemies of the American institutions to be gaining ground in the island, and the work of the American Federation of Labor is each time made more difficult." As the situation stood, "the producing class of Puerto Rico represents three-fourths of the population, an element of major importance to the island, but also an element to which no consideration or protection is given." Unless immediate reforms were instituted, the effort of the Free Federation of Labor to "uphold American institutions" would fail miserably.

Hence the Executive Council proposed the quickest possible adoption of 16 proposals demanded by the majority of Puerto Rican workers. These included an increase in the appropriation "for the maintenance of public schools in the island, so as to provide education to about 300,000 children, that are today debarred from the benefits of instruction"; workmen's compensation laws to furnish compensation for injuries sustained by workers during their work, the "law to be plain and precise in its provisions," creation of housing provisions for laborers in the principle industrial and manufacturing centers to put an end to "the veritable congestion of residents" which was undermining the health of the working class; "absolute abolishment of convict labor on public works, this labor being utilized in Puerto Rico in competition with free labor"; "eight-hour law reform, inasmuch as this law as interpreted in Puerto Rico is practically null"; provision for comfortable seats in shops and factories for women and children, "so that they may rest whenever it is necessary for them to stand"; a law prohibiting the employment of children under sixteen years of age in the factories and in the fields; levying of a tax upon capital taken out of the country which should be invested in schools and municipal sanitation; ending the practice of government support for strikebreaking by employers, "and other measures of recognized benefit of progress and well being of all the people of Puerto Rico."[108]

Not only did authorities fail to meet these requests, but they even intensified their support of strikebreaking. Governor Arthur Yager, appointed in 1913 by President Woodrow Wilson, openly recruited and protected strikebreakers for the Puerto-Rican-American Tobacco Company in its battle with the Puerto Rican Cigarmakers' Union. So blatant was the government-supported strikebreaking that Samuel Gompers, George W. Perkins, President of the Cigar Makers' International Union, and Daniel Harris, President of the New York State Federation of Labor, visited Governor Yager in San Juan to urge an end to the practice. Yager arranged a conference between the AFL leaders and the Puerto Rican-American Tobacco Company, but nothing came of the discussions. Yager made no attempt to mediate or seek an equitable settlement. Strikebreakers continued to be brought into plants and strikers continued to be beaten by police, arrested, and imprisoned. Only financial support from unions in the United States, especially the Cigar Makers' International Union, which furnished strike benefits totaling $38,675, enabled the strikebreakers to hold out for seventeen weeks and achieve a settlement that included increased wages, shorter hours, and improved working conditions.[109]

However, Prudencio Rivera Martínez, representative in Puerto Rico of the Cigar Makers' International Union, pointed out that unfortunately, "the employers refused to live up to the terms of the settlement, and, in this, they were supported by officials on the island." While the employers were willing to sign agreements, "they were afterwards unwilling to stand by them, and prefer accusing the workingmen as disturbers of the peace, fire-brands, and 'scallywags'." Moreover, they had "official support at their disposal to perpetuate this state of labor wretchedness."[110]

During his second visit to Puerto Rico in March 1914, Gompers found basically that conditions had hardly improved for the island workers in the ten years since his first trip. It was 15 years since United States rule had begun and twelve years since Santiago Iglesias had assured the American governor in San Juan that his mission was to elevate the Puerto Rican workers through the *americanización obrera* (Americanization of the working class), in accordance with the "pure and simple unionism" of the AFL. Yet Puerto Rico was still, as Gompers put it, "a great factory exploiting cheap labor for the benefit of large corporations in the United States."[111] The *Federación Libre* spelled this out more specifically in an appeal "to all laboring people of America and the rest of the world." The AFL affiliate noted that nothing had been done to adopt any of the 16 proposals its Executive Council had presented to the government, and the situation in the island could be summed up as follows:

> Corporations carry away from the island over 60 percent of the profit we produce.
>
> Hunger and misery abound everywhere.
>
> Lack of schools for 300,000 children results from reduction of the budget to half its requirements so that the corporations might pay less taxes and obtain larger profits.
>
> Death rate is increasing.
>
> Sanitation is in the hands of masters and politicians.
>
> In sum: the producing masses are oppressed and trampled upon, and absolutely restrained from fighting the monster monopolies. And as a result the reign of industrial tyranny and oppression is supreme over life and labor.[112]

Gompers had assured the Puerto Rican workers before he left the island that his influence with the Wilson Administration would produce an end to the oppression they suffered. On his return to the United States, however, he did nothing to fulfill the promise, and Iglesias gently reminded him of his statement which had "created a deep interest" in the minds of Puerto Rican workers. He assured Gompers that his failure to act was understood as not due to his unwillingness to stand by his pledge, "but that only great reasons are preventing you from taking immediate action in behalf of the suggestions you proposed to make after your last visit to the Island."[113]

What made the situation worse was that conditions were deteriorating even further on the island since Gompers' second visit. In the spring of 1915, Gompers did try to get to President Wilson to discuss the situation in Puerto Rico. But Wilson was too absorbed with other foreign policy matters to comply with his request. So Gompers had to settle for a meeting with Joseph Tumulty, Wilson's Secretary. At the meeting on June 6, 1915, he was accompanied by Santiago Iglesias and Prudencio Rivera Martínez, and all three conveyed to Tumulty the necessity of calling the President's attention to "the fact that fundamental rights are being violated

. . . [and] that the liberties of many of the people of Porto Rico, particularly the working people are in jeopardy and . . . in consequence of this, the essential, normal activities of the workers are being crushed in the interests of the powers that be in Porto Rico. . . ."[114]

Before the group left Tumulty's office, Gompers handed Wilson's secretary a petition prepared by Iglesias and Martínez. It declared that the rights and liberties of the workers of Puerto Rico were placed in jeopardy by the "maladministration of the laws" under Governor Arthur Yager, and it urged the President to appoint a commission to investigate labor conditions on the island and the responsibility of the government for these conditions.[115]

Following the visit to Tumulty, Iglesias and Martínez prepared to return to Puerto Rico. Gompers assured them that the failure to see President Wilson was not too serious, "You will agree with me that the expressions of Mr. Tumulty were strongly sympathetic and that at the earliest possible opportunity it would receive the very earnest consideration of the President and I am in strong hopes that the tangible relief and reform of existing conditions in Porto Rico will soon ensue." He urged Iglesias "that upon your return to Porto Rico you will carry the message to the working people of the Island that they be not depressed but to take courage and hope for the attainment of justice and right. . . ."[116]

When nothing happened as a result of the visit to Tumulty, Gompers wrote to President Wilson calling for an investigation into the "terrible oppression that has fallen upon the workers of Porto Rico." "There is a calm there," he conceded, "but it is a calm that results from hunger, fear, and lethargy. The fact that the workers are no longer clubbed, that the meetings are not disbanded, that they no longer make protests against violation of constitutional rights, does not mean that justice prevails now in Puerto Rico but it means that these oppressed human beings are living in terror if not despair."[117]

Again nothing came of the suggestion.

· VI ·

U.S. INTERVENTION
IN CENTRAL AMERICA

Roosevelt
Corollary, too?

B etween 1903 and 1914—first under Theodore Roosevelt's "Big Stick" policy, then under William Howard Taft's "Dollar Diplomacy," and then under Woodrow Wilson's version of a combined "Big Stick" and "Dollar Diplomacy" policy—three Central American nations experienced the military presence of the United States. These were Panama, Nicaragua and Colombia (which included Panama until 1903 and was historically part of what is now Central America).* The main, though not the only object of intervention in these countries, was the achieve-

---

*The "Big Stick Policy" was given this name after a speech by Theodore Roosevelt in Chicago in which he advocated that the United States "Speak softly and carry a big stick." Applied mainly to foreign affairs, the first part of the phrase tended to be forgotton since it was rarely practiced. "Dollar Diplomacy" was basically a tactic of U.S. imperialism. A concept developed during President Taft's administration, it emphasized increasing bankers' loans to various countries, and intervention with the armed forces of the United States to protect U.S. investments. The U.S. also intervened, as we have seen, in Cuba during this period as well as in Haiti, San Domingo, Honduras, and Mexico. The Mexican intervention is discussed below.

In a thoroughly misdirected case of hero worship, Richard H. Collin argues that Theodore Roosevelt was anything but a "war mongering imperialist," and insists: "The big stick is the straw man of the Roosevelt era." It simply never existed, he argues, and "Strategic necessity, not imperialism, not the big stick, caused American intervention in the Philippines and Panama." This presentation may be found in Richard H. Collin, *Theodore Roosevelt, Culture, Diplomacy, and Expansion: A New View of American Imperialism* (Baton Rouge, La.: 1985), pp. 18, 32–33. For an earlier defense of U.S. imperialism, see Richard M. Abrams, "United States Intervention Abroad: The First Quarter Century," *American Historical Review* 79 (February 1974): 72–102. For an even more undisguised defense of U.S. imperialism, see Lewis Feuer, *Imperialism and the Anti-Imperialist Mind* (Buffalo, N.Y.: 1987).

ment of an isthmian canal under total U.S. control, and the economic and political domination by U.S. imperialism of the countries surrounding the canal.

"What did the Federation [AFL] think about this trend toward intervention by the United States in Latin America?" asks Delber Lee McKee in his study of the AFL and U.S. foreign policy. His answer is that for the most part the AFL "showed little concern" over these developments.[1] The same could be said for the Railroad Brotherhoods and the Socialist Party.

Prior to November 1903, the AFL passed only one resolution on the subject of an isthmian canal. Adopted in 1898, it concerned what was then a proposed Nicaraguan canal. What was of importance to the AFL was solely whether or not American labor would be used in the event a canal was undertaken, and whether guarantees would be included providing that "workingmen may be supplied with all possible safeguards as to hygienic living, hospital conveniences and surgical service, and otherwise protected by reasonable hours of labor, and by all other safe conditions which will give them a chance to labor and live with every possible degree of comfort." How the canal would affect Nicaragua and its population was of no concern to the Federation.[2]

Thereafter, the AFL remained silent on the subject until the late fall of 1902. Comment, however, did appear during these years in the labor press. The *Locomotive Firemen's Journal* urged that an isthmian canal be built, calling it "essential" for foreign trade and national defence, while the Socialist-inclined *Cleveland Citizen* said the building of the canal would be "a steal by the capitalists." The *Coast Seamen's Journal* warned that the opening of a canal promised only disaster for the Pacific Coast. Unwelcome immigrants would overflow the region, glut the labor markets, and crush the wage scale while increasing unemployment. As a consequence, capital would triumph and reduce labor to servitude. The organ of the Seamen's Union of the Pacific urged workers who were "hollering themselves hoarse" in favor of the Nicaraguan canal to stop and consider "what will be the possible effect on the labor market when the canal is opened and in full operation."[3]

In 1901–02, developments took place that would lead to the canal becoming a major issue for American labor. Up to then, under the Clayton-Bulwer Treaty of 1950 the U.S. had shared with Great Britain equal rights in any canal constructed across Central America. But now Britain, deeply involved in the Boer War in South Africa, yielded to U.S. pressure and agreed to scrap the old treaty. Under the new Hay-Pauncefote treaty of 1901, the United States received a free hand to build, control and, by implication, to fortify the canal. The following year, on June 28, Congress passed and President Roosevelt signed the Spooner Act specifically designating Panama as the preferred site for the canal rather than Nicaragua, which had been the other possible choice.[4]

When the subject of a canal later came up at the 1902 AFL convention, discussion centered on a resolution criticizing the project of a canal through either Panama or Nicaragua. The resolution was proposed by Andrew Furuseth of the Seamen's Union of the Pacific, a leading trade union opponent of imperialism, and it saw the canal question in terms of war and colonial expansion. If the United States were to build the canal, the resolution said, it would have to defend the area. But defense, would necessitate "the conquest and annexation . . . of all territory lying between the Rio Grande and the canal in order to keep communications open."

The resolution sought further to lay down the principle for guiding the AFL in its future policy toward Latin America. Not only should it oppose the building of a canal by the United States, but it should also be "unalterably opposed to any encroaching upon the independence of any Latin American states . . . feeling that it must lead to war, bloodshed and hatred, in and through which the workers must be the chief sufferers."

Rejecting this argument, the Gompers'-dominated Committee on Resolutions reported adversely on the resolution. Although Max Hayes, Cleveland socialist, and Ed Rosenberg, Pacific Coast AFL representative, supported Furuseth in the ensuing debate, a group of Executive Council members defended the position adopted by the Committee on Resolutions. In the end, Furuseth's resolution was tabled, and the AFL refused to go on record as being "unalterably opposed to any encroaching upon the independence of any Latin American states. . . ." by the United States.[5*] Between the 1902 and 1903 AFL conventions, there was a series of startling events related to the canal issue. Panama was part of Colombia then, and Colombia was recognized by the U.S. under an 1846 treaty as having sole sovereign rights to the Isthmus of Panama—which the United States preferred as the site for a canal. By holding the alternative of a Nicaraguan canal over the heads of Colombia's negotiators John Hay was able to drive a hard bargain with Tomás Herrán of Colombia in a treaty approved by the United States in March 1903. The treaty stipulated that $10 million initially and $250,000 annually were to be paid to Colombia for the rights to a canal zone six miles wide across the Isthmus of Panama. When the Colombian government tried to revise some of the terms Herrán had agreed to, Hay curtly refused. Thereupon, the Colombian Senate rejected the treaty in August 1903, by a vote of 24 to 0.

Many believed that the United States would now shift its attention to the alternate Nicaraguan route. Instead, President Theodore Roosevelt, an ardent imperialist, assisted in organizing a "revolution" in Panama, which broke that area loose from Colombia. United States warships prevented the Colombian army from quelling the uprising. On November 3, 1903, three days after the "revolution," the new government of Panama was recognized by President Roosevelt, and in ten days its envoys were received in Washington. The treaty for the canal was soon framed along the lines the United States wished. Meanwhile, any attempt by Colombia to interfere was taken care of in the manner described by the *New York Times* correspondent in Panama:

> A company of marines from the United States auxiliary cruiser *Dixie*, under the command of Capt. Kirt McCreary, were landed here this morning [December 8], and took a train from Colon to Empire, a town on the railroad

---

*The Sailors' Union of the Pacific adopted Furuseth's resolution at their own convention the following month, but added the statement that the building of a Nicaraguan or Panama canal would be detrimental to American workers because it would bring in its wake, unlimited cheap, competitive labor. *Coast Seamen's Journal*, Jan. 14, 1903.

near Panama, where a camp was established in the Canal Company's buildings.* Another company of marines, to the number of fifty, from the *Dixie*
left on the afternoon train for Empire.

The stated official purpose of this movement is to give the marines practice
in the building of camps and to relieve them from their long confinement
on the vessel.

The actual purpose of the United States Government in landing the marines
is, however, believed to be connected with the precautionary measures now
being carried out on both sides of the Isthmus. . . .

It is considered significant that the point selected for the encampment of
the *Dixie's* marines, while it is the highest and most sanitary on the line of
the Panama Railroad, is also on the trail most frequently used in the past for
the movement of troops overland from the Cauca district into the Chiriqui
district.

If Colombia troops should succeed in obtaining a foothold in the rich
Chiriqui district, it is generally conceded that after predatory raids on the
countryside they could retreat to the mountain fastness from which it would
be most difficult to dislodge them.

There is no doubt that naval authorities took into consideration the moral
effect on the Colombian Government of the establishment of a marine camp
at Empire.[6]

With Colombia prevented from removing his "Big Stick," Roosevelt arrogantly
boasted: "I took the Canal Zone and let Congress debate; while the debate goes on
the canal does also." Even historian Samuel Flagg Bemis, usually an apologist for
American imperialism, could not swallow Roosevelt's arrogant conduct, and calls
the seizure of the canal "the one really black mark on the Latin American policy
of the United States."[7] We have already seen, and shall soon see, other "black
marks."

On November 6, 1903, only three days after Roosevelt recognized the Republic
of Panama and assumed the role of protector of the new Isthmian republic, the AFL
met in convention. In a desperate effort to arouse American public opinion to oppose
Roosevelt's role in seizing Panama and to support a policy of strict American
neutrality which might enable Colombia to suppress the Panamanian rebellion,
Colombian representatives in the United States sought to persuade the AFL to
oppose the Roosevelt policy. Their major argument was the AFL tradition of opposition to imperialism, and that the dismemberment of Colombia would strengthen
"Yankee Imperialism."[8]

Unfortunately, the assumption that knowledge of the true facts would bring

---

*Years before, a French canal company, led by Ferdinand de Lesseps, had gone bankrupt
trying to dig a canal through Panama. But a successor corporation, the New Panama Canal
Company, had acquired the assets as well as an extension of its concession of canal rights
from Colombia until 1904. The United States bought out the assets of the New Panama
Canal Company. It was Philippe Bunau-Varilla, the lobbyist for the French company, who
fomented the revolution in Panama against the Colombian government, but only after he
had been assured by President Roosevelt and Secretary of State John Hay that the United
States would prevent Colombia from suppressing it.

support for the aggrieved victim showed how little Colombians understood the changes that had occured in the AFL on the issue of imperialism.

At the 1903 AFL convention, Furuseth re-introduced his resolution condemning the building of the canal, but with a new provision. In addition, Furuseth denounced Roosevelt's policy and argued that building a canal should also be opposed because it would lead to interference with the sovereignty of Central American states and to the acquisition of territory in the surrounding area. "Our greed for sovereignty over the country which the interoceanic canal must pass," read Furuseth's outspoken indictment of Roosevelt's actions, "has already caused this country to disregard the sovereignty of sister republics in Central America."[9]

This time Furuseth's resolution was not tabled. Rather, a substitute resolution, completely reversing the action he called for, was offered by the Committee on Resolutions. The new resolution did not discourage the building of the canal, but urged Congress to employ workers from the United States on the proposed project. The resolution called attention to the fact that since an industrial depression seemed imminent, and naturalized southern Europeans, particularly Italians, were available who could cope with the Panama climate, it was the AFL's purpose to demand only that union labor be used in the canal's construction.

Several delegates bitterly attacked the scuttling of Furuseth's indictment of American imperialism in general, and the dictatorial action of President Roosevelt in disregarding the sovereignty of Colombia, a sister-republic in Central America. But Gompers and other top AFL leaders defended the Panama Canal seizure which, Gompers argued, represented "the organized expression of the American people." The fact that the naked imperialism revealed by the canal seizure had shocked the peoples of Latin America did not disturb the AFL leadership.

As the final vote of 99 to 47 approving the substitute resolution indicates, there was an important minority who could not swallow Roosevelt's aggressive policies.[10] Unfortunately, less than half of the delegates at the convention voted on the question. Evidently the Gompers' leadership was afraid to publicize the real views of those who did voice opposition to Roosevelt's policies. John B. Lennon, AFL treasurer, for example, was reported in the *Boston Evening Transcript* to have severely criticized Roosevelt and to have stated that he thought "the President and some of his friends had stirred up the revolution . . . in the interest of the schemes of some capitalists."[11] Yet he was innocuously paraphrased in the official AFL *Proceedings* as having said "that he was not opposed to the building of the canal, but he was opposed to this convention taking action which could result in an injury to the working man of the country."[12]

In any event, Roosevelt and the pro-imperialist press hailed the action taken by the AFL convention as evidence that organized labor was a partner in the building of the "New American Empire," and promised that rewards to American workers flowing from this stand would amply justify their position.[13] Actually, in the case of the Panama Canal, the rewards were fairly limited. The AFL, after great exertion, was able to prevent the use of Chinese labor in the construction of the Panama Canal, but it was not able to block a measure which exempted aliens who worked on the canal from the eight-hour day law. Since the AFL feared that this exemption would result in foreign laborers—when available—being employed instead of American workers, Gompers wrote to Roosevelt asking him to veto the bill. His efforts were in vain.[14]

Despite the "Big Stick" methods used by President Roosevelt to acquire the Panama Canal, not a few socialists welcomed the construction of the canal as paving the way for the expansion of capitalistic methods in Latin America and the Orient, to be followed by socialist revolutions. Furthermore, the construction of the canal was evidence of "splendid feats of engineering" possible under a state-directed undertaking, and proved what could be achieved on an even greater scale under socialism.[15] A member of the Socialist Party, who described himself as "A Comrade Who Has Been Engaged in the Work for Nearly Four Years," praised working conditions in the canal zone, and had only words of commendation for the U.S. Army Engineers for their management of the construction. "The incomes of the men in charge of the Isthmian Canal do not depend upon making slaves of us," he noted, "and we are really one of the happiest bunches of workingmen in the world." He concluded with the lyrical outburst: "We feel as though we had temporarily escaped the driving lash of Capitalism . . . and are enjoying a fore-taste of what life will be for all the workers in the Wonderful Days A-Coming."[16]

On the other hand, a member of the Industrial Workers of the World (IWW)* sent a vivid description of the hazardous conditions involved in building the Panama Canal, which the *Industrial Union Bulletin* of the IWW published on its first page. "I would advise no working man to come to the zone," the letter concluded.[17]

For years many Nicaraguans had believed that the isthmian canal would go through their country instead of Panama. Indeed, the government under General José Santos Zelaya had granted unusual concessions to American capitalists in the hope that this would influence the United States to choose a Nicaraguan route for the trans-isthmian canal. Naturally, the final arrangement with the Republic of Panama came as a great shock to the Nicaraguans. Zelaya turned to other nations for support. In January 1909, he negotiated a loan with a London banking syndicate instead of with Wall Street firms. He was also said to be ready to offer Japan exclusive rights to construct a canal across Nicaragua. In addition, he cancelled some of the business concessions previously granted U.S. capitalists.

All of these actions were guaranteed to cause relations with the United States to

---

*The Industrial Workers of the World was founded in Chicago in June 1905 by the leaders of various radical trade unions and political parties, such as the Western Federation of Miners, the United Metal Workers, the Socialist Party of America, and the Socialist Labor Party. The IWW brought together workers who believed in the class struggle and were dissatisfied with the class collaborationist, craft unionist ideology of the American Federation of Labor. It was organized along industrial rather than craft lines and believed in the organization of all workers regardless of skill, sex, color, or religion. On this basis and militant strikes and free speech fights, the IWW attracted thousands of unorganized workers.

Among the many studies of the IWW are Philip S. Foner, *History of the Labor Movement in the United States*, vol. 4 (New York: 1965); Paul F. Brissenden, *The I.W.W.: A Study of American Syndicalism* (New York: 1920); Melvyn Dubofsky, *We Shall Be All: A History of the Industrial Workers of the World* (Chicago: 1969); and Patrick Renshaw, *The Wobblies: The Story of Syndicalism in the United States* (New York: 1968).

deteriorate rapidly. Since the United States considered that it had a right to determine and guide policy in Central America, Zelaya's days were clearly numbered, especially since his dictatorial regime was hated by most Nicaraguans, and had spawned a host of enemies determined to remove him from power.[18]

On October 10, 1909, anti-Zelaya Liberals led by General Juan J. Estrada and Conservative forces led by General Emiliano Chamorro and Adolfo Díaz launched an assault on Bluefields, the capital of the Mosquito Coast of Nicaragua. The United States had been warned of the attack but concealed the information from Zelaya. The American Consul at Bluefields even told the rebels that Zelaya's ouster would be welcomed by the United States since it would bring many new opportunities for American business interests.[19]

Zelaya reacted swiftly to the rebellion, and sent three thousand men against the insurgents. When Estrada's expectation of a mass uprising against Zelaya proved to be an illusion—the fact that the dictator had incurred the hatred of the United States worked in his favor—he asked for American intervention to protect the lives and property of foreigners in Bluefields. Using as a pretext the execution by Zelaya of two Americans who were fighting with the insurgents, President William Howard Taft sent 400 marines to Bluefields. This action was followed by the breaking of diplomatic relations with Zelaya and the establishment of unofficial contact with Estrada. Realizing that with U.S. support, the rebels would soon be in power, Zelaya resigned on December 17, 1909.[20]

The Liberal-controlled Congress thereupon appointed a new president but the United States, which wanted Estrada in that post, refused to recognize the government. With American military assistance, Estrada continued his campaign to become president. After occupying the port of Bluefields, the U.S. Navy handed over the collection of customs, the principle source of government revenue, to Estrada. Then it was only a matter of time before Estrada would oust the Liberals and assume the presidency.

Once he was appointed President, Estrada agreed to the terms of a treaty presented to Nicaragua by Philander C. Knox, Secretary of State under President Taft and the father of "Dollar Diplomacy." Under those terms, Nicaragua granted the United States exclusive rights in perpetuity to construct an interoceanic canal across that country in return for a payment of $3 million in gold.* It also gave the United States a 99-year lease on a naval base in Fonseca Gulf and two small islands in the Caribbean. Another feature was a loan to Nicaragua by the American bankers Brown Brothers and J. & W. Seligman & Co, of New York. The money was to be used to pay off the loan extended by British bankers, build a railroad and establish the gold standard. U. S. bankers took charge of Nicaragua's finances.

On December 31, 1910, the United States recognized the Estrada government. Their mission completed, the Marines were withdrawn from Nicaragua.[21]

But the U.S. Senate, charging that the terms smacked too much of "Dollar Diplomacy," refused to ratify the treaty Knox had negotiated with Nicaragua.

*Colombia had rejected the offer of $10 million cash and $250,000 annually so the U.S. was now getting a real bargain.

Meanwhile, internal dissension tore the Estrada administration apart, and after declaring martial law in February 1911, Estrada resigned in favor of Vice-President Díaz and went into exile. The United States immediately recognized the Díaz government. But without support of his own, Díaz was widely viewed in Nicaragua as a figurehead for the United States. As opposition mounted to the puppet regime, the United States sent an entire battalion of marines to occupy Bluefields. Led by Major Smedley Butler, "Old Gimlet Eyes," the Marines landed on August 16, 1912, bearing a note from Washington which read:

> The United States has a moral mandate to exert its influence for the general peace in Central America, which is seriously menaced. . . . American purpose is to foster true constitutional government and free elections, and to this end strong moral support will be given to established governments against revolutions based upon the selfish designs of would-be despots.

The official United States Marines' study, "The United States Marines in Nicaragua," put it more succinctly and frankly: "After urging Americans to invest in Nicaragua, the United States government could not stand idly by and see their properties destroyed." The hope was that the Marines would end the turbulent events that threatened American property in Nicaragua. By October 1914, there were 2,700 Marines in various parts of Nicaragua.[22]

After the Marines had put down the rebellion against Díaz, they were again withdrawn, except this time the U.S. retained a 100-man contingent in Nicaragua to maintain the peace and protect the property. Those Marines remained in Nicaragua until August 1925, propping up the increasingly unpopular regime that had first moved the United States to intervene.

The last phase of the occupation of Nicaragua by a full contingent of U.S. Marines occurred during the administration of Woodrow Wilson, It was during this period that the Bryan-Chamorro treaty was drawn up between Emiliano Chamorro and William Jennings Bryan, Secretary of State in the Wilson administration.

The Bryan-Chamorro Treaty was actually a revised version of the treaty Knox had proposed to Nicaragua which the U.S. Senate had rejected. The new treaty retained features of Knox's version, such as the exclusive, permanent right of the United States to construct an interoceanic canal in return for $3 million, and the 99 year lease to the base in Fonseca Gulf and two islands. But the revised version included a number of startling new features. Nicaragua agreed to bind herself to the following terms:

(1) Not to declare war without the consent of the United States

(2) Not to negotiate any treaties with foreign governments which, in the eyes of the United States, would tend to destroy her independence, or that would give those governments a foothold in Nicaragua

(3) Not to contract a public debt beyond the ordinary revenues of the government

(4) To grant the United States the right to intervene at any time it deemed

it was necessary to preserve Nicaraguan independence or to protect life or property.

These terms, Bryan frankly told the Senate Foreign Relations Committee, would extend the principles of the Platt Amendment to Nicaragua and establish a U.S. protectorate over the Central American republic. "A new policy toward Nicaragua," reported the *New York Times* the following day, "virtually involving control of the affairs of that republic by the United States through a protectorate similar to that now exercised over Cuba, was announced today by Secretary Bryan at a private conference with the Senate Foreign Relations Committee."[23] Small wonder that the *Times*, usually a staunch defender of American imperialism in Latin America, declared editorially that compared with the proposed treaty under President Wilson, the original treaty negotiated under President Taft, "which had been rejected by the Senate because it savored of dollar diplomacy, more nearly resembled ten-cent diplomacy."[24]

"Where shall we stop, once we have begun a policy of this kind?" The *New York Evening Post* angrily asked when the terms of the Bryan-Chamorro Treaty were made public.[25] The answer was not long in coming. A headline in the *New York Times* soon read, "A PROTECTORATE OF LATIN AMERICA. WILSON PLANS TO HAVE NICARAGUA TREATY TERMS EXTENDED TO ALL CENTRAL AMERICAN REPUBLICS." Testimony by administration spokespersons before the Senate Foreign Relations Committee made it clear that the Nicaraguan treaty would indeed be the forerunner for a U.S. protectorate over Central America as a whole.[26]

The Díaz puppet government did its duty by the nation that had put it in power in Nicaragua and kept it there, by ratifying the Bryan-Chamorro Treaty. But opposition to the outrageous provisions mounted among all sections of the populations. A mass protest meeting held in Parque Central in Managua, the capital of Nicaragua, heard Sofonias Salvatierra deliver "The Protest of Nicaragua." Calling the treaty a "bill of sale," which had delivered Nicaragua lock, stock, and barrel to the United States, and guaranteed for it the "sad fate that has fallen Cuba under the Platt Amendment," the "Protest" declared:

In this treaty we Nicaraguans lose everything—material and moral integrity, and the nights of a free and autonomous people. Everything falls into an abyss; our economic and national future grows dim, and in the end, there will remain not a country, but a name Nicaragua and a national emblem, an emblem without dignity and sovereignty.

Continuing, the "Protest" noted that Nicaragua would be "forced down the same path as Cuba, as Colombia, as Panama, and other nations in Latin America which have fallen under the claws of the American Eagle. Shall we wait for nature to rise up against this source of iniquity, or shall we Nicaraguans act in time to prevent our Republic from sharing the fate of the other victims?"

"And what," Salvatierra asked, "about the people of the United States? Especially those who still cherish the principles of their founding fathers, and of the Declaration of Independence which proclaimed the right of all people to life, liberty and the pursuite of happiness, without outside interference? Will they remain silent while another independent Republic is deprived of its independence by the very nation which gave the Declaration of Independence to the World?"[27]

This appeal reached few people in the United States, although it did reach many in Mexico when it was published in *Acción Mundial* of Mexico City. The same was not the case, however, with the *Public Appeal of Nicaragua to the Congress and People of the United States* published in English as a 185-page pamphlet, and distributed in various parts of the United States. The pamphlet was written by Dr. Rosendo Agüello, Dr. Salvadore Lejarza, and Carlos Martínez, all of whom had been expelled from Nicaragua."[28] They had been expelled, as they put it, for the "crime of being Nicaraguans," and specifically for having risen "in resentment against the scandals that have given place in the country by certain personages in the United States, in consort with the so-called Nicaraguans." They had not abandoned the struggle for a free and independent Nicaragua, they said. Since, however, "the material pressure of the United States impedes our overthrowing by arms a treacherous and insensate government," they had decided to appeal to public opinion in the United States, for they recognized that the success of U.S. policy toward Nicaragua "is owing in the first place to complete lack of acquaintance with the real conditions in that country." Before going into further detail, they summed up the situation succinctly as follows:

> Intervention is made as an act of war or at the solicitation of a people. The United States had had no war with Nicaragua, and the people of this republic not only have not asked for intervention, but protest against it; they reject it actively and consider it a solemn, culpable attack upon their national sovereignty. That the so-called Nicaraguan government should have asked the aid of a foreign army is no just nor legal motive for granting it, for it is patent that in the act itself of presenting such an unheard-of-request it has confessed its impotence and loss of prestige and is only worthy of universal contempt.Who aids the government, so-called, of Nicaragua?Abroad, a co-terie of New York bankers who have carried on with the republic transactions of the most unworthy character and who hope to continue them.
>
> At home, a body of soldiers of the United States navy, who, under the pretext of protecting North American interests, which no one has even threatened, occupies the Field of Mars (Campo de Marte), a military fortress of Nicaragua, at which are kept the war supplies.
>
> And the people?
>
> They are in rags, with muzzles on their lips, protesting against the foreigner and anathematizing the traitors.[29]

The *Public Appeal* traced the "shameful history of U.S. intervention in Nicaragua" from 1909 to 1913, and then published the full text of "the treaty of sale and tutelage" signed by Chamorro and Bryan and ratified by "the puppet government of Nicaragua." It also described the protests raised against the treaty by the Nicaraguan colony in New Orleans, and other actual letters of protests from Nicaraguans in Managua and other parts of the country sent to the U.S. Senate, President

Wilson, and Secretary Bryan. Since the U.S. Senate had rejected the treaty negotiated under President Taft as "reeking of Dollar Diplomacy," they were hopeful that, with public support, their current protest and appeal would have the same result.[30]

Among the many documents included in the *Public Appeal* were the "Collective Protest of Latin Americans Against Military Occupation of Nicaragua," and "Opinions of Some Honorable Citizens of the United States." The first document, dated September, 1912, was addressed to the U.S. Minister in Costa Rica, and appealed to him to bring to the attention of his government the mounting evidence that enabled the petitioners to predict that

> far from obtaining peace, the military coercion on behalf of the American Government would only succeed in propagating war, fierce and sanguinary war, as all would unanimously fight to the end against a regime which is repelled by public opinion and which could not be maintained unless by means of the establishment of permanent quarters of American soldiers in the country.
>
> Under what pretence does the Government of the United States intervene? For the sake of Humanity?
>
> But then the means do not correspond to the end. The State Department should know that in such cases International Law indicates recourse to good offices or to proceedings of a purely diplomatic order. Outraging a Nation by landing foreign soldiers is not the way of showing sentiments of humanity towards that country. Central America is not yet placed under the auspices of the Platt Amendment. . . . We beg you, Mr. Minister, to submit to the Washington Government our vigorous protest on account of the military occupation of Nicaragua by North American soldiers, and our patriotic request that they be withdrawn fron Central American Soil for the greater tranquility of these war-beaten countries.
>
> Peace will never be obtainable in the violent shape of military occupation, Let the State Department know, Mr. Minister, that the trampling of foreign legions upon Central American Land reaches through the whole Continent; that we do not want to be the Poland of America, and that the maintenance of amicable relations between both Nations, demands from the United States a respectful impartiality and obliges them to discontinue protecting with troops of the American Army a Government which has been disauthorized as traitorous and the continuation of which could not only be obtained drowning in blood and exhausting and extermination the sentiments of patriotism of the people who repel such a regimen.
>
> For the sake of Humanity, Justice and Righteousness, we hope that your Government will listen to our outcry of protest and our just plea, in this hour of deep anxiety for Central America.

The "Collective Protest" was signed by "Nicaraguenses," "Guatamaltecos," "Salvadorenos," "Hondurenos," "Cubanos," "Venezolanos," "Colombianos," "Ecuatorianos," a "Peruano," and a group of individuals whose countries were not listed.[31]

"Opinions of Some Honorable Citizens of the United States" opened with an anonymous, heretofore unpublished document, entitled, "American Intervention in the Republic of Nicaragua, and who personally knows our affairs. . . . " In the course of his article, the author noted: "The American Government occupied the territory of Nicaragua with armed forces to insure peace in that revolt-stricken country, and to give to all its inhabitants 'guarantee of life, peace and the pursuit of happiness.' This is a very laudable American intervention, and one worthy the name. But how does it work out in practice?" He answered:

> Our marines are stationed in Nicaragua, not as a guarantee of peace, but rather as a menace to assist a group of bankers and piratical politicians in selling the very birthright of the people. This is not a very laudable purpose, nor one worthy of the name of American intervention.[32]

This piece was followed by a previously-published article, called "The Truth about Nicaragua: The Early History of Nicaragua," by Theodore Lippincott. It traced the history of U.S.-Nicaraguan relations from the landing of William Walker, the notorious filibuster, who arrived in Nicaragua in 1855 with about 56 American soldiers of fortune, established himself as president and ruled until he was overthrown in 1857.[33]* Lippincott conceded that intervention by the United States produced some benefits, but insisted that "the benefits accrue principally to foreign capitalists, politicians and the upper ten. The working classes seldom benefit in any material manner, and the political situation remains the same, "with veneer of decency, but rotton to core with corruption, graft and favoritism." But, bad as had been previous interventions by the United States, that which had taken place under President Woodrow Wilson—exemplified by the Bryan-Chamorro treaty—exceeded them all in its tragic impact on Nicaragua. Lippincott wrote:

> Secretary Knox, in his wildest moments, never conceived such a diabolical use of the almighty dollar as has the present administration in Washington.
> There is a method of accomplishing things, that has been successfully used in the time gone by, by other powers with axes to grind. That method was diplomacy. It gave no offense and aroused no criticism.
> Dollar Diplomacy? No! Loan Shark Diplomacy.[34]

Another of the "Some Honorable Citizens of the United States" was John Kenneth Turner, the famous socialist author of *Barbarous Mexico*. The *Public Appeal* reprinted Turner's article, "U.S. Navy Aids Wall Street Pirates," which had originally ap-

---

*Walker's regime in Nicaragua was recognized by the Pierce Administration, ever mindful of the interests of the Southern slaveholders. In a message to Congress on May 15, 1856, President Franklin Pierce actually boasted that the new government of Nicaragua had been established with "the assistance and cooperation of a small body of citizens of the United States." On September 22, 1856, Walker revoked the decree abolishing slavery in Nicaragua and reopened the slave trade. In the end, Walker was crushed by the greatest banker of the day, Cornelius Vanderbilt, who feared and resented Walker's interference with the lucrative shipping operation from New York to California. Vanderbilt was aided by four other Central American states and the British. Walker was captured by the British who surrendered him to the custody of Honduras, where, on September 12, 1860, he met his death before a firing squad. William O. Scroggs, *Filibusters and Financiers* New York: 1916, pp. 220–70.

peared in the most widely circulated socialist journal in the United States, the *Appeal to Reason*. Beginning with the observation that the United States was "prepared for war with Nicaragua" if it became necessary, Turner traced the history of U.S. aggression towards Latin America. He began with the war on Mexico of 1846, which he called "an affair of spoliation carried out in the interests of Negro slavery." Then came the war with Spain in 1898, a "war, while carried on in the name of humanity—in the name of oppressed and exploited Cubans—was in reality plotted and fought in the interests of the American sugar trust and its allies." This war was followed by Wall Street's rule of Cuba. The president of Cuba was a "mere puppet," with the United States pulling the strings under the Platt Amendment. "Cuba Libre" had become a country whose "wealth . . . is rapidly being gobbled up by Americans," inhabited by a people who were "coming to feel that it would have been less costly to remain a subject of Spain than to be 'Libre' under the financial domination of the United States."

The Platt Amendment was followed by the domination of the economic and political life of the Philippines and Puerto Rico by Wall Street, the "scandal" surrounding the seizure of Panama from Colombia, and other examples of the "Big Stick" policy of Theodore Roosevelt and the "Dollar Diplomacy" of William Howard Taft. All of it was climaxed by "naked aggression against the independence and integrity of Nicaragua." Turner warned that if the United States succeeded in converting Nicaragua into a semi-colony of the United States as it had already done in the case of Cuba, it would not be long before nearly all of Central America would be reduced to this servile status.[35]

None of the protests against the Bryan-Chamorro Treaty made any impression on President Wilson. On January 20, 1914, Wilson wrote to Bryan: "No, I have not changed my opinion as to the advisability of the Nicaraguan treaty. . . ."[36]

Readers of the *Public Appeal* might have drawn the impression from the inclusion of the article by John Kenneth Turner in the *Appeal to Reason*, that the Socialist Party and its press vigorously opposed U.S. intervention in Central America in general and in Nicaragua in particular. This however, was not the case. As we have seen, the Socialist Party had no words of condemnation for Roosevelt's "Big Stick" policy in the Panama Canal episode. Apart from the article by John Kenneth Turner, the *Appeal to Reason* published only one other attack on U.S. intervention. In its issue of January 28, 1911, the *Appeal* condemned Washington's decision to act as customs collector in Honduras on the basis of the "Roosevelt Corollary" of the Monroe Doctrine.* It charged that "Under plea of enforcing the Monroe Doctrine . . . the U.S. has deprived an American republic of its independence of action and

---

*In his message to Congress on December 6, 1904, President Theodore Roosevelt set forth what is known as the Roosevelt Corollary to the Monroe Doctrine. Under the Corollary, "the United States would exercise . . . an international police power," and intervene in Caribbean and other Latin American republics which failed to pay their international debts. The first application of the Roosevelt Corollary came in 1905 when the United States intervened in the Dominican Republic and took over control of the Customs Collections, allocating a percentage of the funds to pay the Dominican debt.

established a protectorate." No further word, however, appeared on the subject, and the intervention in Nicaragua received no attention in the *Appeal's* news or editorial columns.

Indeed, only one article appeared in the Socialist press specifically relating to events in Nicaragua. It was an editorial in the *New York Call* of August 24, 1910, entitled, "America, Nicaragua and Mexico." After briefly tracing the hostility of the U.S. government toward Zelaya, its support for Estrada, and the use of American warships and marines to help Estrada achieve the presidency, the *Call* commented: "From the standpoint of international law the interference of our government in the internal affairs of Nicaragua was most unwarranted. But Nicaragua is a small and feeble republic and its rights may be violated with impunity." The article then contrasted the difference between the U.S. government's attitude towards Zelaya in Nicaragua and Porfirio Díaz in Mexico. While doing everything it could to oust Zelaya, the U.S. government did everything possible to help Díaz remain in power:

> The reason for this difference is very simple. Zelaya resisted the encroachments of foreign capital, while Díaz has become the partner of the international exploiters. And our government, like all existing governments, is nothing more than an agency of capital.

This was the sum and substance of the socialist approach to U.S. intervention in Nicaragua. No call was issued for protest meetings or for petitions denouncing the military intrusion and demanding the immediate withdrawal of the Marines. Indeed, the *Call* took the position that all such actions were useless since the events that had occured in Colombia, Panama, and Nicaragua were all "decided by small cliques of powerful capitalists. Our government merely does their bidding, and in Congress there is no one to cross their purposes. And thus it will continue until the workers send representatives of their own to Congress, men pledged to the Socialist platform, who will insist on the enforcement of the rules of honesty and equality also in our international relations."[37]

While the *Public Appeal* included one article which had appeared originally in a Socialist publication, it did not reprint a single article or editorial from a trade union publication in the United States or a single statement by an American labor leader protesting the intervention in Nicaragua. There simply was no such document or statement to reprint. The publication and leaders of the AFL and the Railroad Brotherhood ignored the events in Nicaragua during the years from 1909 to 1914.[38]

"The outstanding instance of Dollar Diplomacy took place in Nicaragua," note Richard Hofstadter, William Miller, and Daniel Aaron in their discussion of U.S. intervention in the affairs of Latin America.[39] But on this "outstanding instance," the U.S. labor movement remained almost entirely silent. However, American socialists and American trade unionists could not and did not ignore the most important event in Latin American history since the struggle for independence from Spain—the great Mexican Revolution.

· VII ·

THE DÍAZ DICTATORSHIP

P orfirio Díaz, dictator of Mexico, came to power in 1876 and, did not relinquish his presidential authority until forced to do so early in 1911. Even though there was opposition to his despotic rule, and he faced several attempts to overthrow him, Díaz dominated political, economic, and social life in Mexico for almost thirty-five years.*

During his years in power, railroads were built, mines opened, factories established and other impressive developments took place. But the benefits of these economic achievements went solely to the upper classes of Mexican society and foreign capitalists. To the peasants Díaz's great economic achievements meant a system of peonage, and in the Yucatan even slavery. To Mexican workers they meant a system that lacked labor laws, opposed real trade unions, and offered wages half those of American working at the same job. Strikes ended in blood and prison for the strikers.[1]

Díaz prided himself on the support he gave to "private enterprises," referring particularly to foreign and especially U.S. investments in Mexico. Leading capitalists—Morgan, Rockefeller, Hearst, Harriman, Doheny—were attracted to Mexico because liberal concessions were granted to foreigners. As a result, U.S. investors controlled substantial mining, timber, ranching, and agriculture enterprises. Some of these capitalists, like southern California publisher Harrison Gray Otis or Arizona rancher and copper king William C. Greene, held extensive properties on both sides of the U.S.-Mexican border. The railroads were not only American-owned and

*The literature of the Porfiriato, as the dictatorship of Porfirio Díaz is called, is immense. A useful summary of recent scholarly trends on the Mexican Revolution is David C. Bailey, "Revisionism and Recent Historiography of the Mexican Revolution," *Hispanic American Historical Review* 58(Feb. 1978): 62–79.

managed, but Americans for the most part were engineers, conductors, telegraphers, and dispatchers. Mexican employment on the railroads was restricted to unskilled, so-called "peon work."[2]

In 1890 the total U.S. investment was around $130 million. At the turn of the century, American capital invested in Mexican enterprises amounted to a little over $200 million. By 1910, according to figures published by the Mexican government, total foreign capital amounted to over two billion pesos, of which 1.2 billion pesos (or over $500 million U.S.) was American. However, the figure described by John Kenneth Turner at that time, in his *Barbarous Mexico*,[3] was $900 million worth of American investments. On April 25, 1914, the *Deseret Evening News* of Utah, in an article entitled "U.S. Large Stake in Mexico," reported that "American-Owned Property There is Estimated at More Than a Billion Dollars." (Both of these figures compare favorably with recent scholarly estimates.) The American Smelting and Refining Company and the Greene Cananea Copper Company were the second-and-third-largest concerns in all Mexico.[4]

Transferring capital into Mexico, and importing Mexican workers into the United States was highly profitable. Morgan-Guggenheim, Standard Oil, American Sugar Trust, Southern Pacific Railroad, and other open-shop employers in the United States could use cheap labor in both countries to undermine the growing power of organized labor north of the border.[5]

Wall Street and Díaz were "business partners," and the relationship that was so beneficial to American capitalists endeared the Mexican dictator to businessmen in the United States and their imperialist government. To Theodore Roosevelt, Díaz was "the greatest statesman now living."[6] His successor to the presidency, William Howard Taft, shared his viewpoint.[7] In fact, for Taft, the need to find new outlets for U.S. capital and goods was even more critical than it had been for Roosevelt. By 1910, U.S. exports of manufactured goods exceeded the foreign sales of raw products for the first time. "To avoid the perils of overproduction and a glutted home market," one scholar points out, "direct government intervention in support of U.S. enterprise was necessary."[8] Thus the cooperation of Porfirio Díaz in furthering U.S. investments was most welcome and appreciated.

In March 1908 *Pearson's Magazine* featured an article by James Creelman entitled, "President Díaz, Hero of the Americas." Creelman painted a picture of a man who was really interested in the welfare of Mexico and Mexicans. The article was instantly translated into Spanish and publicized in the pro-Díaz press, which meant practically all of Mexico's newspapers and magazines.[9] But it did nothing to solve the grievances of Mexican workers or to halt their mounting discontent.

In 1873 the participants in one of Mexico's large strikes protested: " . . . there are workers who receive a weekly salary of sixteen cents and this cannot be denied. The working day exceeds from 5:15 A.M. to 6:45 P.M. in the summertime . . . in the wintertime from 6 A.M. to 6 P.M. . . . the foreman only concedes five minutes daily to the workers in order for them to eat."[10] Conditions did not improve much in the decades that followed. In 1901, a labor paper usually friendly to Díaz lamented:

What has the proletariat of the country gained with the increase of agriculture? Nothing, the status quo continues with the same demands and humiliations of two centuries ago. What have the mining workers gained with the immeasurable development that the mining industry has received? Nothing. Only stagnation and lowering wages. . . .[11]

At the same time this report appeared, and for several years thereafter, the working day in the factory or mine began before sunrise and ended after dark. Textile workers spent fourteen hours in the mill for which they received a top wage of 1.25 pesos a day. For a 12-hour day in the mines of Cananea, which offered the highest wages in Mexico, the miner received 3 pesos. Skilled craftsmen in Mexico City, such as carpenters and masons, received between 2 and 3 pesos a day for their work. Women in textile factories received as little as 25 centavos a day, and many of the women, Ramón Eduardo Ruiz points out, "were no more than children." They spent the same number of hours at work as men, but received a pittance in wages.[12]

From their meager wages, Mexican workers often had deductions made to pay for civil and religious festivals and for fines imposed for unsatisfactory performance on the job—"a judgment made only by employers."[13] For some workers commercial and industrial development did bring higher wages. But the rise in the cost of living robbed the wages of real value. "If the progress of Mexico brings about a rise in the value of everything," asked the textile workers of Orizaba in 1906, "including the cost of housing, food, and clothing, and if that progress adds to the profits of industry, why should wages of workers, who contribute greatly to the wealth of business, lag."[14]

Inferior housing characterized by squalid, makeshift abodes; widespread disease; and an enormously high rate of industrial accidents were additional grievances of Mexican workers. Then there was the *tienda de raya* (the company store). The factory or mine owners either ran the store or sold the concession to an entrepreneur. Employers often paid wages in chits or scrip that workers exchanged for food at the store. Here, inferior goods cost more than ordinary supplies in the usual stores. Because the company store gave credit, most workers eventually accumulated debts that employers passed on from father to son.[15]

Blue-collar and white-collar workers in Mexico shared one common grievance— that foreigners received higher pay and had a monopoly on the better paying jobs. Mexican workers were paid half of the wages of Americans who were, in addition, paid dollars or gold. On the railroads, as we have noted, Mexicans usually worked as track hands or janitors, or did other menial tasks. On rare occasions, some became conductors or engineers on the trains. To do so, they had to join the Railroad Brotherhoods in the United States, because no Mexican equivalent existed.[16]

Years later Carlos Lovera y Chirinos, the Cuban novelist and revolutionist who became chief of the Department of Labor of Yucatan, told a group of reporters in the United States:

Until the revolution, employees on the railroads with $100 a month were all Americans. For thirty or forty years the Mexicans did all the track work and the hard labor, under the command of the Americans. No matter how bright or capable a Mexican might be, he could not be promoted. The American employees were paid in gold. The Mexican got silver, they got about one-half or one-fourth of what the Americans used to get. It was the same in the mines.[17]

To change these labor conditions was not easy. The Mexican penal code threatened anyone who used either moral or physical force to raise or lower wages with a fine or imprisonment. Not surprisingly the slogans "equal pay for equal work—Mexicans and foreigners" and "Mexico for Mexicans" became popular chants during the Mexican Revolution.

Devoted to encouraging capitalist development in Mexico, Díaz saw that a cheap and submissive labor force was essential to attract foreign capitalists. Before 1906, the dictator was successful in coping with all industrial disputes by a combination of unrestrained violence against militant workers and co-optation of radical leaders who were bought out and became well-rewarded collaborators and vigorous promoters of Díaz's policies.[18]

Although the urban proletariat of Mexico was slow to develop, a working class movement began to emerge as a powerful force. Earlier in the 1800's, advanced political, social, and economic ideas had flowed into Mexico and spurred a growing militance. From Spain anarchist activists joined with a group of anarchist Mexican students in the 1860's to give organizational impetus to the Mexican labor movement. Socialism and Syndicalism gradually replaced the mutualism and cooperativism of the Mexican labor movement. Founded in 1872, on the heels of the Paris Commune, the Circulo de Obreros de Mexico had its organ *El Socialista* which published the *Communist Manifesto* by Marx and Engels in 1888.[19]

The two decades after 1890 saw a significant increase in the number of Mexican industrial workers, along with the proletarianization of many artisans forced out of their shops by industrial competition.[20] Though disputes occurred, they were dominated by leaders who sold out to Díaz, and Mexican labor appeared relatively docile in comparison with the contemporary labor movement in the United States and Europe. Yet below the surface unrest was simmering as long-standing grievances were compounded by the onset of a severe recession, aggravated by the depression of 1907 in the United States. With the fall of real income, open conflict erupted in 1906, "the year of the strikes."[21]

Three strikes are landmarks: the 1906 uprising of the miners at Cananea; the confrontation between textile workers and their employers at Rio Blanco in 1907, and the railroad dispute of 1908.

The uprising at Cananea, Sonora, in 1906, was against Colonel William C. Greene's mining empire which had been set up with the aid of Porfirio Díaz. Díaz enthusiastically encouraged Greene's Sonoran enterprise with a multitude of incentives, even though Greene openly discriminated against Mexican miners. U.S. miners working side by side with the Mexicans received up to three times their pay for identical work.[22]

The strike against the American-owned Greene-Cananea copper interests, began on June 1, 1906. The following day Colonel Greene asked for the aid of the Arizona Rangers, who had already proved themselves adept at breaking strikes. Walter Douglas of the Phelps Dodge Mercantile Company who armed the Rangers free of charge from the company's stores in Bisbee, Arizona, responded to the request affirmatively. Colonel Thomas Rynning of the Rangers fell back on an old arrangement which allowed the Arizona Rangers to cross the border in case of "hot pursuit." However, since it was clear that breaking a strike was different from pursuing a criminal, especially when the strike involved Mexican workers and took place 50 miles from the border, Governor Rafal Yxable of Sonora swore the entire ranger contingent into the Mexican Army as "volunteers."

The miners raised the cry of equality of work and pay and appealed to Díaz for sympathy and support. The dictator, however, not only sent in Mexican *rurales* (rural guards) to shoot down the strikers, but allowed 275 Arizona State Rangers to help mow them down. It is impossible to determine how many workers were killed during the three days before the strike was crushed. Estimates range from twenty to 200.[23]

On January 7, 1907, a strike at the Rio Blanco textile mill was bloodily suppressed by Mexican troops. As many as 200 workers may have been killed, twice that number imprisoned, and many more wounded. In April 1908, the Grand League of Mexican Workers began a full scale attack against the Ferrocarriles Nacionales de Mexico (National Railways) over its promotion policies, citing continued discrimination against Mexicans. The League demanded the discharge of American supervisors and, failing to achieve this, precipitated a walkout of nearly all Mexican workers on the railroad. The strike seriously affected company operations, prompting the managers to appeal to the Mexican president. Díaz's response was to dissolve the League and imprison its leaders.[24]

The brutal suppression of these strikes, and the fact that in the case of the battle at Cananea, it was put down by the joint action of Mexican and U.S. military forces, made them important symbols of the struggle by Mexican workers for justice and dignity. Most of these workers were by now totally alienated from a regime so obviously the puppet of foreign capitalists, so obviously hostile to the interests of the Mexican working class, and so unwilling to deal with their justified grievances. In the years that followed, Mexican workers were to be frequently involved in bitter struggles against their employers and a government which served only the interests of their enemies.[25]

Recent scholarship has emphasized that the mounting labor conflicts of the last half decade of Díaz's rule were the results of the influence of socialism, syndicalism and anarchism, and the agitation of their proponents. As a corollary to this thesis, other scholars have maintained that the *Junta Organizadora del Partido Liberal Mexicano* (*PLM*), or Liberal Party, was the vehicle by which these doctrines were disseminated among the Mexican masses, enlisting widespread working class support.[26] Still other scholars have denied both of these assertions.[27] But it is generally conceded that of all revolutionary groups, the PLM was the best organized and most effective. Its leader was Ricardo Flores Magón, who has been called the "precursor" of the Mexican

Revolution and is generally believed to be the man and thinker who cleared the way for the final overthrow of Díaz.

Born in Oaxaca, Mexico in 1873, and educated in Mexico City, Ricardo Flores Magón became a lawyer, but left his law career to become a revolutionist. He founded *Regeneración* and the *Partido Liberal Mexicano* to combat the Díaz dictatorship, and was imprisoned for his actions in 1902 and 1903. A convert to anarchism, Flores Magón became a leading exponent of anarchist thought, and influenced the *PLM* with his voluminous writings on it.[28] For a long time the role of Ricardo Flores Magón and the party he created were neglected in histories of the Mexican Revolution. But a reappraisal began a few years ago, and is still under way.

The *Partido Liberal Mexicano* held its first Congress in the city of San Luis Potosi, Mexico on February 5, 1901 and adopted a broad program of land distribution, social betterment of the masses, and anti-clericalism, It sought the overthrow of Díaz, and the end of U.S. economic domination of Mexico. Its initial leadership consisted of Ricardo Flores Magón (President), Juan Sarabia (Vice President), Antonio L. Villareal (Secretary), and Enrique Flores Magón, Ricardo's brother (Treasurer). The PLM somehow managed to survive five precarious years in Mexico before it was broken up and its leaders exiled to the United States in 1906.

Party headquarters were established first in St. Louis, Missouri, but soon afterward moved to Los Angeles, California. Wherever they were situated in the United States, the Flores Magón brothers spread anti-Díaz propaganda, aided by Juan Sarabia, Antonio I. Villarreal, and other exiled leaders of the PLM. *Regeneración* was published in San Antonio, St. Louis, and Los Angeles, and sent through U.S. and Mexican mails to subscribers along the border and into the Mexican interior.[29]

On July 1, 1906, the PLM issued a manifesto from St. Louis, Missouri, which proclaimed both opposition to Díaz and a desire for much needed social, economic and religious reform in Mexico. The PLM came out strongly for labor unions and the redistribution of hacienda lands; stipulated that landowners had to be or become Mexicans; advocated an end to the Mexican military draft, replacement of parochial schools with a secular system, and nationalization of all clerical and unworked landholdings. Debt peonage would be abolished; foreigners, both workers and investors, would face severe restrictions; U.S. workers would not be paid more than Mexicans for equivalent work; company stores would be banned; child labor would be outlawed; and Mexican workers would receive a specified minimum wage, work an eight-hour day (with Sundays off), and receive their pay in cash. All this would be accomplished with the overthrow of the Díaz regime and the establishment of a government under the leadership of the PLM.[30]

It was a progressive, anti-imperialist program. (The only anti-progressive feature was the provision that Chinese immigrants be barred from entering Mexico.) It attracted support for the PLM not only among Mexican workers but Mexican-American workers in Arizona and Texas.[31]

Then, in a second manifesto issued in the spring of 1909, PLM indicated that its strategy had changed, and that the organization had evolved from a traditional liberal, anti-clerical movement into a radical anarchist one. "Mexico's revolution," the second manifesto declared, "is not purely a political revolution—it is a social problem which relates to us directly. We are compelled to meet with force, for so the tyrant Díaz has decided. We did not seek strife, we were driven to it. We have learned the lesson so ably expressed by a great thinker—Better a handful of force than a bag of rights." As an anarchist organization, the PLM now sought to overthrow not only the Díaz dictatorship but the entire structure of capitalist society and the state apparatus. At the same time, the 1909 manifesto reiterated the demands set forth in the 1906 manifesto.[32]

The 1909 manifesto noted sadly that "not only in Mexico are we tracked by the police agents; in the United States we are also hunted like wild animals. Mexican homes in this country are entered without warrant, the patriots manacled and hurried to the United States jails, while others are secretly taken to the border and delivered into the hands of the waiting rurales. . . ."[33] This was not in any sense an exaggeration. It is clear from recent studies[34] that state and federal officials in the United States engaged in a variety of activities in order to destroy or weaken allegedly dangerous radical anti-Díaz groups, especially the *magonistas*,[35] as the followers of Ricardo Flores Magón were called. In the process, the vicious, pro-imperialist, anti-democratic conduct of the United States government aroused the bitter and angry opposition of many, especially radical Americans, and brought the struggle in Mexico close to the U.S. labor and socialist movements.

Probably the first contact between the U.S. trade unions and the Mexican occurred on the eve of the bloody 1906 strike of the miners in Cananea. "Before the strike," an American labor organizer recalled later, "I had been collecting the dues of some of our Western Federation of Miners' (WFM) boys who were working in Cananea and when I went over the border, the Mexican miners would ask me, 'Why can't we get the same wages you Americans get?' I told them they could if they'd organize. So they went to it." But it was Mother Mary Harris Jones, the union and socialist organizer, who was the first North American to be deeply involved in the Mexican cause. "Mother," noted a WFM leader, "with her white hair, had single-handed, commenced the fight for the imprisoned Mexican political refugees in the time of Díaz."[36]

At the time, Mother Jones—then 77— was assisting the WFM in organizing a strike against the Phelps Dodge copper mine interests in Douglas, Arizona. One evening when she returned to her hotel after a street meeting, the editor of *El Industrio* burst into her room, screaming, "Oh Mother, they have kidnapped Sarabia, our young revolutionist." On learning that Mexican officials, working hand-in-glove with authorities, had pirated Manuel Sarabia across the border, Mother Jones immediately telegraphed the territorial governor—Arizona was not yet a state—and President Theodore Roosevelt. Then she started a publicity campaign through the Douglas *Daily Examiner*, and scheduled protest meetings. Mother Jones told all who gathered to hear her:

> That's got to stop. The idea of any blood-thirsty pirate on a throne reaching across these lines and stamping under his feet the constitution of the United

States, which our forefathers fought and bled for! If this is allowed to go on, Mexican pirates can come over the border and kidnap any one who opposes tyranny.

Through her various activities, Mother Jones was successful in having Sarabia returned to Arizona in eight days from a penitentiary in Hermosillo, Mexico.[37]

In her *Autobiography*, Mother Jones recalled that "kidnapping seemed to be in the air just about that time. The Idaho affair was on." She was referring to the kidnapping of William D. ("Big Bill") Haywood, Charles Moyer, and George Pettibone in the aftermath of the murder of the ex-governor of Idaho. These men, leaders of the Western Federation of Miners (WFM) and of the recently-organized Industrial Workers of the World (IWW), had been abducted from Colorado to stand trial in Idaho on the basis of the confession of an informer. In this case, Clarence Darrow successfully defended the accused and completely exposed the frame-up.* But the Idaho affair had made kidnapping a popular issue for all who believed in constitutional rights. It had demonstrated that mass protests could bring success, and the rescue of Manuel Sarabia confirmed this view.[38]

Ricardo Flores Magón, Antonio Villareal, and Librado Rivera, all PLM leaders, were arrested, and lodged in the Los Angeles jail in August 1907 on the charge of violating U.S. neutrality laws. Mother Jones immediately began a campaign to have them released. "They were patriots," she told the American people, "like Garibaldi and George Washington—these Mexican men in jail fighting against a bloodier tyrant than King George against whom we revolted."[39]

The three men remained in prison for a year and four months before their trials opened in Tombstone, Arizona. To meet the costs of the trial, Mother Jones raised $4,000, $1,000 of which she persuaded the United Mine Workers to contribute, with the remainder coming from the WFM and other unions.[40] In addition, she wrote articles in the *Appeal to Reason*, the mass circulation socialist weekly, and distributed the leaflet, *Oh! Ye Lovers of Liberty!* in which she called for the working people of the United States to respond to the needs of "our comrades and brave brothers" who were crying from the "bastille of capitalism in Los Angeles." "You have saved Moyer and Haywood, she concluded, "and now you have got to save our heroic Mexican comrades."[41]

"Throughout 1910," writes W. Dirk Raat, "she [Mother Jones] continued her fund-raising for other PLM members like Antonio de P. Arujo and Jesus M. Rangel, and aided in opposing the extradition of half a dozen others. She also visited *revoltosos* in Leavenworth and sent letters of moral support to the political prisoners in Yuma and Florence."[42] Writing from prison, Flores Magón, Villareal, and Rivera saluted Mother Jones as a "noble example . . . teaching a lesson humanity should not forget." They went on to say: "You, an old woman, are fighting with indomitable courage; you, an American, are devoting your life to free Mexican slaves. And they will be freed in the near future, and they will learn to call you Mother."[43]

*For the case, see Philip S. Foner, *History of the Labor Movement in the United States*, vol. 4 (New York: 1965) pp. 40–59.

Others besides Mother Jones were active in the campaign to defend the Mexican exiles. The *Miners' Magazine*, organ of the WFM, cried out in anger and anguish:

[T]hey [Flores Magón. Villareal, and Rivera] have heard the groans of agony and the moans of pain that have come from thousands of Mexican hovels and because they have lifted up their voices against Cossack barbarism in Mexico they are hounded by the vultures of capitalism with no more consideration than wild beasts of the jungle.[44]

The Los Angeles IWW insisted that the imprisoned men and their comrades represented a "working class movement and nothing else, and it is for us who are revolutionists to help them in the fight." Clear across the country at a meeting of Local No. 212, Pittsburg IWW's resolved:

That we as citizens of the United States of America, demand that these three men, R. Flores Magón, Antonio Villareal and Liberado Rivera, now confined in jail at Los Angeles . . . be given a fair and impartial trial and that they shall not be deported to Arizona where it would be an easy matter for them to be kidnapped and taken to Old Mexico and there shot.[45]

"Big Bill" Haywood, fresh from victory in his own case, sent a telegram to the *Appeal to Reason*, reminding all socialists, Wobblies, and AFL unionists that Flores Magón, Villareal, and Rivera were "your comrades, men who dared to speak for liberty, men who were fighting for political freedom and struggling to overthrow the system of peonage." "Do for them as you did for me," he appealed.[46]

At its Convention in Chicago in May 1908, the Socialist Party of America unanimously passed a resolution supporting the three imprisoned Mexican rebels. Eugene V. Debs, who had sponsored the resolution, also wrote an article for the *Appeal* that was later reprinted in pamphlet form in English and Spanish. In this pamphlet, entitled "This Plot Must Be Foiled" (*Emplot que es necessario desbarratar*), Debs argued that:

Ricardo Flores Magón, Antonio L. Villareal, Librado Rivera, and Manuel Sarabia are our comrades in the social revolution! They have been doing in Mexico what we are doing in the United States and by practically the same means. If they ought to be shot so ought we. The truth is that they are four reformers in the highest sense of the term, highly educated, cultured, pure in mind, exalted in thought, noble of nature and lofty of aspiration. They are victims of a foul conspiracy between two capitalistic governments to put them to death.[47]

Meanwhile, Mother Jones had organized one defense committee and John Murray, a Los Angeles socialist and labor leader, had established the Mexican Revolutionists Defense League. Jones and Murray worked together to convince Samuel Gompers, president of the AFL, to support the cause of the Mexican exiles. Indeed, Murray resigned as editor of the *Los Angeles Citizen*, the official organ of the city's Central Labor Council, to devote the rest of his life to the Mexican cause.

Murray convinced Gompers that the PLM 1906 manifesto showed that the movement was essentially liberal. He argued effectively that the AFL would not be wise to allow the IWW and the Socialist Party to get all the credit among workers in Mexico, and Mexican-Americans in the U.S. Southwest, as the only ones to speak out against the persecution of the Mexican exiles.[48] Persuaded, Gompers in turn influenced the 1908 AFL convention to adopt a resolution which extended sympathy "to Magón, Villareal, Rivera, et al., and commends to all affiliated organizations the consideration to proper means for their defense."[49]

Despite all the support from organized labor and the Socialist Party, Flores Magón, Villareal, and Rivera were found guilty in May 1909, and sentenced to months in jail.[50] Immediately, the *Appeal to Reason*, the *New York Call*, and other socialist papers called upon President William Howard Taft to pardon the three PLM leaders. The *Appeal* printed in full the text of a petition which argued that "the ends of justice have already been served by the long time that the defendants have already remained in jail." Since the three men had already been imprisoned for 21 months, longer than their 18-month sentence, the petitioners urged leniency.[51]

Mother Jones did not rely on petitions alone. She requested and was granted an interview with President Taft in the White House. Jones urged Taft to "pardon the patriots that languished in our jails," and reported the following dialogue after the interview:

> "Mother Jones," said the President. "I am very much afraid if I put the pardoning power in your hands there would not be anyone left in the penitentiaries."
>
> "Mr. President," said I, "if this nation devoted half the money and energy it devotes to penitentiaries to giving men an opportunity in life, there would be fewer men to pardon out of jails."[52]

But the governments of the United States and Mexico were too closely linked in protecting American capital investments to free the men in prison to continue their work for the overthrow of Díaz. At Díaz's request, Taft became the first U.S. president to visit Mexico. He also met the old dictator at El Paso, Texas, and bestowed his blessings on him. Taft believed that U.S. support for the dictator would "strengthen him with his own people and tend to discourage revolutionists' attempts to establish a different government."[53] Given all these forces in operation, neither Mother Jones nor any of the other petitioners could prevail, and the three men remained in prison.

In the spring of 1910 a coalition of progressives, AFL unionists, and opponents of the Taft administration initiated congressional hearings on the Mexican political prisoners. It is difficult to determine whether it was John Murray or Samuel Gompers who convinced William B. Wilson, labor Congressman from Pennsylvania and a former leader of the United Mine Workers, to introduce a resolution asking Congress to investigate harassment of Mexican political refugees.[54] In any case, the House Rules Committee debated Wilson's resolution, calling witnesses familiar with the subject. The hearings lasted for five days between June 10 and 14, 1910, with Congressmen Wilson in the chair.

Congressmen heard the reading of a letter submitted by Samuel Gompers (originally sent to President Roosevelt) in which the AFL president condemned the Díaz dictatorship and defended the PLM leaders still in prison in Arizona. Gompers' letter pointed out that "in Mexico men, women, and children alike are working from fourteen to sixteen hours per day for wages ranging from 10 to 40 cents per day, and nearly one-third of the population is held under a system of peonage which makes them virtually slaves." For years, he continued, reformers had tried to work "for the uplift of the working people of Mexico through peaceful means." Their "liberal clubs" had been broken up without trial, and they themselves had been sent "as slaves to work on the plantations of the Tropics or condemned to rot in dungeons of prisons that are below the level of the sea. Men, women, and children have been shot down in the streets for joining in unarmed parades in favor of popular elections, and the man who wishes for liberty or justice has to whisper that wish below his breath."

The Mexican Government, Gompers argued, was not content with merely killing or imprisoning the revolutionary leaders they caught on Mexican soil. "It reached out after the men who had sought refuge in the United States." The Díaz dictatorship had had the exiled leaders imprisoned with the aid of the U.S. government and they were still in prison. In the name of the AFL Executive Council, Gompers asked President Roosevelt to "take such action as in your power to safeguard the great Anglo-Saxon concept and right of political refugees who seek the asylum and protection of our American Republic." Roosevelt ignored the appeal, and Gompers made it public through the hearings of the congressional committee.[55]

The hearings continued with the testimony of Lazaro Gutierrez de Lara, John Murray, and John Kenneth Turner. All three presented evidence of the horrors of life in Mexico under the Díaz dictatorship, and the persecution of the dictator's opponents by U.S. officials in collaboration with the Mexican authorities. Mother Jones was the last witness. She told the story of the kidnapping of Manuel Sarabia and how his return from Mexico was achieved. Jones condemned the U.S. authorities for collaborating with the Mexican dictator, accusing the Taft administration of suppressing civil liberties and engaging in corrupt practices to assist Díaz.[56]

The evidence presented before the congressional committee—that local, state and national officials, and private detective agencies in the United States were cooperating with Díaz agents in persecuting Mexican political refugees—received attention in the commercial press as well as in the labor and socialist journals. Excerpts from that testimony were carried by the United Press and by major dailies such as the *New York Times*, the *Baltimore Sun*, and the *San Francisco Daily News*, despite efforts by the pro-Díaz faction on the committee to keep the testimony secret. This publicity contributed to the growing American disenchantment with Díaz and with the policies of the Taft Administration in aiding the dictator. "The testimony," commented the *Chicago Daily Socialist*, "is proving anew the fact that Díaz is only the tool of American capital." The *Socialist* continued:

> It is the copper trust, the rubber trust, the Standard Oil and railroad trust that is really ruling Mexico. . . . We read of men and women whipped to death, shot down by the hundreds in the streets, cast into foul jails without

trial, murdered by wholesale, in almost every possible manner. These brutalities are not simply condoned by those who rule this country. If it were not for American support these atrocities would cease.[57]

The Congressional investigation was a major factor in the release of the three PLM prisoners. Flores Magón, Villareal, and Rivera went free almost five months before the expiration of their sentences.[58]

Although Mother Jones did the most work on behalf of the Mexican rebels being persecuted in the United States, John Kenneth Turner did more than any other American to expose the evils of the Díaz dictatorship and the role of U.S. imperialism in sustaining it. Son of a printer, Turner became interested in socialism as a youth and when he became a reporter for the *Los Angeles Express*, he joined the local Socialist Party. It was in Los Angeles that Turner interviewed Ricardo Flores Magón in prison. Flores Magón convinced Turner that Díaz was "a monster," and the young socialist reporter determined to prove it. He was particularly anxious to demolish the image cultivated by the commercial press of Díaz as the efficient, benevolent ruler of a peaceful country.

Turner traveled to Mexico with Lazaro Gutierrez de Lara, an important member of the PLM, who acted as his interpreter. Turner posed as an American businessman exploring investment opportunities in Mexico, and in this way collected a tremendous body of information. The two men were able to penetrate deeply into the slave labor areas of Valle Nacional and the Yucatán, and thus expose the widespread use of slavery on both Mexican and U.S.-owned plantations.

Turner spent the next decade of his life exposing the Díaz dictatorship and promoting revolution in Mexico. He wrote numerous articles for capitalist and socialist publications, but it was his book, *Barbarous Mexico*, which has been called "the *Uncle Tom's Cabin* of the Mexican Revolution,"[59] that made him famous.

Barbarous Mexico, issued by Charles H. Kerr, the socialist publishing house in Chicago in January 1911, was a revised and expanded version of articles Turner had published in *American Magazine*, the *International Socialist Review*, the *Appeal to Reason* and the West Coast socialist journal, the *Pacific Monthly*.* Turner exposed and denounced the existence of slavery on plantations owned by Americans and Mexicans. Recalling the bloody four years of the Civil War to end slavery in the United States, he wrote angrily: "The United States is a partner in the slavery of Mexico. After freeing his black slaves, Uncle Sam, at the end of half a century, has become a slaver again . . . in a foreign country."[60]

After describing how investors from the United States had taken over control of the Mexican economy and government, Turner raised an issue which was of special concern to U.S. trade unions. "American capitalists," he wrote, "support Díaz because they are looking to Mexican cheap labor to help them break the back of organized labor in the United States, both by transporting a part of their capital to Mexico and by importing a part of Mexican laborers in this country."[61]

*After Turner had published three articles in the *American Magazine* exposing the evils of the Mexican dictatorship, the *American* suddenly ceased publishing any of his additional pieces. Turner published his remaining articles in the *International Socialist Review* and the *Appeal to Reason*.

Here was an argument that was guaranteed to gain a sympathetic response from organized labor in the United States. Under the Díaz dictatorship, conditions of Mexican labor were deteriorating so rapidly that more and more workers were being forced to cross the border into the United States in search of better living conditions. In the last two decades of the nineteenth century and the opening decade of the twentieth century, Mexican workers played a vital part in the development of the Southwest's railroad system and in the agricultural economy of the Southwest and Far West, as well as, in the mines of Arizona and other southwestern states. In 1909 nine western railroads employed about 6,000 Mexicans in their "maintenance of way" departments. Agricultural, railroad, and mine journals noted that the fear of being sent back to Díaz-ruled Mexico, if they complained of unequal pay, made the Mexicans "satisfied with very low social conditions."[62]

AFL unions near the Mexican border complained that cheap, non-unionized Mexican laborers were direct economic competition for workers already in the United States.[63]

"The cheap peon labor of Mexico," the California State Federation of Labor declared in 1909, "is one of the greatest detriments which the organized workers of America face today." And it maintained that the "uplifting of the Mexican working people is as necessary to Americans as it is to Mexicans."[64]*

The Pan-American Press noted that both the Western Federation of Miners and the United Mine Workers actively opposed the "tyranny in Mexico and the persecution of the Mexican political refugees," and that Mother Jones, a leading opponent of the Díaz dictatorship, was associated with both of the miners' unions. While international labor solidarity played a very important role in these developments, the Pan-American Press observed:

> It is well known that the great mineral belt running through Arizona crosses the border into the state of Sonora, Mexico, and that an economic menace to American miners is fast developing through the starvation wages paid Mexican miners whose product compares with the output of American ore. Western Federation of Miners are well aware that miners in Mexico would immediately organize and raise their standard of living if it were not for the guns of Díaz's rurales ready to shoot them down at the slightest pretext.

Once they were organized and raised their wages to decent levels, Mexican workers would no longer be a threat to the wage standards of miners in the Southwest of the United States. "But," concluded the Pan-American Press, "the necessary precondition for all this is the overthrow of the Díaz dictatorship."[65]

---

*Another concern voiced by the California State Federation of Labor was that the police and U.S. government repression of Mexican political exiles in the United States could easily be turned against U.S. labor organizers. *Proceedings of the Tenth Annual Convention of the California State Federation of Labor*, 1909, p. 34.

· VIII ·

OVERTHROW OF DÍAZ
AND THE BAJA CALIFORNIA EPISODE

E arly in August 1910, Ricardo Flores Magón, Antonio I. Villarreal, and Librado Rivera were released from prison. They immediately established the headquarters of the PLM in Los Angeles and, with the financial assistance of socialists, as well as AFL and IWW unions in the city, renewed the publication of its official organ, *Regeneración*. In the very first editorial, Ricardo Flores Magón predicted:

> We come to tell the Mexican people that the day of the liberation is near. Before our eyes is the splendid dawn of a new day; the noise of the liberating tempest . . . echoes in our ears; that rumbling is the revolutionary spirit; the entire Nation is a volcano on the verge of spouting forth the fire within its entrails. . . . Mexicans to war![1]

It was an eloquent and accurate prediction. Within a year the hated dictatorship of Porfirio Díaz would be ended. The mantle of revolution, however, fell not to the radical, anarchist Ricardo Flores Magón and the *magonistas*, but to the aristocratic and politically moderate Francisco Madero and the *maderistas*.

Madero, a wealthy landowner and industrialist, and candidate of the Anti-Reelection party, was jailed for daring to oppose Díaz and then released on parole. By rigging the elections in his favor with the aid of the *porfirista* political machine, Díaz won the general elections of July 1910. The official election results stated that Madero received only 196 votes against the customary millions for the aged dictator![2]

Breaking his parole, Madero fled to San Antonio, Texas, where he issued the Plan of San Luis Potosi in October 1910, calling on Mexicans to join him in an armed revolt.[3]

The revolt began on November 20, 1910, and by early May, 1911, the armies of Madero's supporters were besieging the major border city of Ciudad Juarez. Díaz resigned on May 25, 1911, left Mexico and lived in exile until he died in Paris in 1915. (His remains have never been returned to Mexico.) His enemies temporarily designated as head of state an old Porfirista, the diplomat and politician Francisco Leon de la Barra. A few months later, on the heels of a resounding triumph at the polls, Madero took the reins of power into his hands.[4]

While Madero triumphed, the PLM splintered. Its leadership originally encouraged Mexicans to join Madero's armies while withholding support for his presidency. The *magonistas* were determined to have a revolution which would not mean the ouster of Díaz with the continuation of foreign domination and the prolongation of misery for the masses. While the *magonistas* fought in the revolution against Díaz as separate guerrilla units, their leader Ricardo Flores Magón soon became thoroughly disillusioned with the revolution led by Madero. "Francisco I. Madero is a Traitor to the Cause of Liberty." This sentence was displayed in a 7-column head on the front page of *Regeneración* of March 2, 1911. It appeared over a 7-column article by Ricardo Flores Magón in which he charged that Madero worked with the U.S. authorities to have the PLM leaders imprisoned for violating the neutrality law;[5] and that he then took advantage of their imprisonment to spread information that he was supported by the *magonistas*, who "accepted his cause as their own." More serious, Flores Magón charged that Madero was not seeking a broadly based social revolution, and that his victory would be nothing more than the traditional coup d'etat. He even charged that Madero was "simply the tool of Díaz, who had used him to divert into the harmless and sterile channels of politics a revolution that was beginning to fill him with alarm." Flores Magón made it clear that he would not support Madero, because the latter refused to go along with the PLM land reform program, as was to be expected since he "himself owns immense estates and is very wealthy." Another reason was that Madero was "hand-in-glove with the clergy," and had made "special promises" to the Church. But above and beyond all this, he opposed Madero because he represented Government, and all governments, Flores Magón emphasized, were

> repugnant to me. I am firmly convinced that there is not and cannot be a good government. They are all bad, whether they call themselves absolute monarchies or constitutional republics. Government is tyranny. . . . Governments are the guardians of the interests of the rich and educated classes, and the destroyers of the sacred rights of the proletariat. I have no wish, therefore to be a tyrant. I am a revolutionist and a revolutionist will I remain until my last breath.

Flores Magón then made his own position clear: "Our salvation lies not alone in the fall of Díaz, but in the transformation of the ruling political and social system, and that transformation cannot be affected by the mere overthrow of one tyrant that another may be put in his place, but by the denial of the pretended right of capital to appropriate to itself a portion of the toilers' product."[6]

To achieve a "real revolution" in Mexico, Ricardo Flores Magón conceived the plan to seize Baja California and spread the revolution from the California peninsula throughout all of Mexico. Baja California, he explained, would be the principal base from which the PLM would carry the "Social Revolution to all of Mexico and to all the world."[7]

This vision caused a split in the PLM. A number of PLM leaders doubted the wisdom of the Baja California venture, and urged Flores Magón to advance the revolution in Mexico by working with Madero and pushing him in a more radical direction. But Ricardo Flores Magón remained adamant, whereupon Antonio Villareal, Gutierrez Lazaro de la Lara, and Enrique Flores Magón (Ricardo's own brother) broke with him and left to join Madero.[8]

This did not deter Ricardo Flores Magón. He now took the surprising step of writing to Samuel Gompers for his help. His appeal, written in March, 1911, was on behalf of "a cause as just and holy as ever history recorded," a revolution "against unspeakably atrocious slavery, forced on us and supported by the American money power" represented by the "Standard Oil Co., the Guggenheims, the Southern Pacific Railway, the Sugar Trust"—in short, the "Wall Street autocracy, the same forces which exploited the working class in the United States." Hence Flores Magón appealed:

> It is time that the workingmen of the United States speak out, and it is for you to give the word, promptly and decisively. The slavery against which we are fighting is the slavery your American Federation of Labor was organized to fight. The chains that the money power has fastened on us are the chains against which you fret. Our cause is your cause, but yours in its extremist, most pitiable and, therefore, most irresistible form. . . .
>
> We repeat that our cause is your cause, and we call on you to give it voice—promptly, clearly and decisively.[9]

Flores Magón did not ask Gompers to support his plan for a "real revolution" in Mexico, and he did not mention Baja California. What he asked was for the the AFL to protest President Taft's action in support of Díaz and his Wall Street allies by the sending of thousands of American soldiers to the Mexican border—an action we will discuss below.

Gompers replied that the purpose of the troop movement was not yet known. But he hoped that fears that they were being sent to support Wall Street's man in Mexico were unfounded, not only because the Mexican people had the right to govern their own affairs but because intervention would be a blow to the integrity of the United States and the liberty of the American people.[10]

Gompers, however, suspected that Flores Magón had other motives in approaching the AFL, and he wanted more information about the movement the Mexican rebel headed: "I think the American people should be told by the authorized spokesman of the revolutionary movement of Mexico, what it aims to accomplish as a constructive power if entrusted with the power of government."[11]

Flores Magón replied that the revolution was war, the purpose of which was to secure to the Mexican workers "possession of the land, reduction of the hours of labor and increased wages" as well as liberty for all. He reminded Gompers that American capitalists were looking to cheap Mexican labor to break the back of organized labor in the United States, both by importing Mexican workers and by transferring capital to Mexico. "If our people can win for themselves industrial liberty they will work out their own salvation. But if American labor stands idly by, and permits them to be crushed by militarism, at the behest of the money power, they will drag with them, to the lowest depths, their immediate neighbors— the American workingmen."[12]

Gompers transmitted this correspondence to the AFL Executive Council but without any recommendation. At first he seems to have been inclined to favor Flores Magón, for he had been pleased by editorials in *Regeneración* in praise of the AFL. But when Gutierrez de Lara and Antonio I. Villareal, who had written these editorials, abandoned the PLM for Madero, Gompers had second thoughts. Moreover, when Flores Magón's anarchist philosophy became crystal clear in his attacks on Madero and in his letter to Emma Goldman—praising anarchism as "clearing the soil of weeds that it may eventually bear fruit"—Gompers decided to submit Magón's letter to the Executive Council without any recommendation.[13]

Many socialists were also turning a deaf ear to Flores Magón's appeals for support. They had welcomed the overthrow of Díaz, and while most socialists were skeptical of Madero's revolutionary credentials, they were not willing to reject him out of hand and ally themselves with Flores Magón.[14] This attitude was greatly influenced by the experience of Mother Jones. The aged socialist and labor organizer visited Mexico in September 1911 together with Joe Cannon of the Western Federation of Miners and Frank J. Hayes, vice-president of the United Mine Workers. Díaz had fled, and Madero was about to assume the presidency. They were taken to see Madero by Jesus Flores Magón, Ricardo's brother. Their mission was to get the consent and protection of the Mexican government "to organize all the miners of Mexico."

Madero, who spoke good English, asked, "What is your interest in the Mexican miner?" The answer was that "the labor movement is international, and to organize the Mexican workers is as necessary for our end as is the organizing of the workers in the United States." The Americans added that they were "compelled to either fight to raise the standard of living of the Mexican miner that lowered our wage scale, or accept lower wages, and we preferred the first to the last." At this Madero said: "Not only will I pledge you my word that no objection will be made by the government to your organizing our miners, but I assure you that we want them organized; we want labor to act collectively; we do not want blind revolt. Come down from the United States and organize all the workers of Mexico—you will be welcomed." Before the interview ended, Mother Jones told Madero that one of the things she hated most about the Díaz regime was the fact that Mexican workers were paid less for the same work than the Americans. To this Madero replied: "That's a condition that will not be tolerated as long as I am connected with the government."

On her return to the United States, Mother Jones told of the group's experience, and declared that Madero's "heart seemed filled with the desire to relieve the suffering in his country." She, Charles Moyer of the WFM, and Frank J. Hayes of the UMW later traveled to Mexico and did begin organizing miners with Madero's blessing.[15]

Many socialist and radical labor leaders, including Mother Jones, urged Ricardo Flores Magón to return to Mexico and work to push the Madero revolution in a more radical direction.[16] But nothing they said could convince him. He was determined to go ahead with the Baja California project as the initial phase of a thorough-going revolution in Mexico, and he viewed any other course as a betrayal of the Mexican workers and peasants.[17]

Ricardo Flores Magón still had support for his plan among radical groups in the United States, such as the IWW, the Anarchists and the Anarcho-Syndicalists, and some socialists. Among the latter were John Kenneth Turner, his wife Ethel Duffy Turner, and Jack London. Turner warned the socialists not to be taken in by Madero's general promises, charging that his movement was dominated by middle-class interests "rather than by the working class." The revolution under Madero's leadership, while constituting a tremendous step forward from Díaz, would not by any means go as far as one under the leadership of Ricardo Flores Magón. Hence Turner and his wife allied themselves with Flores Magón, and helped raise men and money for the Baja California venture.[18]

Jack London also helped raise funds. The socialist novelist prepared a manifesto to be read at a meeting in Los Angeles. It was addressed "Dear Brave Comrades of the Mexican Revolution," and London expressed himself as being "with you heart and soul" along with other "Socialist, anarchists, hobos, chick thieves, outlaws and undesirable citizens of the U.S. . . ." After hailing "the gallant band that took Mexicali," London described himself "a chicken thief and revolutionist."[19] As we shall see, the victory at Mexicali was an event in the Baja California expedition.

Jack London also published a short story which dealt with the effort to raise money for the Baja California venture. In his story, a poor Mexican hobo named Felipe Rivera, joins a revolutionary junta in the United States (clearly the PLM in Los Angeles). When the junta needs $5,000 to purchase arms and munitions, Rivera attempts to obtain the money by fighting a professional boxer. Rivera defeats the professional and turns over the purse to the revolutionary junta for the purchase of arms for the Baja California expedition.[20]

It was to the Wobblies, as members of the IWW were called, that Ricardo Flores Magón mainly turned for support. Nor is this surprising. From its formation in 1905, the IWW had been a steady ally of the *magonistas*; indeed, the PLM revolutionary paper *Regeneración* was viewed by U.S. authorities as the Spanish-language IWW weekly.[21] The Wobblies regarded Madero as simply "a fake," a "gentleman millionaire and a slave owner himself." Only the PLM stood for the "real revolution."[22]

On April 22, 1911, *Solidarity* (an IWW organ) published a "Stirring Appeal" from the PLM Junta, pleading for "MONEY, MONEY AND MORE MONEY for the support of the Social Revolution in Mexico." Signed by Ricardo Flores Magón, the appeal read:

Our cause is yours: it is the cause of the silent slaves of the soil, of the pariah of the workshop and the factory, of the galley slave of the sea, of the hard-labor convicts of the mines, of all those who suffer from the inequality of the capitalist system.

Our cause is yours: if you remain inactive while your brothers meet death embracing the red flag, you will give with your inaction a rude blow to the cause of the proletarian. . . .

Comrades! comply with your duty.

When the news reached the IWW that the *magonistas* had begun fighting for a "real revolution" in Baja California, *Solidarity* as well as the IWW's *Industrial Worker* and the *The Agitator* (then still an IWW organ) hailed the information. Then called upon all Wobblies and sympathizers not only to send money to Ricardo Flores Magón in Los Angeles, but for recruits to join the military revolutionary campaign "to TAKE back the millions of acres of rich soil that has been given away by the Butcher Díaz to Hearst, Otis, Morgan and their like. . . ."[23]

Lowell L. Blaisdell has told the full story of the Baja California fiasco. As he tells it, Ricardo Flores Magón and a number of his PLM supporters, operating from their base in Los Angeles, instituted a military campaign to develop anarchist strongholds in northern Mexico. These were to expand and embrace all of Mexico in a social revolution.[24]

Along with a small group of Mexicans, the Baja California campaign attracted a host of North Americans. What it did not attract were many Mexicans. *Regeneración* enjoyed a significant readership among Texas Mexicans. But hardly any of them joined the Baja California venture.[25] Rather, a large proportion of the "Mexican Revolutionists" were North Americans, many of them with ties to the IWW. "There are a great many I.W.W.'s in our ranks and I presume that more will arrive daily," wrote a Wobbly correspondent from Baja California. Among the Wobblies who joined the Baja revolution were Joe Hill (the famous IWW songwriter), Frank Little, John Bond, Luis Rodríguez, Simon Berthold, and Jack Mosby, along with groups of nameless members of the IWW.[26]

Arms for the expedition—inadequate at best—were furnished by John Kenneth Turner who sent rifles, pistols, and cartridges across the border packed in boxes that bore the label "Agricultural Implements," and by the IWW which shipped arms from Chicago to San Diego; they were then carried to Mexico by wagon.[27]

From San Diego, Wobbly poet Laura Emerson sent an appeal for more arms for the Baja California fighters, and included her poem "Revolution" which began:

> *They are rising by the millions*
> *In the land of Mexico*
> *Slaves and peons long down trodden*
> *Dare to strike their tyrant foe.*
> *Weak and trembling from starvation*
> *Yet with spirit fierce and brave*
> *They unite to break their fetters*
> *And a dying race to save.*

And she appealed:

> *Workers of the world, awaken!*
> *Your comrades call from Mexico.*
> *They care not for one grey haired tyrant*
> *A system damned they'll overthrow.*
> *Class with class in deadly conflict*
> *As it is throughout the land,*
> *Rise! ye millions, as a unit*
> *And the wealth you've made demand.*[28]

The first military success of the Baja revolt was the taking of Mexicali on January 28, 1911 by a band of 13 Mexicans and one Wobbly, John Bond, all led by Fabian Socialist José Maria Levya. *Solidarity* reported that "a rifle squad of 75 I.W.W. men" had "put to rout over 300 Federal soldiers," and hailed the victory as a "Good argument for direct action."[29]

Another argument came a week later when a Canadian Indian by the name of Stanley Williams led 30 men in taking the small village of Algodones. But in March came the first split in the ranks of the Baja revolutionists. Levya arrested Williams and expelled him from Mexico. Thereupon 40 of Williams' followers left Levya to fight for Madero in Sonora. That same month, however, a group of 18 men under the fanatical Wobbly Luis Rodríguez captured the village of Tecata. In April came the death of Simon Berthold, subchief of the Baja California revolutionaries. Another Wobbly, Jack Mosby, took his place by a vote of non-Mexicans. At this, Levya abandoned the Baja revolt to fight for Madero in Chihauhua.

Rys Prices, a Welshman, led his army of Wobblies (mostly from San Diego), Irishmen, Italians, Germans, and a handful of Mexicans in capturing the border town of Tijuana on May 9. The victory, achieved almost without opposition, was greeted in the Wobbly press as promising the early triumph of "the true revolution" in Mexico. "REDS GAIN A GREAT VICTORY" was the headline in the *Industrial Worker*. The sub-head read: "Turning Point in Revolution—Many Deeds of Bravery—I.W.W. Boys in Insurrecto Army." The story that followed was dated Tijuana, Baja Cal., May 10, and was headed "Special to the 'Worker!" It opened:

> At last the victory of social revolutionists in Lower California is assured. The workers of America and Mexico are awakening, and brave men are sacrificing their lives for the cause of Freedom, another sacrifice shall not be in vain. . . .
> The fall of Tijuana means the turning point in the campaign against Díaz tyranny in Baja California. The rebels now control the whole peninsula excepting the capital of the state. Ensenada, and the acquisition of Tijuana gives the "red army" an excellent base of supplies and a military headquarters from which to conduct the rest of the campaign.[30]

It did not take long for this optimistic prediction to be proved wrong. In June, Price suddenly departed the Baja area, leaving Mosby in charge of the Tijuana army. On June 22, 1911, Mosby's troops were pushed out of Tijuana by Mexican *federales*, now serving under Madero. Díaz, it will be recalled, had fled Mexico in May.

Mosby fled across the border, and, on June 26, was interned with his men by U.S. military authorities at Fort Rosecrans in San Diego.[31] The *New York Times* reported that "100 rebels, under Gen. Jack Mosby . . . laid down their arms at the international boundary line . . . and marched across as prisoners of United States troops."[32]

Most of the one hundred men were eventually released, but Mosby, even after he had turned informer for the government and testified against Ricardo Flores Magón, was sentenced to prison for desertion from the Marines. He was killed en route to jail when he allegedly tried to escape.

Despite these developments, the IWW press clung to the hope that the Baja escapade would turn out well. As late as June 8, 1911, the *Industrial Worker* published an appeal from the IWW Brigade in Tijuana: "Hold meetings, read this letter, collect money and come. Don't believe the capitalist press when they tell you there is peace in Mexico because Díaz has resigned. There will never be peace in Mexico until the Red Flag flies over the workingmen's country and capitalism shall have been overthrown." A month later, however, the Wobbly organ was forced to concede that the Baja revolt had been crushed, defeated by factionalism and traitors, as well as by the Mexican *federales* and U.S. troops.[33]

Thus ended Flores Magón's "desert revolution." The last episode on Mexican soil in this bizarre episode of the Mexican Revolution came when Dick Ferris, an actor and promoter, proclaimed the separate Republic of Baja California with himself as self-appointed president. The last episode on U.S. soil came in June 1912. Hoping to have rapprochement with the *magonistas*, Madero sent Ricardo's brother, Jesus, along with Sarabia and Levya, on a peace mission to invite Ricardo to return to Mexico and take a place in the revolutionary government. But Ricardo Flores Magón refused to budge, and condemned his older brother and former friends as traitors. The mission failed. On June 4, the four leading junta members—Ricardo and Enrique Flores Magón, Librado Rivera, and Anselmo Figueroa—were arrested and jailed, with bail fixed for Ricardo Flores Magon at $5,000.[34]

The Junta leaders were indicted on five counts of violating sections 37 and 10 of the U.S. criminal code, that is, "conspiracy to hire and retain the services of foreign people as soldiers."[35] "Although the prosecution went through the motions of proving the neutrality violation," notes W. Dirk Raat, ". . . the unwritten and real charge was the *magonista* alliance with American radicals, especially the hated I.W.W."[36] On June 22 the inevitable verdict of guilty was handed down. The rebels were sentenced to serve the maximum sentence—23 months in prison—and were not released until January 19, 1914.[37]

In retrospect it appears that the Baja California revolutionists won one or two "revolutionary battles," held the towns of Mexicali and Tijuana, and then the movement fell apart. While the odd collection of North American Wobblies, socialists, anarchists, adventurers, fortune-hunters and misfits of all sorts fought together with a small array of Mexicans, the leader—Ricardo Flores Magón—never took to the field but remained practically in hiding in Los Angeles. Thus an army, headed by and made up largely of non-Mexican adventurers and soldiers of fortune, never properly equipped or adequately supplied, conducted the military "revolution." The Mexican forces, slow to take the initiative and not too effective when they did, finally drove that "army" back into the United States. Blaisdell concludes his study with the observation that although Ricardo Flores Magón was an extremely significant thinker, "as a leader of men his incompetence was truly breathtaking."[38]

For Ricardo Flores Magón the Baja California fiasco proved to be tragic. He lost much of his support among American radicals and Mexicans, who now viewed him more as a "filibuster" than a revolutionist. Indeed, in both Mexico and the United States, the view prevailed for a long time that the movement led by Ricardo Flores Magón was in actuality nothing but an American filibustering scheme aimed at Baja California. It was even argued in Mexico that North American financial and industrial interests, many of them owners of property in Mexico, supported Flores Magón in the Baja California operation. This alone was enough to make him a traitor to his country.[39] Finally, it was bluntly stated that the whole Baja California venture was only a conspiracy by the U.S. government and private financial interests to deprive Mexico of Lower California and annex it to the United States.[40]

In recent years this view has been rejected in both Mexico and the United States. Lowell L. Blaisdell, who has examined the Baja California episode in great detail, concludes that "as a matter of record neither the United States government nor American business had conspired with the Magonist revolutionaries." The only real "filibuster" threat to Mexico was that of the "still born Ferris Republic" which Blaisdell correctly describes as "largely a comedy."[41]

Today the memory of Ricardo Flores Magón is honored throughout Mexico. His remains rest in the Rotunda of Illustrious Men in Mexico City. Streets and squares in all parts of the country bear his name, and Mexicans pay him homage as a great "precursor" of their Revolution. Yet he is still criticized in some historical circles for having failed to return to Mexico to help push the Madero administration further to the left.

This is not a new criticism at the time of Díaz's resignation and Madero's ascent to power. The most severe critics of Flores Magón in this connection were Mother Jones and Job Harriman. Mother Jones probably did more for the Mexican Revolution and the Mexican refugees in the United States than any other North American apart from John Kenneth Turner; Job Harriman, California socialist lawyer, had defended PLM members in federal trials. But by late 1911, both were denouncing Ricardo Flores Magón for remaining in the United states after Madero's victory instead of returning to Mexico and helping to advance the revolution among the Mexican masses.

In October 1911, Mother Jones and Job Harriman visited the Flores Magón brothers in Los Angeles. In two letters, one to Madero's Secretary of Justice and the other to Ricardo Flores Magón, Mother Jones explained the break with the *magonistas*. She pointed out that she and two other AFL organizers had visited Madero shortly after his election. Upon her return to the United States, Mother

Jones fulfilled a promise to the new Mexican Secretary of Justice and tried to convince Ricardo Flores Magón and his allies at *Regeneración* to return to Mexico. She met twice with Flores Magón, urging him to take advantage of new civil liberties under the Madero government and to organize a new and real Mexican labor movement. In fact, Mother Jones believed Flores Magón was legally and morally bound to leave the United States, for

> when men are granted the rights to agitate within the border and under their own government, I don't consider that they have any right to come and do that agitation at long range, across the border under another government.

Mother Jones reported that she and Flores Magón and his associates had discussed politics for over an hour, but the PLM leaders insisted that Madero was insufficiently radical, that "they believed only in direct action," "the taking over the lands," and "charged everyone with being a traitor but themselves." At the end of her second meeting, Mother Jones presented Ricardo Flores Magón with an ultimatum:

> You cannot go into Mexico by force and take the lands, for the United States is a friendly nation to Mexico. They will not uphold any violation of International laws. There is one of two things before you. You will either go into Mexico . . . or you will be arrested by the American Government and handed over to the Mexican Government.

After the meetings, Job Harriman told Mother Jones that he could not continue to be the lawyer for the PLM leaders "or have anything to do with them." Hence, when these men were tried by the federal government in June 1912, Job Harriman refused to defend them, and they were defended by "a young and inexperienced lawyer who was unable to develop a convincing defense."

Mother Jones felt so betrayed and frustrated by her dealings with Flores Magón and the PLM that she urged trade unions not to render them any further aid. She told Flores Magón that "Neither my colleagues nor myself shall ever again insult you by taking any money from the American Federation of Labor to defend you if you should again get into the clutches of the law." She visited AFL leaders in the Los Angeles area, securing promises from them not to render any future aid to the *magonistas*. She summed up her attitude in her letter to Madero's Secretary of Justice:

> I consider them one and all a combination of unreasonable fanatics, with no logic in their arguments, and when people tell me these fanatics are honest I cannot agree with them. Fanaticism has never won anything permanent for humanity's cause.[42]

This must have sounded strange coming from someone who had been repeatedly accused of fanaticism in the cause of of labor and socialism. But one must keep in mind that Mother Jones was also fanatical about the need to work inside mass organizations where the workers were assembled; about the need to play a role in pushing such movements in a more progressive direction rather than to isolate oneself with a "pure, revolutionary program" which reached only those who agreed with the revolutionists. The fact that Ricardo Flores Magón had the enthusiastic support of the IWW did not impress Mother Jones. Although herself a charter member of the IWW, she had long since decided that the isolationist policies and anarchist tendencies within the Wobbly movement made it impossible for it to influence the mass of American workers.[43]

Eugene V. Debs agreed with Mother Jones in her criticism of Ricardo Flores Magón's views and policies, but he respected the *magonistas* for sponsoring a real revolution whereas Madero was "but a revised edition of Díaz."[44] Announcing his belief that the forces represented by Flores Magón would still triumph, Debs called for their defense in their forthcoming federal trial:

> Personally I am not in agreement with all the plans and tactics of these leaders, but I am bound to admit their honesty, their sincerity, and their unselfish devotion to their enslaved people, and I am under obligation to fight for them against these fresh outrages perpetrated upon them by the hessian hirelings of American capitalism to the full extent of my power.[45]

Debs, however, did agree with Mother Jones that the PLM leaders in the United States should help advance the Mexican Revolution by working inside Mexico, and indicated approval of those *magonistas* who had joined Madero for this purpose. As he put it: "there is no road to successful revolution except through education and organization."[46]

Ricardo Flores Magón never doubted the correctness of the course he had followed. He explained his position in a letter to the American people which the Wobbly press published under the heading "WHY MAGÓN FIGHTS." He wrote of the visit by Madero's emissaries, among them his own brother, to win his support; "I refused and the arrest of the Junta of the Mexican Liberal Party followed." "Madero," he noted, "had the support of the money power of the world, rebel though he was. He had the support of the United States army. . . . All the assistance that money and influence could give him was at his command, regardless of national boundaries. For he had made his peace with the money power."[47] Then by way of contrast:

> How different is it with us! Because we stand for the people; because we wish to see them in possession of the necessities of life and we do not want them cheated with fine words; because we insist that their blood and hard-won, inexpressibly hard-won earnings, must not be allowed to have spent in vain; because we will not give up their cause, we find ourselves again in prison— to break up the one movement that seriously threatens the money power in Mexico and promises to lift the masses out of the unspeakable misery into which plutocracy has plunged them.

"How can we help fighting on," Flores Magón concluded. "How, so long as we retain a vestige of honor and self-respect, CAN we give up the ship? . . ."[48]

· IX ·

U.S. INTERVENTION, 1911–1914

In March 1911, as the anti-Diáz revolt led by Francisco I. Madero, gained momentum, United States Troops were mobilized along the border. The action by the Taft Administration in calling out the troops was immediately regarded in Mexico as the prelude of an impending invasion to keep the aged dictator in power. The goal of such an action would be to protect the large sums that U.S. businessmen had invested in Mexican factories, mines, railroad, oil fields, and other enterprises during the Díaz period—investments which would lose much if not all of their value if a thorough-going Revolution triumphed.[1]

It will be recalled that Ricardo Flores Magón wrote to Samuel Gompers, president of the AFL, asking for the Federation to protest President Taft's action. Gompers, it will also be recalled, had replied that the purpose of the troop movement, was not yet known but he hoped that fears that they were being sent to support Díaz were unfounded. He made it clear that he opposed intervention not only because it would interfere with the Mexican people's right to govern themselves, but it would also be a blow to the integrity of the United States and the liberty of the American people.

When Gompers transmitted Flores Magón's request to the AFL Executive Council, he recommended no action and instead waiting to see what developed before taking a stand. The members of the Executive Council took this advice, with John Mitchell of the United Mine Workers voting against it. Mitchell, of course, represented a union which was particularly confronted by competition from low-paid Mexican workers.[2]

While the AFL leadership did nothing, the Socialist Party of America decided to act. It was conscious of how closely associated were the Díaz dictatorship,

American business, and the administration in Washington, in fact, long before the intervention crisis of 1911, the socialist press, raised the danger that the U.S. government would use troops to crush any embryonic revolution.[3] By the end of 1910, as the anti-Díaz forces increased in influence, the *New York Call* made the slogan "Hands Off Mexico!" a feature of every issue. In a front-page editorial on November 24, 1910, it appealed:

Hands off Mexico! must become the slogan of the American labor movement. For starvation wages in Mexico are a perpetual menace to the living conditions of American workingmen, and political tyranny in Mexico tends to bring about a similar state of affairs in adjacent countries. Hands off Mexico! must be the demand made by the united working class upon the government in Washington. The Socialist party, the American Federation of Labor, and all other labor organizations have a common interest in this matter, and should combine to act in common. Hands off Mexico! you rulers in Washington, and in the border states as well, and let the tyrant contend unaided against the spirit of revolt he himself has unchained. Hands off Mexico! also you capitalists and financial magnates. And if you come to the aid of the tryant with your money bags, be warned before hand. The American people will not aid you to recover your money from a successful Mexican revolution. Hands off Mexico!

"Three times during the past two years," John Kenneth Turner wrote in the *International Socialist Review* of December 1910, "the United States government has rushed an army to the Mexican border in order to crush a movement . . . against the autocrat of Mexico."[4] The next time, a powerful military force would cross the border to crush a successful revolution—unless the people, especially the trade unions and the Socialists, mobilized immediately to prevent it.[5]

This danger caused the 1910 national convention of the Socialist Party of America to pass the following resolution without objection and discussion:*

Resolved, That we, the members of the Socialist party of the United States, demand that the government of this country shall not interfere in the affairs of Mexico and other Latin American countries. That we are unalterably opposed to the powers of this nation, being used to buttress any foreign despotism.[6]

*Twenty-five minutes, however, were allowed for a Mexican comrade, Lizáro Gutierrez de Lara, to explain why the resolution was important. In the midst of his remarks, de Lara reported that "many of you have told me of your great hopes that Mexico would be annexed to the United States," *Proceedings of the First National Congress of the Socialist Party of America* [Chicago, May 15–21, 1910], pp. 3–4, 6. No delegate commented on this statement, and Wilfred H. Peterson concludes that "it seems unlikely that many Socialists were sincere advocates of American expansion to the south," "Foreign Policy and Foreign Policy Theory of the American Socialist Party," p. 31. Peterson, incidentally, calls the resolution the first clear stand taken by the Socialist Party on a current foreign policy issue. The meeting was called a "congress" to distinguish it from the regular quadrennial conventions, but its funtions were essentially similar.

On March 10, 1911 the United States dispatched 20,000 troops to the Mexican border, and sent several American warships to Mexican ports in both oceans. The action provoked an immediate response from the Socialist Party's National Executive Committee. At 10 A.M. on March 11, John Spargo moved at the NEC that Morris Hillquit prepare a statement on the troop movements. By the morning of March 12, the Committee had approved the motion, and issued a proclamation entitled, "Withdraw the Troops!" The proclamation informed the American people of the dangers involved in the military movements and gave a brief history of the Díaz dictatorship, and of U.S. capitalist backing for the despotic regime. It also decribed how Díaz, whom it called the "evil genius" of Mexico, had "destroyed the freedom of suffrage, speech, press and assembly," and had "exiled, imprisoned and assassinated" many patriots who sought to restore popular rule. The proclamation closed with the assertion that "the mission of the American army at the Mexican border and the American warships at the Mexican coasts" was nothing but a strategy "to save the regime of Díaz and quell the rising of the Mexican people."

> Against this unspeakable outrage the Socialist party of the United States, representing six hundred thousand American citizens and voters lodges its public and emphatic protest. Let the voice of the people resound from one end of the country to the other in loud and unmistakable tone, "Withdraw the troops from the Mexican border."

The proclamation was designed to gain support from "labor unions and other bodies of progressive citizens" as well as from socialists. It was sent to all SPA locals with instructions that

> It is now in order for every member and sympathizer of the Socialist Party to move as one man. It is war, or the threat of war, for capitalists only. The workers as usual are to play the role of food for cannons.
>
> Arrange for protest meetings at once. Local speakers must be pressed into service. Our daily papers will carry plenty of information to equip such speakers for an intelligent discussion of the subject.
>
> YOUR TOWN SHOULD BE THOROUGHLY PLACARDED, AND AT ONCE, WITH THESE PROCLAMATIONS.[7]

The National Secretary was ordered to prepare petitions supporting the proclamation which the local branches were urged to circulate. The petitions were to be sent to Congress through Representative Victor Berger, Socialist Congressman from Milwaukee.[8]

Hundreds of SPA locals, labor unions, and various citizens' groups and individuals responded. In the archives of of the Adjutant General's office, there are 305 such petitions: 128 were from SPA locals, 116 from mass meetings of citizens, and 58 from labor unions.[9] While most of the petition more or less followed the language of the SPA National Executive Committee, there were some interesting variations. The Christian Socialist Fellowship of Boston declared that the money used to move troops "ought to have been devoted to the abolition of child labor, safeguarding workers employed in the mines . . . and a thousand other efforts at protecting the lives of the workers of the country." The Herrin, Illinois local of the United Mine Workers observed that "should our Army and Navy be the cause of stopping [*sic*] this revolution in Mexico, that it will force thousands of Mexicans into this Nation for safety of their lives and in competition with American labor that are now in idleness by the thousands."[10]

Two of the petitions are worth quoting at length as reflecting the views of the Socialist locals and the trade unions which responded to the appeal of the SPA National Executive Committee.

The first is from the petition of the Dubuque, Iowa local of the Socialist Party:

Whereas, the people of Mexico are at present rising in rebellion against a despotic government which has kept them for more than a generation without even a semblance of democratic government; and

Whereas, At the behest of American capitalists, who fear the loss of profit on a billion and half of capital invested in American industries, President William H. Taft has sent to the frontier of Mexico twenty thousand United States troops, with the avowed purpose of putting an end to the rebellion of an oppressed people; therefore, be it

Resolved, That we, residents of Dubuque, Iowa and members of Local Dubuque of the Socialist Party in meeting assembled, do hereby protest against this action of President Taft and do promise to those who have risen against oppression in Mexico all the support which is in our power. . . .[11]

The second is from the Barre, Vermont branch of the Granite Cutters' International Association. It read:

Believing that the sudden massing of American troops on the Mexican border is intended to intimidate, impede, and harass the people of Mexico, now in actual revolt to maintain their human rights against the despotic rule of a President, who through illegal and unconstitutional methods has now assumed the role of a cruel dictator; that the massing of such troops may precipitate wanton war and bloodshed between the people of two American republics, who have no just cause for hostilities, and that it was undertaken for the purpose of protecting the private property interests of a ring of American capitalists and spectators, We the Barre, Vt. branch of the Granite Cutters International Association protest against the executive order for the movement of troops toward Mexico, as a degrading and unworthy attempt to bolster up predatory interests. Thereby ignoring the human rights and aspirations of a liberty loving people. We therefore request that you withdraw the American Army now on the Mexican border, and let the despot Díaz and the revolutionists fight it out.[12]

"LABOR RAPS TAFT FOR MEXICO MOVE" was the headline in the *Chicago Tribune*. The story described a meeting of the Chicago Federation of Labor. An anti-intervention resolution introduced by the Teachers' Union stirred up a controversy between male and female delegates. After Margaret Haley introduced the resolution on behalf of the teachers, mainly a paraphrase of the SPA's national proclamation,

Delegate Charles Frey of the Machinists' Union objected and proposed that an all-male committee investigate the question. "This brought every woman delegate to her feet clamoring for recognition," the *Tribune* reported. In the end, only two delegates voted against the resolution. Copies were sent to President Taft and Samuel Gompers.[13] Thus, while the AFL leadership remained silent on the amassing of U.S. troops on the Mexican border, Federation affiliates did speak out against intervention and for withdrawal of the troops.

On April 5, 1911, freshman socialist Congressman Victor Berger, in office less than a month, introduced a resolution demanding the withdrawal of military forces from the Mexican border. A few weeks later, he presented Congress with a petition for troop withdrawal bearing 90,000 signatures.[14]

Responding to an appeal from the national headquarters of the Industrial Workers of the World in Chicago, Anti-Interference leagues were organized by IWW locals in several cities. The leagues called on all Wobblies, socialists and revolutionists "to send telegrams to Washington, to the president, to the department of state, and to congressmen, DEMANDING that the American troops be called away, from the Mexican border, and demanding that the insurrectos or rebels be recognized as belligerents by the U.S. government. We also call on you to hold protest meetings everywhere, and have the actions of our capitalist politicians advertised to the workers everywhere."[15]

Wobblies also distributed leaflets at Army and Navy recruiting offices reading: "Don't enlist in the American Army's and Navy's capitalist war against the Mexican peons. Enlist in the class war against American, Mexican and all other capitalists."[16] "What is to be done?" asked a leaflet distributed by Wobblies at factory gates in the state of Washington. The answer followed:

Warn the masters at Washington in the most emphatic manner that THE INVASION OF MEXICO WILL MEAN A GENERAL STRIKE IN THE UNITED STATES.[17]

As the protests mounted, the Taft administration announced that the purpose of the American troops at the border and the warships at the Mexican ports was solely to prevent the smuggling of arms to the Mexican insurgents seeking to overthrow Díaz, and also to protect American lives. The protesters were hardly convinced, and continued to insist that the real aim was to protect U.S. investments in Mexico, and that the troops would be ordered to cross the border if it became necessary to achieve this goal.[18]

Then when the troops were removed from the border without having actually invaded Mexico, Socialists, Wobblies and AFL affiliates—those who had protested—insisted that their opposition had upset Taft's plan and headed off a full-scale invasion.[19] However, recent scholarship has rejected this view, and upheld the Taft administration's claim that it had called out the troops primarily to limit filibustering and protect American lives. The troop movement, in short, was not another manisfestation of "outright Dollar Diplomacy," characteristic of foreign policy under Taft,[20] but part of the administration's efforts "to meet the obligations of a neutral."[21]

It is true that Taft did not view the prospect of military intervention with glee.[22] It is also true that Taft, after first favoring the idea of a joint Mexican-U.S. military expedition proposed by Harrison Grey Otis (wealthy publisher of the *Los Angeles Times* and one of the biggest investors in Mexico), yielded to the advice of the Army Chief of Staff against the project on the ground that it would unite Mexicans against the invaders.[23] But the fact that Taft failed to invade Mexico to save the Díaz dictatorship does not mean that he would not have done so if he felt it essential to protect the interests of American capitalists.

Taft explained the real reason for the dispatch of American troops to the border in a confidential note to the army chief of staff, General Leonard Wood. He informed Wood that he had acted after learning from Henry Lane Wilson, U.S. Ambassador to Mexico, that Mexico was about to explode like a volcano. There would be a general insurrection, Wilson had said, that would injure or destroy "American investment of more than a billion dollars" as well as endanger the lives of 40,000 or more Americans. Troops were to be positioned so that if revolutionary conditions demanded it, they could be sent into Mexico to "save American lives and property."

In the meantime, the presence of American troops would help prevent insurrectionary attempts from American soil and provide encouragement to Díaz and his backers.[24] "In other words, it was designed to enable Díaz to stem the tide of insurrection," wrote W. Dirk Raat, who does not accept the conclusion of recent scholarship.[25]

That no U.S. soldiers actually entered Mexico *en masse* at this time was particularly due, as the socialists, Wobblies and other protesters claimed, to opposition to the presence of the troops at the border and the loud demands for their withdrawal. But other factors played a role. Most significant was the growing disillusionment with Díaz of a key number of U.S. capitalists. The Rockefeller interests were clearly angered when Díaz began to favor British petroleum interests, while American mining groups were antagonized by the dictator's reluctance to grant further concessions in order to attempt to hold back the growing opposition to his policies. New York bankers were angered by the fact that Mexico began seeking loans and credit in Europe instead of in the United States. On top of this, Díaz refused to provide the United States with a permanent lease on Magdalena Bay, Baja California, site of an American naval station. It was actually reported that Japan and Germany were to be favored with concessions in the area of Magdalena Bay.[26]

The die was cast on May 12, 1911. After meeting with Secretary of State Philander C. Knox and Attorney General George W. Wickersham, Taft issued an order to the Department of the Treasury permitting the passage of guns and ammunition from El Paso to Ciudad Juárez, where two days earlier Díaz's troops had been defeated by the *maderistas*. In his order Taft stated that the mere sale of supplies to Mexicans, "whether insurrectos or supporters of the Government was not a violation of international law or U.S. statutes." Anticipating that this policy would be seen favoring the *maderistas*, he announced that it probably would help them but the situation grew out of the weakness of the Díaz government, for which the United States was not responsible.[27]

The Taft administration was now ready to accept the inevitable. The long dictatorship of Porfirio Díaz, the old friend of American capitalists, was about to end. Within two weeks of Taft's decision, Díaz resigned the presidency. The next step was also inevitable. Given the choice between the upper-class reformer Madero and the anarcho-syndicalist Flores Magón, the administration, which so faithfully served the interests of U.S. Big Business, decided to back the reformer. But within limits.

On the one hand, the administration would deny the radical revolutionaries the use of American soil in their attempt to prevent the *maderistas* from taking power,[28] and all federal charges against Madero's followers for violating the neutrality law would be dropped. But, at the same time, Madero would be informed U.S. intervention would follow if he did not favor that U.S. capitalists over European and Japanese competitors. The time had passed to save Díaz. Intervention was now a club to be used to force Madero to see the proper light.[29]

Madero got the message, and U.S. troops did not intervene in Mexico. But they did act as roving patrols along the border to prevent the *magonistas* from carrying on an effective opposition to Madero. Moreover, Mexican troops were permitted to cross the border into the United States and suppress the *magonistas*. Secretary of State Knox justified this practice because "this movement of troops is designed, among other things, to secure adequate protection of American life and property in Mexico."[30]

Madero was thus given a free hand to carry through a limited revolution without endangering American business interests in Mexico. But even a limited revolution was too much for certain interests in the United States. Conditioned by years of profitable business activity in Mexico during the long dictatorship of Porfirio Díaz, and by the fact that they continued to hold investments in Mexican land, railroads, and mines, these U.S. capitalists exhibited hostility to all aspects of the Mexican revolution from its inception. They yearned for a return to the stability and the friendly economic climate of the Porfirian period. Considering Mexican revolutionaries of whatever stripe to be "bandits" or terrorists," they began immediately after the overthrow of Díaz to plan for military intervention by the United States to restore the *status quo ante*.[31]

These capitalists gained the support of a group of trade unions in the United States who also yearned for the return of the days when they enjoyed special privileges in Mexico. Chief among them were the Railroad Brotherhoods: Brotherhood of Locomotive Engineers, Brotherhood of Locomotive Firemen and Enginemen, Brotherhood of Railroad Trainmen, and Order of Railway Conductors.*

*Of the four Railroad Brotherhoods, only one local of the Brotherhood of Railroad Trainmen (Subordinate Lodge No. 175) sent a protest to President Taft against the placing of the troops at the Mexican border and urged their withdrawal. The message supported the Mexican revolutionists, stating: "We recognize the Justice of the Revolt of the Insurgents (or Poor People) of Mexico against the tyrannical rule of Porfirio Díaz, and whereas "We recognize the unjust stand that our Government has taken to intimidate the Insurrecto and whip them into submission to a life of abject slavery to American Capital and Mexican Tyranny and oppression.

"Therefore be it resolved by the Brotherhood of Railroad Trainmen, Subordinate Lodge

Pressured by Mexican unions, the Madero administration took steps to end the special privileges enjoyed by U.S. railroad workers at the expense of the Mexicans. Enraged, the Railroad Brotherhood fought to restore the situation that existed under Díaz.[32] The chief of the Order of Railway Conductors complained that Madero was ruining "the only effective government that Mexico ever had," and he called for military intervention by the U.S. government. "Every American who has been in touch with the situation," he cried, "and every citizen of other civilized countries sees the necessity of adding the 'big stick' to the Monroe Doctrine, and the only question is, 'When it will be done.' "[33]

Representatives of the Brotherhood of Locomotive Engineers and the Order of Railway Conductors called at the U.S. Embassy in Mexico City to express their alarm at the anti-American manifestations in the Mexican Revolution. They were met sympathetically by Ambassador Henry Lane Wilson, who not only demanded of Madero that actions against U.S. railroad workers be rescinded, but urged President Taft to reconsider the question of sending the troops across the border.[34]

Charging a "determined attitude of the Mexican government to displace Americans," the Railroad Brotherhoods declared a general strike on the divisions of the National Railways of Mexico on April 17, 1912. Although the strike was a failure in forcing the Madero administration to retreat, the Brotherhoods made use of it to spread propaganda in the United States that the Madero government was increasingly anti-American and to campaign for intervention to stem the tide of anti-Americanism.[35]

But the Brotherhoods did not gain the support of the American Federation of Labor in their campaign. Lazáro Gutierrez de Lara, the former *magonista* but now a follower of Madero, was sent to the United States by a commission of Mexican revolutionists for the purpose of offsetting the pro-interventionist campaign and to appeal to the AFL to protest publicly against any plans for military intervention. The AFL Executive Council heard his appeal, and agreed to issue a protest against military intervention in Mexico.[36]

But it appeared that the promise would remain a paper one, for the Mexican issue was not raised by Gompers or the Executive Council at the 1912 AFL Convention. But Andrew Furuseth of the Sailor's Union of the Pacific along with T.A. Hanson, of the same union, called for a positive stand by the AFL. Specifically they asked the convention to extend cordial greetings and best wishes to all in Mexico who were "now struggling to abolish age-long wrongs," and to oppose with determination any intervention in Mexico by the United States government. The resolution was unanimously adopted by the convention.[37]

No. 175, that we extend our Full Sympathy and encouragement to the Mexican Insurrectionists; that we DEMAND of our National Government at Washington, D.C., that immediate and full recognition be made of the belligerency of these combatants. We further DEMAND that U.S. Troops be immediately withdrawn from the border of Mexico, and that the excuse offered of 20,000 troops will not be accepted by us or by Organized Labor as a whole. The truth is that it is the old story of CAPITAL versus LABOR." March 7, 1911, Old Military Records, Division Record Group 94, Adjutant General's Office, 1763058, National Archives.

For the first time the AFL was in advance of the Socialist Party on the Mexican issue. After the March 1911 crisis, the Socialist Party had remained silent on matters relating to Mexico. In October 1911, as a member of the National Executive Committee, "Big Bill" Haywood, urged the Party to "call upon the membership . . . and working class generally to take immediate steps to prevent war with Mexico." The motion was defeated by a margin of three to two, with two members not voting. In January 1912, Haywood repeated his request to the National Executive Committee, again urging that it should call upon the party membership and the working class generally to "take immediate steps to prevent war with Mexico." Again this was rejected, and when Haywood raised the demand at the 1912 national convention, he was ruled out of order by the chair.[38]

Thus there was the unusual situation that in 1912 the convention of the American Federation of Labor unanimously voted to oppose any intervention in Mexico by the United States government, and the convention of the Socialist Party would not even discuss such a proposal. The Socialist Party continued to maintain an official silence on the Mexican issue. But it broke the silence with a bang when American troops actually intervened later, in 1914.

In February 1913, in Mexico, a counterrevolutionary group, engineered a coup d'etat that culminated in the murder of President Madero and Vice-President José Maria Pino Suarez. Victoriano Huerta, who had betrayed his commander-in-chief, was appointed provisional president.[39]

Originally Ambassador Wilson had believed that Madero would favor U.S. capital over European investors and even that Madero, as time passed, would be forced "to revert more and more to the system implanted by General Díaz." He expressed the firm conviction that "Madero will do justice to American investors." But enraged by Madero's mounting anti-Americanism, Wilson became deeply involved in the coup. To be sure, it is an oversimplification to blame Wilson for Madero's assassination since, as Friedrich Katz puts it: "In the last analysis the large American companies in Mexico and the American government stood behind Ambassador Wilson and it is there that the roots of American opposition to Madero must be uncovered." But while the administration in Washington stood behind Wilson, it did not go along with his pleas that it cooperate with the new government. Despite the urgency of his ambassador, President Taft took no action towards recognizing Huerta. His reason for leaving the problem of recognition as a bargaining weapon to settle disputes with Huerta's government, which Taft considered the only force capable of "preserving order and protecting foriegn interests," he meant U.S. interests since American capitalists had been increasingly worried by Madero's friendly gestures towards British, German, and Japanese capitalists.[40]

Great Britain, Germany, Spain, France, Russia, Belgium, Italy, Portugal, Japan, and Denmark granted *de facto* recognition to Huerta on the conventional principles of international law. But Woodrow Wilson, who succeeded Taft at this time, departed from the traditional U.S. policy of recognition of *de facto* governments. Wilson refused to extend recognition on the basis of a newly declared policy of upholding only constitutional government based on the "moral" factor of govern-

by the consent of the governed. He declared he would refuse recognition to those who seized the machinery of state by means of "blood and iron."[41]

As he took office on March 4, 1913, Wilson announced that one of the chief objects of his administration was "to cultivate friendship and deserve the confidence of our sister republics of Central and South America."[42] But what Wilson said must be viewed in light of what he did.[43] Hailed as a champion of "anti-imperialism," and the supporter of a new and more idealistic Latin American policy, Wilson intervened militarily in Latin America more frequently than any other American President. His administration saw U.S. Marines intervene in Nicaragua, Haiti, Cuba, the Dominican Republic, and twice in Mexico. Moreover, as J. Fred Rippy points out, Wilson "under the doctrine of constitutionalism denied the right of revolution not only to the five republics of Central America but to all the rest of Latin America."[44]

In seeking to achieve his goal of ousting Huerta, Wilson engaged in the policy of "watchful waiting," meanwhile employing a variety of tactics from persuasion, loan proposals, and mediation efforts to ultimatums and threats of force.[45] As the U.S. government waited, Venustiano Carranza challenged Huerta's leadership, and declared himself *ad interim* president of Mexico at the end of March, 1913. Carranza, the elderly governor of Coahuila, provided the civilian leadership for the Constitutionalists, the major anti-Huerta forces. By mid-1913, Carranza had tacit support in the South and the formal loyalty of northern armies led by Francisco "Pancho" Villa, Alvaro Obregón, and Pablo Gonzáles. The Constitutionalists controlled northern Mexico by the end of 1913, and they began to close in on Central Mexico in early 1914.[46]

In his attempt to control the situation in Mexico, Wilson forbade the export of arms and munitions to either side in the civil war. At the same time, Wilson played one revolutionary chieftain against another, favoring Villa by lifting the embargo on arms shipment to him at one point, and supporting Carranza at another. But there was one revolutionary leader with whom Wilson would have nothing to do. That was Emiliano Zapata.

Embittered and disapointed by Madero's action in rejecting the demands for return of the expropriated lands to the peasants, Zapata rose against Madero on November 25, 1911, and proclaimed the Plan of Ayala. It demanded the return of all expropriated lands to the villages, the distribution of one-third of the hacienda lands among the landless peasants, and the expropriation and breaking up of all haciendas whose owners had fought against the revolution.[47]

Although Zapata and his peasant followers had little in common with Ricardo Flores Magón other than demanding the distribution of land among the peasants, he did attract the support of the remaining *magonistas* and the Wobblies. He also incurred the hostility of the Wilson administration which sought to do everything possible to weaken and destroy the *zapatistas*.[48]

The first opportunity came after Jesús M. Rangel, a *magonista* and Wobbly, organized a guerrilla force in Texas (known as the "Red Flaggers") to join the Zapata peasant movement in Mexico. Several of the guerrillas, led by Rangel and

Charles Cline, were militant members of the IWW. Rangel was a veteran Wobbly organizer who had already served two sentences in prison for his strike activities. Cline had been active in Portland and Denver, and helped to organize lumber workers in Louisiana. "Both these men," a labor paper reported, "together with others, took up the cause of the Mexican peon, when he started on his heroic effort to take back the land which had been stolen from him."[49]

On September 11, 1913, led by Rangel, 14 men attempted to cross the border near Carrizo Springs, Texas. While camped on the U.S. side, they were intercepted by Texas authorities and the U.S. cavalry. In the scuffle that followed, two guerrillas and one patrolman (a Mexican by the name of Ortiz) were killed. The remaining guerrillas were taken into custody and charged with the murder of Ortiz. While awaiting trial, they remained in prison.[50]

A defense campaign was immediately launched, and even some who drifted with Rangel, Cline and their followers, called the case one that "demands the serious consideration of every revolutionist."[51] The Rangel-Cline Defense Committee, with headquarters in Los Angeles, sent appeals to locals of the Socialist Party, the AFL, and the IWW pleading for funds, reminding socialist and non-socialist alike:

> The men involved, fourteen in all, have been active in the labor movement for many years, carrying the propaganda of working class solidarity to the toilers in the southwest. That is the real "crime" for which they will be tried, and unless you rally to their assistance at once, for that "crime" they will be convicted and sentenced to death.[52]

Leaders of AFL unions in Los Angeles joined the defense campaign, and a mass meeting was held in the Labor Temple, hall of the AFL unions of the city, to hear Defense Attorney Fred H. Moore, veteran IWW defense lawyer, tell the whole story "of the terrible miscarriage of justice." Moore was introduced by Anton Johannson, general organizer for the United Brotherhood of Carpenters, and the meeting was chaired by C.F. Grow, president of the Los Angeles local of the International Association of Machinists. Moore insisted that the "real crime of the men in prison" was that they had been active for years in "educating vast numbers of unorganized, helpless workers in the Southwest who, as a result, are at the point of revolting against the state of peonage which has oppressed them for years." Their second "crime" was that they were seeking to "organize the workers of Mexico into labor unions, to take possession of the industries and lands stolen from the workers by the rich politicians and foreign speculators." For these "crimes," they had been singled out to be put to death by capitalists in the United States, and President Wilson was merely doing their bidding.[53]

The *Los Angeles Citizen*, a socialist weekly, devoted considerable space to the defense efforts, and published the full story of the "frame-up" under the title, "Facing the Gallows in Texas," which was reprinted as a pamphlet and widely distributed in the Far West and Southwest. Unfortunately, apart from the *Halletsville Rebel* of Texas, no other socialist paper joined the defense campaign. Nor did the Socialist Party. Only after the revolutionaries were tried, found guilty, and sentenced to long terms in prison—Rangel and Cline being given life imprisonment and the others receiving sentences ranging from 25 to 99 years—did the Socialist Party make an issue of the case. Eugene V. Debs went to Texas in 1915 for a mass meeting for the release of all prisoners.[54]*

To Wilson's annoyance, Huerta was holding out much longer than the President had expected. Although Huerta badly needed recognition from the United States—without it European bankers might refuse him loans—he refused to yield to Wilson's ultimatum that he promise early free elections in which he (Huerta) would not be a candidate. Meanwhile, American financial interests and owners of mine and oil leases in Mexico were pressing for intervention in order to establish "order" in Mexico, especially an "order" that did not favor British and other European interests.[55]

By the summer of 1913, deeply resenting Huerta's recalcitrance, Wilson had decided that military intervention would be needed to bring him down. On August 27, 1913, Wilson addressed Congress on the Mexican question, noting Huerta's inability to establish order, and urging Americans to leave Mexico immediately. There were about 15,000 Americans in Mexico at this time, including 4,000 Mormon colonists in Sonora and Chihuahua. At this time, too, U.S. capitalists controlled 78 percent of Mexico's mining industry, 22 percent of the oil industry, 68 percent of the rubber industry, and far exceeded in their holdings the total investments of other foreigners.[56]

In August 1913, also on Wilson's order, the War and Navy Departments made tentative plans to raise and transport 40,000 troops for an invasion of Mexico to oust Huerta. In October, Wilson proposed to Carranza that U.S. troops occupy a large part of Mexico while the Constitutionalists did the actual fighting against Huerta. Carranza refused.[57]

All that was now needed was an incident that would give Wilson the excuse to send an expeditionary force. The incident came when President Wilson seized on a trivial slight to American "honor" at Tampico, Mexico.

An officer and seven crew members of the American cruiser *Dolphin*, anchored in the Mexican harbor of Tampico, were sent ashore to purchase fuel. When they landed, they were arrested by Huerta's troops on the pretext that the port was in a state of emergency and that no unauthorized persons were allowed on shore. Two hours later the Mexican commanding general at Tampico learned of the arrests, and he immediately had them released. The Americans were marched two blocks through the streets and back to their boat. The Mexican general expressed his regret over the incident.

The American admiral, Henry T. Mayo, demanded an apology, assurance that the Mexican officer responsible for the arrests was himself placed under arrest, and a twenty-one-gun salute to the American flag within 24 hours. The ultimatum was to expire at 6 P.M.[58]

The commander of the Tampico garrison sent an official apology and had the

*After thirteen years in prison, the survivors, including Rangel and Cline, were pardoned by Governor Miriam ("Ma") Ferguson of Texas.

responsible officer arrested, but requested an extension of the deadline with regard to the twenty-one-gun salute because the question could only be decided by the president himself. Huerta, for his part, offered to submit the Tampico affair to the Hague Tribunal, but this the United States refused. Huerta then agreed to the salute, provided the United States would fire simultaneously. When this was rejected, he offered to fire five guns instead of twenty-one. This, too, was refused.[59] It is difficult to disagree with Arthur S. Link, the leading Wilson scholar, that the "minor incident" at Tampico would have ended peacefully, "had not the Washington administration been looking for an excuse to provoke a fight."[60]

Ten American battleships were hurried to Tampico, April 14, 1914, with a regiment of Marines. Tension continued to mount, and on April 20, 1914, Wilson addressed a joint session of Congress, misrepresenting the facts surrounding this and other two incidents.[61]

One such incident concerned a misunderstanding due to language differences between an American and a Mexican mail orderly. The two disputants accompanied a policeman to the nearest station, where the difficulty was ironed out and settled. "The incident is without significance," Admiral Fletcher reported four days before Wilson's address to Congress. Still the President did not hesitate to cite the incidence as evidence "that the Government of the United States was being singled out . . . for slights and affronts in retaliation for its refusal to recognize the pretensions of General Huerta. . . ." He asked Congress to sanction his right to use armed force, couching the request in typical Wilsonian language:

> There can in what we do be no thought of aggression or of selfish aggrandizement. We seek to maintain the dignity and authority of the United States only because we wish always to keep our great influence unimpaired for the uses of liberty, both in the United States and wherever else it may be employed for the benefit of mankind.

On the same day. April 20, the Senate by a vote of 70–13, and the House without debate (337–37) adopted a resolution which asserted that "the President is justified in the employment of the armed forces . . . for affronts and indignities committed against the United States." As a sop to opponents of the first part of the resolution, the following was added: "That the United States disclaims any hostility to the Mexican people or any purpose to make war upon them."[62]

Wilson's next move for intervention came on the morning of April 21, 1914, when Secretary of State William Jennings Bryan telephoned him that a German ship, the *Ypirango*, carrying arms and ammunition for Huerta, would arrive at Vera Cruz about 10 A.M. Without waiting for Congressional sanction, Wilson ordered the Navy to occupy Vera Cruz. In carrying out this command, the Mexicans suffered 126 killed and 195 wounded and the Americans suffered casualties of 19 dead and 71 wounded.[63]

The capture and occupation of Vera Cruz provoked anti-American demonstrations throughout Latin America. Mexicans considered this another example of "Yankee Imperialism," and were not impresed by Wilsonian rhetoric in support of the imperialist aggression. United States flags were torn down all over Mexico; American business houses were stoned, and American citizens were threatened. Villa expressed tolerance if not enthusiastic approval, but Carranza joined Huerta in denouncing Wilson's action, and called the seizure of Vera Cruz "an invasion of our territory" and a violation of Mexican sovereignty.[64]

Writing in *The Independent,* historian Albert Bushnell Hart observed bitterly: "Are we to tell our children in years to come that in 1914 the people of the United States had no better reason for entering a neighboring country and killing its people than a dispute about a salute?" But the *New York Times* urged critics of Wilson's action to remember that there were "those who insisted that we should ignore the destruction of the *Maine,*" and it maintained that there were ample reasons for armed intervention against Mexico. The *Times* urged the American people not to listen to critics of the President's action, but to "trust the just mind, the sound judgement, and the peaceful temper of President Wilson."[65]

One section of the population needed no such advice. "The five hundred or more business men who attended the luncheon of the Members Council of the Merchants Association of New York," reported the *New York Times,* "jumped to their feet yeaterday when William C. Breed, the toastmaster, called upon those present to express their loyalty to President Wilson 'to whatever course he shall determine necessary to restore peace, order and a stable government in the Republic of Mexico.' "[66]

Yet the *New York Times* itself contributed to the criticism of Wilson's action by publishing an article by John Reed in which the Socialist journalist, who had just returned from four months in Mexico, warned that if U.S. soldiers entered and occupied Mexico, it would do so to destroy the real desires of the Mexicans and to protect the investments of American capitalists, "many of them obtained by sheer bribery, and all of them rich in the blood and sweat of the peons." As for the argument that the U.S. occupation of Mexico "will benefit the Mexicans by forcing our institutions upon them," Reed predicted that just the opposite would occur; that "if we can ever withdraw from that distracted country we will leave things worse than they were before—an exploiting class firmly entrenched in the places of power, the foreign interests stronger, because we supported them, the great estates securely re-established, and the peons taught that wage slavery and not individual freedom is the desirable thing in life."[67]

At almost the very moment that American naval guns were firing at Vera Cruz, the guns of Colorado militiamen were firing on striking coal miners and their wives and children in Ludlow, Colorado. A telegram from the United Mine Workers at Denver, sent to the labor and socialist press, told of the attack which began on the morning of April 20:

> Ludlow tent colony, which housed 1,200 Colorado striking coal miners, burned to the ground after four men, three women and seven children were murdered. One hundred and fifty gunmen, in militiamen's uniform and with State equipment, have with six machine-guns kept up a constant attack on men, women and children since daybreak Monday morning. . . . Will you,

for God's sake, and in the name of humanity call upon all citizens of the United States to demand of the President and both Houses of Congress that they leave Mexico alone and order troops to Colorado to save those miners, their wives and their children, who are being murdered by the dozen by the mercenaries of the mine owners.[68]

Across the country a cry arose that "the war in Mexico and Colorado are both Standard Oil wars." Rockefeller owned the Colorado Fuel and Iron Company against which the miners were striking, as well as the Standard Oil Company, and Wilson was the puppet of Rockefeller, seeking through intervention to oust Huerta who favored British oil interests over those of Rockefeller.[69] This cry arose especially at meetings sponsored by the Socialist Party of America which was the first and the most active in the protest movement against the invasion of Mexico.

On April 22, Walter Lanfersiek, executive secretary of the National Executive Committee of the Socialist Party, sent the following telegram to President Wilson: "I am instructed by the National Executive Committee of the Socialist Party and in behalf of its membership to protest against the unwarranted invasion of Mexico. The workers of the United States have no quarrel with the workers of Mexico."[70] In a "Proclamation on the Mexican War," the National Executive Committee followed up the protest. It denounced the American military expedition as being solely for the profit of German, English, and especially American capitalists. Just as the Mexican Revolution was close to achieving success

the great American republic, controlled by sinister capitalist interests and without a declaration of war, lands an armed force on Mexican soil. No nation in modern times has ever begun hostilities upon a pretext so shallow as the flag incident at Tampico.

The concluding section stated the Socialist position on the war it assumed had already begun:

The Socialist Party is opposed as a matter of principle to every war of aggression. We believe that there is but one justification for war and that is to fight for freedom. Our freedom has not been assailed by the Mexicans. There is no reason why American men should leave their homes and families to have their bodies mangled on Mexican battlefields. In the name of two million American Socialists, in the name of thirty million Socialists throughout the world, we protest the war with Mexico.

The National Executive Committee called on all state and local Party groups to protest the invasion of Mexico through leaflets, resolutions, telegrams to the President, and mass meetings.[71]

The response came swiftly. The State Executive Committee of the New York Socialist Party called upon President Wilson "to recall the armed forces of the United States from Mexico, and extend the protection of the federal government to the women and children of the miners of Colorado."[72] The Texas Socialists voiced their opposition in the party's state platform, declaring that the United States should keep its hands off Mexico's internal affairs and that "the custom of one nation landing a portion of its war forces upon the soil of another nation in the pretense of safeguarding mythical interests of the citizens . . . should be abolished."*[73]

"We will not bear arms against our brother workers of Mexico," the Boston Socialist Party resolved, as it extended "fraternal greetings to the working class of Mexico—which itself is enslaved not alone by the Mexican, but by the American as well."[74] It was a sentiment widely shared in the Socialist Party. Socialists mocked the soldier "patriots" who enlisted for service in Mexico, and the *International Socialist Review* used the folowing verse to make the point:

THE PATRIOT

I am a brave young soldier,
With sawdust in my head,
I want to take my rifle
And shoot the Greasers dead!
They're mostly good for nothing.
They'd rather loaf than work;
Employers all declare they
Are always on the shirk!
They fuss because the Standard
Has gobbled all their oil,

They're not protecting property,
They want to keep the soil.
So I will take my rifle,
I love My Country so,
And save Poor Johnnie's oil wells,
Way down in Mexico!
So bring the good old flag! If
You've sawdust in your head,
And you will shoulder muskets
And shoot the Greasers dead![75]

Right and left-wing socialists united in denouncing the invasion of Mexico, and agreed, too, that the purpose of the intervention was mainly to benefit John D. Rockefeller.[76] Indeed, only one prominent socialist supported the occupation of Vera Cruz—Jack London. It will be recalled that he had addressed a letter to the "dear brave comrades of the Mexican Revolution" in February 1911, expressing his support for their revolt against Díaz, (See Chapter 8) and he had opposed the Taft Administration's dispatch of troops to the Mexican border. He expressed confidence at that time that while an invasion of Mexico by U.S. troops "might end the revolution, it would not crush the revolutionary spirit in Mexico."[77]

Imagine then the surprise of many socialists and others in the anti-war camp to read London writing in *Collier's Weekly* from Vera Cruz in praise of the "humane" occupation of the city by the U.S. Army,‡ and hailing his countrymen for accepting

---

*The Texas pro-Mexican Socialists were led by T.A. Hickey who edited the militant *Halletsville Rebel* which claimed a circulation of 25,000, most of the subscribers being white tenant farmers in Texas. Hickey applauded the Mexican revolutionaries who favored land confiscation. (Paul Estrada, "Border Revolution: The Mexican Revolution in the Ciudad Juarez-El Paso Area, 1906–1915" [M.A. thesis, University of Texas, El Paso, 1975], pp. 63–66.)

‡*Collier's Weekly* offered London eleven hundred dollars weekly to cover the Mexican Revolution. He left on April 17, 1914, before the Tampico incident, but was delayed in arriving in Mexico because he was detained by military officers at the border who accused him of having written the ant-militarist piece, "The Good Soldier." His vigorous claims that he did not author the attack on the military, enabled him to get to Vera Cruz where he remained until June except for a brief trip to Tampico.

their white man's burdens to uplift the "inferior" Mexicans. "Mexico," London insisted, "must be saved from the insignificant portion of her half-breeds who are causing all the trouble." He lamented that "all native and foreign businessmen are being injured and destroyed." The revolution had been betrayed, and could be rescued only by the United States. London even ridiculed "stay at home Americans" who were thrilled by the phrases and slogans of the Mexican Revolution, and he denied that the revolution was an expression of the people's hunger for land.[78]

London's support of the American invasion infuriated his socialist colleagues. The Oakland branch of the Socialist Party denounced it's most famous member, and went on to endorse a resolution against intervention and invasion of Mexico, calling even for a general strike to halt further penetration of Mexican soil.[79] (It appeared to be the only socialist local to take such a stand.) John Kenneth Turner published a strong reproach to London in *Appeal to Reason* in which he implied that the Socialist author had been subsidized by the oil interests. "Socialist London," he wrote bitterly, "turned out a brief for what Mexicans call 'Yankee Imperialism.' "[80] The liberal *Nation* put it well when it said: "The extremely readable letters from Mexico in *Colliers'* are not written by 'Yours for the Revolution' Jack London but plain 'Jack London.' "[81] It could have added that the letters in *Colliers* were proof of London's increasing contradictions.

But Jack London stood alone in the ranks of the Socialist Party. Later, Morris Hillquit reported to meetings of the Second International in Vienna that SPA opposition to the invasion of Mexico had been unanimous.[82]

It was at public meetings that this opposition was voiced most vehemently and dramatically. "On to Carnegie Hall tonight, in Protest Against War!" was the heading of a leaflet distributed by Socialists in New York City on April 27, 1914. The call urged all workers of the city and all who opposed both the invasion of Mexico and the "Ludlow Massacre" to attend the meeting sponsored by the Socialist Party, the purpose of which was to protest "against the war of American capitalist interests to gobble the resources of Mexico," and also to protest "against the outrages in Colorado, where the same capitalist interests have turned the guns of the militia against the striking workingmen and their helpless wives and children."[83]

Charles Edward Russell opened the meeting with a statement that brought the huge audience to its feet cheering. Under no circumstances would he fight in the war against Mexico, he declared, and if drafted, he would refuse to serve. "And if this sedition make the most of it. And if that is not patriotism, make the most of that too. I stand for a much higher kind of patriotism than that, one which knows no national limits; that reaches around the whole world and that will some day right these hideous wrongs being continually inflicted on the workers and the producers of the world's goods. They'll never get me to go to war!"

Denouncing Wilson for the invasion of Mexico, Russell urged that he be known therafter as "Sixteen Gun Woodrow," in recognition of the fact that the issue over which the fleet was sent to Mexico was "whether Huerta should fire twenty-one guns, or sixteen more than was provided for in his offer to fire five guns." But the real issue was that Huerta favored British oil interests against U.S. oil interests.

"Supremacy of oil interests—that's the game and nothing else," Russell cried, and to all who were stupid enough to enlist for military action in Mexico, he offered the following epitaph:

> *In whatever stress and strife*
> *Or bloody battle's toil,*
> *He cheerfully gave up his life—*
> *His heart beat true to oil.*

And it was a specific oil company that Russell charged with being responsible "for the present war—the Mexican war and the Colorado war are both run from 26 Broadway." That was the headquarters of Rockefeller's Standard Oil Company and Colorado Fuel and Iron Company.

"Let us see what this American flag is, that has been insulted," was the opening remark of Fred Warren, editor of the *Appeal to Reason,* who was the next speaker. He then explained what he thought the flag stood for:

The White—The cowardice of a capitalist class.
Capitalism is not today, nor was it ever, in the fighting ranks.
Red—The blood of the martyred dead sacrificed on the alter of mammon.
The stars, on their limitless field of blue—The limitless ambition of John D. Rockefeller and his gang of free-booters.And you tell me that a flag like that can be insulted!

There was a simple way to end the war in Mexico, Warren insisted. "I would make the President who declared war to go to the front and fight. I would make every Congressman who voted for war go down there and shoulder a rifle. Every preacher who prayed to his God for the success of our army in Mexico would have to go and fight. And every newspaper editor who shrieked war would go down too, where the bullets flew thickest and the dead fell by the scores. And that would be the end of war."

Morris Hillquit called attention in anger and sadness to the fact that "representatives of organized labor in this city, delegates and officials of the Central Federated Union, were narrow-minded enough, cowardly enough to refuse to take part in this demonstration." But he assured the audience that filled Carnegie Hall that these "so-called labor leaders" did not represent "the sentiments of the laboring masses" who were "all further advanced in solidarity and class consciousness than their so-called leaders."

The resolutions adopted (with only one dissenting vote) at the Carnegie Hall meeting described a war between the United States and Mexico as promising to "benefit only capitalists and corrupt politicians," and proceeded to denounce both the invasion of Mexico and the "Ludlow Massacre." The resolutions called upon

all working people and all citizens . . . to join with us in a nation-wide demand that hostilities in Mexico be at once brought to an end in order that public attention may be turned to the vital question of maintaining constitutional government at home and making it possible for the working class to emancipate itself without resort to violent measures.[84]

In Cleveland the Socialist Party announced that the 1914 May Day celebration "will be an anti-war demonstration. Speeches against the United States engaging in wholesale murder in Mexico will be made," and a declaration against the invasion of Mexico would be presented by Charles E. Ruthenberg.[85] Following a march of thousands through Cleveland's Public Square, the May Day demonstrators gathered at Acme Hall and shouted approval of the Ruthenberg declaration. "The struggle for markets," he began, "in which to dispose of vast amounts of surplus products which are produced through exploitation of the workers, and the everpresent necessity of re-investing their profits, bring the ruling class of one nation in conflict with that of the other." In the conflict "the workers are sent forth to murder each other . . . in order that there might be more profits for the capitalist class." The "present armed intervention in Mexico" was but

another example of a ruling class willing to plunge a nation into war to protect its investments and extend its commercial power. It is to protect the interests of American capitalists that American workingmen are to give up their lives in Mexico and Mexican workers are to be murdered. At the same time that the capitalist class is forcing this nation into a bloody war in Mexico, its gunmen and military hirelings are murdering workingmen and their wives and children in Colorado.

The same lust for profits which is forcing this nation into a war with Mexico is responsible for the massacre at Ludlow.

The Declaration then extended "fraternal greetings to the downtrodden people of Mexico," and declared "sympathy with them in their struggle to overthrow their oppressors, whether they be Mexican land owners or American capitalists."[86]

At the AFL convention in November 1913, a resolution was introduced which read:

The American Federation of Labor condemns the attempts being made by American and foreign corporations, and certain jingo newspapers, to force armed intervention by the United States government in Mexico, and urges upon the president of the United States, the continuance of the policy looking to a peaceful adjustment of the conflict among the Mexican people, and that the president and secretary of the American Federation of Labor be instructed to transmit the position of the Federation on the matter to the president of the United States.

Gompers opposed the first part of this resolution. Madero, he told the delegates, had represented the best interests and aspirations of the Mexican people, and had been overthrown as part of a plot to restore the old regime. If the bloody Huerta regime was permitted to strengthen its hold on Mexico, it would take at least another generation before the people could inaugurate another revolution. The Monroe Doctrine was also at stake, Gompers argued. The doctrine's objective of making the American continent secure so it could work out *its* own salvation through self-government could be maintained only if the American nations gave reasonable protection to foreign investments. Otherwise, despite protests from the United States, foreign governments would interfere and the Monroe Doctrine would be destroyed. Hence the AFL should strengthen Wilson's hand in trying to find a peaceful solution of the problem,

> but I do not believe we should resolve under any and all circumstances to denounce intervention and thus bring comfort and hope into the hearts of Huerta. I do not think we ought to encourage him to say that the labor movement of America . . . will not permit intervention and he may go on carrying out his bloody record.

The clause of the resolution condemning armed intervention in Mexico was thereupon withdrawn, and the remainder adopted unanimously.[87]

On July 25, 1914, in a private letter to a representative of Carranza in the United States, Gompers boasted that "We helped in sustaining the government of the United States in its refusal to recognize Huerta up to the present hour." The implication was that this included the invasion of Mexico and the occupation of Vera Cruz. James Duncan, AFL vice-president, was not so subtle. He openly proclaimed that the AFL supported the invasion of Mexico, and that if a war with Mexico followed, it would support that as well. Duncan drew an incredible distinction between the situation confronting the labor movement in Europe, "where wars are generally gotten up for the benefit of the fellow who does not do much of the fighting" and therefore labor "was justified in its antagonism to such wars"; and the situation confronting the labor movement in the United States, "where wars are forced upon us by injustice and insult" which required labor's patriotic endorsement and full support. Such a situation was the President's action in ordering troops to Mexico and in occupying Vera Cruz. Thus the AFL's support of the President was both logical and necessary.[88]

This was the policy of the majority of the AFL affiliates. As Morris Hillquit noted at the Carnegie Hall meeting, the Central Federated Labor Union of New York City refused to participate in the protest. Similarly, the city central labor unions of Cleveland, San Francisco, and a number of other cities refused to participate in protest meetings called by locals of the Socialist Party. (In most cases, thousands of union members attended these protest meetings anyway.)[89] The reason why the New York Central Federated Union refused to participate became clearer when its Executive Committee went on record approving President Wilson's action in Mexico, and, in addition, voted to uphold his stand in any action necessary to "preserve the honor of the American flag and the dignity of the United States."[90] This was actually giving the administration a "blank check" to do anything it wished in Mexico.

Most of the AFL affiliates actively supported the invasion of Mexico after "Big Bill" Haywood gave the official IWW response to the intervention at a Carnegie Hall meeting. In the course of his speech, Haywood declared that if President Wilson and Congress declared war against Mexico, the IWW would "automatically start the greatest general strike this country has ever known," and that its stand would win wide support, especially among members of the United Mine Workers and the Western Federation of Miners. In fact, the miners had already made up their minds to halt production in case of war.

> You must say that this action of the mine workers is traitorous to the country, but I tell you it is better to be a traitor to a country than to be a traitor to your class.[91]

Immediately headlines in the nation's press screamed: "HAYWOOD OPENLY STIRS SEDITION," and newspapers reported that government officials were carefully studying Haywood's speech to see if he could be indicted for "treason."[92] The press also ran interviews with labor leaders throughout the country about their reaction to Haywood's opposition to the invasion of Mexico and his suggestion of a general strike in the event that war followed. As might be expected, the leaders of the Railroad Brotherhoods were all in favor of the invasion and of war if necessary. Warren F. Stone, Grand Chief of the Brotherhood of Locomotive Engineers, furnished the press with a copy of a telegram he had just sent President Wilson informing him that the Brotherhood

> stands ready to furnish locomotive engineers to handle all troops trains that may be needed in Mexico. These men are thouroughly familiar with Mexico and know every foot of railroad there. They, like the rest of us, are Americans and may be relied on.[93]

AFL leaders were not far behind in voicing their support of the President and horror at Haywood's proposal. Ernest Bohm, Secretary of the Central Federated Union of New York declared: "The loyalty of the members of the unions as a body to the Government is as strong as it was in the Spanish-American War. . . . Many union men will volunteer in Uncle Sam's Army."[94] The press quoted statements of labor leaders in Philadelphia, Pittsburgh, San Francisco, Boston, and Austin, agreeing with Bohm. But the newspapers gave special space to the statements of UMW leaders who indicated they "stood behind the President," that Wilson had been "patient, painstaking, and careful in handling the Mexican situation and that he is entitled to the support of every American." Speaking for the three anthracite districts of the UMW in Pennsylvania, Roger O' Donnell declared: "The organization stands back of the Wilson administration in the Mexican matter, for it is the belief of all that President Wilson has made the best of a delicate situation. Haywood's threat does not mean anything to us. He does not represent us, and therefore cannot speak for us."[95]

But even the jingo press could not hide the fact that there were dissenting AFL voices. As might again be expected, unions influenced by the socialists, even while not endorsing Haywood's threat of a general strike, did voice opposition to the invasion of Mexico. John Weaver Sherman, whom the press described as "long active both in the Socialist Party and the labor movement," told reporters that "one can be sure that the labor leaders who are beating the drums for war with Mexico do not represent the views of their members."[96] "The Jewish workers have nothing against their Mexican fellow workers," declared the United Hebrew Trades of New York City, an organization of 300,000 workers. "It won't be the jingoists or the capitalists who are stirring up war against Mexico who will go to war. Organized labor has always stood for universal peace, and we favor peace with Mexico at all costs."[97]

While Edgar Wallace, editor of the *United Mine Workers' Journal* would not endorse Haywood's statement, he also rejected the views of the UMW leaders who told the press that they supported the invasion of Mexico:

> We can't see how we would profit in any way through war with Mexico. . . . We look upon the present war scare as a preconcerted scheme to conserve the interests of those who have money invested in Mexico and which we, as laboring people are not interested. As to the insult to the flag, we can't see how the action of a man whom this government has never recognized can be regarded as an insult to the nation. Why punish Mexico for the act of a man who, according to our theory is not the representative of any government at all? It does not seem to us that this is a ground for war.[98]

George H. Ulrich, president of the Philadelphia Central Labor Union, criticized the press for including his organization among those in the labor movement who supported the invasion of Mexico because one or two of its leaders expressed themselves "in favor of the President's stand." Ulrich said firmly that the Central Labor Union took the position "that war should be avoided at any cost, as it meant the protection of commercial interests in Mexico by the rank and file of the laboring men. These men should have to shoulder muskets and do the real fighting, while the autocrats who own the interests in Mexico stayed home."[99]

The *New York Times'* Chicago correspondent reported that "labor heads here are opposed to war with Mexico." The Chicago Federation of Labor proved him correct by unanimously adopting a resolution, introduced by Mary O'Reilly, opposing the invasion of Mexico and calling upon President Wilson "to prevent the United States from becoming involved in the struggle with Mexico."[100]

Two thousand miles west of Chicago, in San Francisco and Los Angeles, mass meetings of trade unions were held to protect "against War and Murder in Mexico and Colorado." Los Angeles trade unionists met in the Labor Temple, heard speakers denounce the plans for war against Mexico, and adopted a resolution which ridiculed the reason given for the sending of troops to Vera Cruz, declaring that it savored "of baronial days and entirely out of harmony with the supposed lofty intelligence and high minded humanity of the present day."

The trade unionists called upon the City Council of Los Angeles to oppose

> any declaration of war upon Mexico for the causes now agitating the diplomats at Washington and that we urge with all our emphasis the continuation of peace between the two nations, knowing as we do the conditions about; and that we further condemn war in any event and in any case because of its barbarities and because of the well known fact that those who bring wars upon us are never those who fight those wars.

Copies of the resolution were forwarded by telegraph to President Wilson and to members of the Senate representing California.[101]

Gradually the headlines dealing with Haywood's "seditious" suggestion for a general strike faded from sight, as did reports that he was in danger of being indicted for "treason." But IWW activities opposing the invasion continued to make frontpage news. Headlines read: "MOB I.W.W. WOMAN TALKER WHO DECRIES WAR"; "I.W.W. SLUR ON FLAG STIRS ANGRY CROWD"; "I.W.W. WOMAN ON HUNGER STRIKE." One of the stories related to the headlines went:

> Becky Edelson, the young saleswoman, who has participated in three I.W.W. riots growing out of her speaking against the actions of the United States in Mexico, and has been twice placed under arrest, was led to the Tombs prison [in New York City] this afternoon after refusing to give a bond to keep the peace.
>
> As the young woman was taken from the Police Court she cried out that she was going on a hunger strike against court sentences taking away from persons engaged in agitations against war the right of speech. Up to a late hour tonight Miss Edelson had not touched a dinner placed before her at 6 o'clock.[102]

When the *New York Times* was asked by a correspondent to condemn the mob which attacked IWW anti-war speakers and to demand that the police protect freedom of speech, the paper refused. "Stop that nonsense about 'free speech,' " it editorialized. "That phrase has a meaning which bears no relation to the vaporings of the mentally defective and morally depraved followers of the I.W.W."[103]

"The Socialists are no better," the *Cleveland Plain Dealer* declared, approving *Times'* editorial, and urging Cleveland Public Safety Director to ban the Socialist Party from meeting in the Public Square to protest the government's policy toward Mexico. The official immediately announced that he planned to put a stop to "all speeches on the public square attacking the United States flag or the attitude of the Government in the Mexican crisis."[104]

Charles E. Ruthenberg, leader of the Cleveland socialists, immediately responded by holding an emergency free-speech meeting on the Square. Ruthenberg notified the press that the subject of the speeches would be the American invasion of Mexico. In spite of the short notice, a thousand people were at the Square. As Ruthenberg mounted the stone block, traditional free-speech rostrum, armed militiamen and recruiting officers appeared at the edge of the crowd and began to edge their way menacingly toward the platform. Ruthenberg began speaking and charged that oil and banking interests were behind the attack on Mexico. "There is no reason," he cried to the cheers of the crowd, "why any man should go down into the hell of war to fight for the dollars of the ruling class!"

As he said these words, the militiamen made a rush for the rostrum, using the butt end of their revolvers to strike down men and women in the audience who got in their way. The crowd defended themselves with their bare fists, and a general fight broke out.

Some of the Socialists went to call the police while Ruthenberg held fast on the block waiting for their arrival. About ten minutes later a half dozen policemen sauntered into the Square. Again Ruthenberg spoke against the invasion of Mexico and the meeting finally ended peacefully.[105]

While the United States continued to occupy Vera Cruz, protracted and fruitless negotiations took place at Niagara Falls under the auspices of the ABC powers (Argentina, Brazil, and Chile). Senator Albert Fall of New Mexico, spokesperson for the oil companies, and Senator Henry Cabot Lodge of Massachusetts, long a leading spokesperson for U.S. imperialism, introduced a resolution in the Senate that would empower President Wilson to dispatch troops throughout Mexico "to protect American life and property." The justification was that the real cause for U.S. military action was the mistreatment of Americans and their property throughout Mexcio. The resolution was defeated in the Senate after Wilson let it be known that he believed the intervention should be limited.[106]

During these developments, the Constitutionalist forces under Carranza gained strength and swept toward Mexico City. By the middle of July, 1914, Huerta's position had become impossible, and he resigned his office and fled to Puerto Mexico. On July 20 he and his family boarded the German cruiser *Dresden* and sailed for Jamaica.[107]

But American troops still remained in Vera Cruz. The Socialist Party praised Wilson for resisting the Fall-Lodge resolution with its aim of expanding the occupation to include all of Mexico. But it could not fail to express disapointment and anger at the continued presence of the troops in Vera Cruz. The Wilson administration's justification for sending the troops had been the need to deal with Huerta, and they should have been withdrawn after his fall.[108]

On November 23, 1914, the long-delayed evacuation of Vera Cruz finally began. American socialists insisted that it was largely due to their protests and those of organized labor against the invasion of Mexico that the occupation had not been expanded beyond Vera Cruz. Furthermore, they claimed that by popularizing the slogans "Hands Off Mexico" and "Withdraw the Troops," these same forces had helped achieve the final evacuation.[109] Arthur S. Link concludes that public pressure (in which he includes thousands of telegrams from trade unions, socialists, peace organizations and church groups to the president) helped in bringing about the evacuation of Vera Cruz. Friedrich Katz agrees, and notes, too, that "pressure from opponents of further intervention in Mexico" was an important factor in "causing the American government to give up its plans."[110]

Woodrow Wilson's Mexican policy is the subject of a vast number of scholarly studies.[111] The prevailing view in most of these studies is that Wilson intervened and interfered in Mexico repeatedly in order to push the Mexican Revolution into a "liberal-capitalist" mold and that he failed in that effort. Several studies (especially those by Arthur S. Link and Kendrick A. Clements) argue that although Wilson would have liked Mexico to follow such a course, he gave up any effort to force it in that direction after early 1914, and that the main aim of his policy after that time was to assure the Mexican people of the freedom to choose whatever course they desired. But a number of scholars, especially those in Mexico, point out that behind the "moralistic" and "idealistic" princples used to justify Wilsonian intervention was the same old imperialism; and that the main motivation was to protect the enormous economic interests of U.S. capitalists in Mexico and prevent Mexico from favoring European, especially British imperialism. Some scholars also argue that Wilson was greatly influenced by the need to assure a flow of oil from Mexico to the United States for the development of foreign trade and U.S. industries and for the building of the Navy. They point out that the conversion of British naval vessels from coal to oil burners at this time made Huerta able to play England and the United States against each other: Mexico was almost the only source of supply for the British Navy. When Huerta gave guarantees that this need would be fulfilled, and when he also showed himself favorable to German and Japanese economic groups, he guaranteed his rejection by Woodrow Wilson, who justified it by saying that he refused to recognize a "government of butchers," which had overthrown a constitutional government by military usurpation.

American socialists, Wobblies, and sections of the American Federation of Labor did not have access to the archives in the United States, Europe, and Mexico. But unlike Gompers and other AFL leaders, they saw and understood enough to realize that behind the Wilsonian rhetoric, U.S. policy toward Mexico had the same old goal of protecting the interests of United States capitalists.

· X ·

CARRANZA, GOMPERS, AND THE MEXICAN LABOR MOVEMENT

F ollowing the resignation and exile of Victoriano Huerta, Samuel Gompers began for the first time to take an active role in U.S.-Mexican affairs and to involve himself deeply in trying to influence the nature and future course of the Mexican labor movement. In order to understand what produced this major change, it is again necessary to see what was occurring in Mexico.

Although Ricardo Flores Magón had suffered a severe setback in influence among Mexican workers as a result of the Baja California fiasco, his ideas still influenced the leading labor organization in revolutionary Mexico—the Casa del Obrero Mundial. The Casa championed a militant doctrine of anarcho-syndicalism, and functioned as a clearing house where union leaders could exchange ideas, agree on general principles, and decide upon tactics. The Casa emphasized apolitical, direct action while stressing the strike as its chief weapon. Several of the Casa's founders were Spanish anarchist exiles who were part of the steady stream of anarchists who left that country for Mexico, and a number were influenced by Flores Magón's writings. The Casa believed that education for the working class would "eliminate slavery" and establish complete liberty. Its "modern schools" for workers' children and women stressed experimentation and the scientific method while scrapping religious dogma and authoritarianism. Unions affiliated themselves with the Casa not necessarily because they accepted all of its ideology, but mainly because its leaders were the most articulate and best organizers, and many of the unions were created by these men.[1]

On May 1, 1913, Mexico had its first May Day rally under the auspices of the Casa del Obrero Mundial. Thousands of workers marched across Mexico City calling for an eight-hour day and six-day work week. Dozens of unions and working class groups enthusiastically supported the May Day festival, and about 20,000 workers listened to fiery speeches demanding an eight-hour day and Sunday rest.

The Huerta government tolerated the first May Day in Mexican history and it took place without incident.[2] But the situation worsened during the rest of Huerta's regime, and by the end of 1913, the working class in Mexico City was in terrible economic straits. When workers protested, the police raided Casa headquarters, arrested its leaders, and destroyed its facilities. Several of the leaders were jailed, some were deported, while others escaped. Still the Casa had enough influence left to defeat Huerta's efforts to win the Mexican people to his side during the occupation of Vera Cruz by U.S. troops. While condemning the invasion of Mexico by the United States as "Yankee imperialism," the Casa printed and distributed a pamphlet entitled, *People, Don't Be Fooled*, which exposed Huerta as the tool of Mexican and British capitalists. "We scattered the pamphlet all through the streets," Casa leader Juan Savinon reported, "and it stopped Huerta's game and killed his last chance of rallying the people to his support."[3]

After Huerta's defeat, the Constitutionalists forces loyal to Venustiano Carranza moved quickly to recruit urban labor support against the forces led by Francisco "Pancho" Villa and Emiliano Zapata who had previously been allies of the Constitutionalists. This was not too difficult to achieve. Villa's revolutionary army did include railroad workers, miners, and a large number of the unemployed but he had no program for the urban working class. Zapata's movement was basically peasant and he displayed, especially in the early years of the revolution, little understanding of the problems of the working class. Like Villa, he never articulated a comprehensive program with specific proposals for the working class. The urban workers themselves had little contact with or understanding of either of these movements. Also, while they respected Zapata's revolutionary zeal, they tended to look with disdain on the religious devotion of Zapata and his followers, and the role of the clergy in the Zapatista movement. Carranza's movement, on the other hand, was fiercely anti-clerical.[4]

Essentially Carranza represented the "new bourgeoisie" which had only recently accumulated wealth, and the urban workers had no illusions about Carranza's "bourgeois alliances." But they were aware that, in contrast to Villa and Zapata, Carranza made a special effort to woo the urban workers. A relatively large number of generals in the Carranza movement came from the working class, and some had been leaders of the copper miners' strike in 1906 and the textile workers' strike in Rio Blanco in 1907—the most important and bloodiest strikes during the Díaz Dictatorship.[5] Moreover, former *Magonista* Antonio I. Villarreal was now a leading figure in Carranza's movement, and he urged the workers to join the Constitutionalists and thereby end their miserable conditions.[6]

When General Alvaro Obregón gained control of Mexico City for Carranza, he provided churches and convents for use as working class headquarters. Amidst great jubilation, the headquarters of the Casa del Obrero Mundial in Mexico City reopened on August 21, 1914, when Carranza entered the capital for the first time. It was now housed in the luxurious House of Tiles.

With Constitutionalist blessing, the Casa began an intense organizing campaign in the factories and shops of Mexico City, Guadalajara, and other industrial centers of the nation. Within a short time, the formerly almost defunct anarcho-syndicalist center for Mexican trade unions represented over 50,000 workers.[7]

By November 1914, Carranza's break with Villa and Zapata had become irreparable. The situation looked desperate for Carranza. He was compelled to evacuate the capital city, and most observers expected his rapid defeat. A few months later, however, the situation had completely changed. In part it was due to the military skill of Alvaro Obregón, who inflicted a series of crushing defeats on Villa's forces from which they never recovered. But to no small extent it was because of the support Carranza recieved from the workers led by the Casa del Obrero Mundial.

The Casa leaders opposed militarism and collaboration with political figures as violating fundamental anarcho-syndicalist principles. But they were convinced they could influence the course of a victorious Constitutionalist government while they would have little power under Villa or Zapata. Hence they decided to join Carranza and mobilize armed workers behind him. The Casa leaders struck an agreement with Carranza's representatives which committed organized labor to the Constitutionalist military effort.

The "Agreement between the Constitutionalist Government and the Casa del Obrero Mundial," signed at Vera Cruz on February 17, 1915, opened:

> As the workers of the Casa del Obrero Mundial are supporting the Constitutionalist government headed by Citizen V. Carranza. We hereby declare that the following terms are to govern the relations between the said government and the workers and between them and it bearing on the manner in which the workers shall collaborate with the Constitutionalist cause. . . .

The terms provided that

(1) The government would enact laws to improve working conditions.

(2) The workers of the Casa would take up arms "both to garrison the towns in possession of the Constitutionalist government and to combat the reaction."

(3) The government would "attend, with all the solicitude it has used up to date, to the workers' just claims arising from their labor contracts with their employers."

(4) The workers would establish occupying forces in towns occupied by the Constitutionalist forces.

(5) The workers of the Casa would furnish the Constitutionalist government with a list of workers so that it "may know the number of workers ready to take up arms."

(6) The workers of the Casa would "carry on an active propaganda to win sympathy for the Constitutionalist government, among all the workers throughout the republic and the working-class world, pointing out to Mexican workingmen the advantages of joining the revolution, inasmuch as it will bring about the improvement the working class is seeking through its unions."

(7) The workers who took up arms in the Constitutionalist government, "and

also the female workers who perform service in aiding or attending the wounded, or similar service, will be known under the one denomination; whether organized in companies, battalions, regiments, brigades or divisions, all will be designated as 'reds.' "

The agreement closed: "Constitution and Reform—Salute and Social Revolution."[8]

Early in March, 7,500 workers headed by a contingent carrying red flags paraded through the streets of Mexico City. They were greeted by General Obregón, and departed for the Constitutionalist military training center in Orizaba, Vera Cruz. They were organized into six Red Battalions. The urban labor forces, including workers' militia from the mines, constituted a massive augmentation for the small Constitutionalist army.

The Red Battalions immediately distinguished themselves in battle by helping Carranza crush the Villa and Zapata forces. The various unions formed specific units after being trained, and fought well at the key battles of El Ebano and Celaya while guarding railroad junctions and garrisoning hotly contested regions. By late 1915 the final outcome of the Revolution's armed conflict stage was over. Carranza's troops controlled most of Mexico. The Constitutionalists had won. With Villa and Zapata smashed, the Red Battalions disbanded.[9]

The working class, having contributed so much to the Constitutionalist triumph with their Red Battalions, now confronted the government with demands for the restructuring of Mexican society in the interests of urban labor. *Unieta*, the official Casa newspaper, featured articles setting forth these demands and carried revolutionary essays by famous European anarchists, including Proudhon, Bakunin, Kropotkin, and editorials from *Regeneración* by Ricardo Flores Magón. *Unieta* also regularly reprinted articles from *Solidarity* and the *Industrial Worker*, and praised the anarcho-syndicalist principles of the IWW, indicating that these were the same ideas as those of the leaders of the Casa del Obrero Mundial.[10]

The IWW watched these developments in Mexico with great interest. It viewed Carranza, Villa, and Zapata as a trio of "working class haters" who could not be trusted to carry out the true Mexican revolution. This could be accomplished only by seizing control of the industries of the country. Hence it looked to the Casa leaders as the representatives of the real Mexican revolution. "They are the real social revolutionists who are preparing to plant the seed of industrial unionism in old Mexico," declared *Solidarity* on July 25, 1914. "They know that the seed will ripen in the soil in the larger revolution that will restore the earth and all its wondrous modern possibilities to the producers."[11]

A year later *Solidarity* maintained that its faith had been justified. The headline on the first page of the July 10, 1915 issue read: "MEXICO HAS LABOR UNION 'MENACE' ORGANIZATION WHICH CAPITALISTS DESCRIBE AS A 'BRANCH OF I.W.W.' SPREADING LIKE WILDFIRE." Written by Charles V. E. Starrett, the article had originally appeared in the *Chicago News* and was reprinted with pride by *Solidarity*. The pride was caused by the statement in the article that the fastest-growing labor organization in Mexico was the "Casa del

Obrero Mundial, said to be a branch of the I.W.W.," and which had been started by a group of Wobblies. The Casa "has spread like a disease among the lower and middle classes, until today it tis estimated that about 30,000 members are enrolled in the southern provinces alone." Not only did workers belong but "a vast number of the soldiers are members of the organization." The writer pointed out that the IWW was a model for the unions launched by the Casa, and he concluded: "Last Labor Day, celebrated in Mexico on May 1, I stood on a street corner in Vera Cruz and watched the obreros parade. In the procession was a new flag that attracted my attention. It was red like the others, but it seemed to bear some sort of inscription. I pressed in closer and was able to read the words. The crimson banner contained a memorial tribute to the anarchists who were hanged in Chicago for complicity in Haymarket riot!"[12]*

During the Haymarket Affair, Samuel Gompers, president of the young American Federation of Labor, had played an active role in the defense of the victims of the tragic "frame-up," and had written: "I am opposed to the execution. It would be a blot on the escutcheon of our country."[13] One might then expect that he would have greeted the report in the *Chicago News* with satisfaction.‡ But nothing was more anathema to Gompers than the prospect of an IWW-dominated Mexican labor movement. The report in the *Chicago News* alarmed Gompers and brought an end to the period when he was only partly interested in events South of the border. Gompers knew that a strong IWW base in Mexico would provide a great spur to the Wobblies' organizing efforts in the United States, especially among the Mexicans of the Southwest, who were anyway more sympathetic to the IWW than to the AFL.[14]

On July 25, 1914, after consulting the AFL Executive Council, Gompers wrote a long letter to Rafael Zubaran Campmany, Carranza's representative in the United States, in which he extended the AFL's "felicitations to the Constitutionalist cause," and expressed hope "for its early and successful consummation." Then, pointing to the contributions he and the AFL had made to the overthrow of Díaz, he praised Madero, and the work he had been doing "for the benefit of the Mexican people"

---

*The reference is to the Haymarket Affair resulting from the explosion of a dynamite bomb in the midst of a squadron of police attempting to disperse a peaceful labor meeting in Chicago on May 4, 1886. Seven police were killed and some sixty wounded. During a wave of hysteria, eight men, all anarchists and alleged anarchists, were arrested and placed on trial. Though no evidence proved their connection with the actual bomb-throwing, they were tried for their opinions only and condemned to death. Four were hanged on November 11, 1887, one committed suicide in prison (or was murdered by prison guards) one was sentenced to 15 years imprisonment. In Mexico the Haymarket Affair is well-known and the Haymarket or Chicago martyrs are highly honored.

‡For Gompers' role in the Haymarket Affair and the story of the events surrounding this episode in American labor history, see Philip S. Foner, *History of the Labor Movement in the United States* (New York: 1955) 2: 105–15.) In his autobiography, published in 1925, Gompers advanced the following significant reason to explain his action in behalf of the framed Haymarket martyrs: "Labor must do its best to maintain justice for the radicals or find itself denied the rights of free men." Gompers, *Seventy Years of Life and Labor*, 1: 187; Stuart B. Kaufman, ed., *The Samuel Gompers Papers* (Urbana and Chicago: 1987)2:53–62.

before his untimely assassination. Citing as a fact that no force in the United States had been so influential as the AFL "in sustaining the government of the United States in its refusal to recognize Huerta and for the success of the revolutionary movement headed by General Carranza," Gompers declared that the AFL thereby had acquired "the right" to suggest how the Constitutionalists should operate. For the moment, he would only recommend that the conflict be brought to a close by granting amnesty "to the Huertists and those responsible for the overturning of the Madero government," and that a definite declaration be issued asserting that "the Constitutionalists will carry into effect a rightful and justifiable division of the lands of Mexico for the working people."[15]

Gompers already envisaged the creation of a conservative bulwark composed of capitalists, *huertistas* and the small peasants who had won their land, to offset any influence of the anarcho-syndicalist, IWW-oriented leaders of the Casa del Obrero Mundial.*

Although Carranza paid no attention to Gompers' suggestions, the AFL president was soon pleased to learn that the Casa had reached an agreement with the Constitutionalist leader in which the labor body would support Carranza against the anti-Carranza factions. This promised to bring the "IWW-dominated" Mexican labor movement under Constitutionalist influence. The information was conveyed to Gompers by John Murray, who was introduced to the AFL president by Santiago Iglesias, Gompers' chief aide and spokesperson in Latin-American, especially Caribbean, affairs.

Murray had been editor of the *Los Angeles Socialist*, had helped raise money for defense of the *magonistas* on trial in the United States, had been himself jailed in connection with his work against Díaz, and, after the overthrow of the dictator, had visited Mexico and established contact with the Casa del Obrero Mundial. On his return to the United States, he met with Iglesias. Both were officially socialists but definitely anti-Marxist and pro-AFL-oriented. Together they decided to persuade Gompers to become actively involved in achieving closer co-operation between U.S. and Mexican labor. AFL influence, they were convinced, could meet and defeat the threat of the IWW.[16]

Murray so impressed Gompers that he immediately accepted him as his chief aide and adviser on Mexican affairs. He promptly agreed to Murray's suggestion that the AFL should enter into some kind of alliance with Mexican labor, and that Gompers should without delay urge President Wilson to recognize the Carranza government.[17]

---

*William G. Whittaker makes the statement that "Following a conference with Gompers, Rafael Zubaran Campmany [a Carranza spokesperson] returned to Mexico and arranged a pact between Mexican labor [represented by the Casa del Obrero Mundial of Mexico City] and the Carranza forces. Under its terms, labor would support the Constitutionalists in exchange for the right to organize." ("Samuel Gompers, Labor and the Mexican-American Crisis of 1916: The Carrizal Incident," *Labor History* 17 (Fall 1976): 554–55.) Whitaker here implies that Gompers played a part in arranging the pact. But there is no evidence in Mexican archives for this assertion. Indeed, Gompers himself does not make this claim in his autobiography, although Whittaker cites it as his major source. *Seventy Years of Life and Labor* 2: 311–12.

On the surface this seemed to be no difficult task. With the aid of the "Red Battalions" of trade unionists, organized by the Casa, Carranza had re-established himself in Mexico City in February, 1915, and to all outward appearances his opponents had been smashed and his position was secure. But President Wilson was in no hurry to recognize him. The idea of a revolution guided by the United States continued to dominate Wilson's thinking, and John Lind, his representative in Mexico, informed him that Carranza was too much of a nationalist to yield to U.S. pressure easily, and that Villa was the best man to lead the kind of a revolution which would satisfy Wilson. Also in Villa's favor was the fact that he expropriated Mexican properties to raise funds for his armies and did not thus have to tax U.S. properties. Carranza, on the other hand, would not tax Mexican properties, and had to rely on taxes from foreign sources, often American, for his income. When the United States protested these taxes, the semi-official Carranza journal *El Pueblo* notified its readers that the U.S. "has still not finished its imperialist expansion," and accused Wilson of supporting "rich traitors, thieves, bankers, and large land-owners." Wilson, it observed, piously urged land reform and a redistribution of wealth but firmly opposed any modification of existing U.S. property rights in Mexican natural resources. Little wonder that on July 8, 1915 Wilson informed Robert Lansing of the State Department that he still regarded Villa as the best presidential candidate for Mexico.[18]

American investors were also making much of the fact that U.S. socialists endorsed Carranza. In an effort to curtail Gompers' activities on behalf of the Constitutionalist leader, Ralph M. Easley, National Civic Federation executive secretary, wrote to the AFL president:

> The Socialists are taking Carranza under their wing, The "Appeal to Reason" last week had a 3000-word cablegram from Vera Cruz, giving an interview with Carranza, which shows that he is ready for the Co-operative Commonwealth. It is also worthy of note that there are one hundred school teachers sent by Carranza to this country who are being more or less chaperoned by the Socialists. Nobody else seems to know they are here.[19]

The American Socialists were indeed "taking Carranza under their wing." During the "affair of honor" at Tampico leading up to the invasion of Mexico, Carranza had opposed U.S. intervention while Villa had practically endorsed it. That action ended whatever support for Villa, much of it generated by John Reed, existed among Socialists. Later the pact between Carranza and the Casa del Obrero Mundial strengthened pro-Carranza feeling among socialists, and this grew when it became clear that Wilson favored Villa over Carranza. Carranza was now pictured as the real revolutionist in Mexico. Although not portrayed as a socialist, he was considered an honest liberal reformer and a sincere nationalist who firmly opposed U.S. intervention. On May 8, 1915, *Appeal to Reason* urged Wilson to recognize the Carranza government. Two weeks later, stressing Carranza's moderation, the *Appeal* reminded Wilson that the Constitutionalist leader had pledged that he would "be more advantageous and . . . afford a wider field for foreign investments than the system of privileges and concessions that existed heretofore."[20]

It was this aspect of Carranza, and not the frightening picture painted by Ralph Easley, that Murray and Iglesias had pointed out to Gompers. They convinced Gompers that Carranza had to make concessions to the radical elements in the Mexican labor movement at this stage of his presidency. Hence Easley's warning did not deter Gompers from working actively to persuade Wilson to recognize the Carranza constitutionalist forces as the legal government of Mexico.[21]

The most immediate problem in the U.S.-Mexican relations was not recognition but the danger that the United States would again intervene to impose on Mexico the president of Wilson's choice. This time, as played up in the interventionist press, the pretext was that starvation was spreading throughout Mexico, and military intervention was necessary to make certain that food shipped to the Mexicans by the American Red Cross would be used to feed them, "and not to enrich Carranza and his supporters."[22]

The first to warn against intervention was the Socialist press. *New York Call's* editor Chester M. Wright sent a message to President Wilson declaring that "American workers are willing to help Mexican workers, but they are not willing to shoot them." He reminded Wilson that organized labor in Mexico was "backing Carranza," and that no patriotic Mexican "will welcome United States soldiers in any guise." "Go slow, President Wilson," Wright concluded. The socialists and working class press in the United States had prevented him from keeping troops in Vera Cruz indefinitely, and with the aid of American labor, they would prevent a new intervention.[23]

Two weeks later, Gompers decided to express himself to Wilson, He had received a telegram from the Comité Revolucionario of the Casa del Obrero Mundial in Vera Cruz, protesting any intervention plans of the United States, and informing him that the Mexican workers were ready to sacrifice themselves to prevent intervention. Gompers sent President Wilson a translation of the telegram, and along with it, a long letter pointing out that Carranza had entered into a agreement with the representatives of the organized workers of Mexico, and that he had "fully carried out" his pledge to the workers of "guarantees of the right of free speech, free assemblage and the exercise of normal activities for the protection and promotion of the interests of the workers of Mexico."[24]

Several weeks later, Gompers received several wires from the Mexican labor movement. One was a telegram from Josquin Correa, Secretary of the Confederación de Sindicatos Obreros de la Republica Mexicana, in which he urged Gompers "to protest reports in the American press which were creating a feeling of humiliation in Mexican labor people" by casting aspersions on their devotion to the revolution and that they were willing to welcome U.S. intervention because they were starving , an utterly false portrayal both of their attitude and of the food situation in Mexico. Gompers also forwarded this telegram to Wilson, and expressed the opinion that it was "a fair assumption that the representatives of the organizations of the working people in Mexico would not enter a protest against representation that the people of the country are hungry if the needs of the people were great." He recommended that a reliable person be sent to Mexico to investigate the situation and determine "the truth of the reports generally published."[25]

A widely publicized telegram came to the *New York Call* from Luis Viveus and Anulfo Zalatón of the United Federations of Orizaba. It demanded a "Hands Off Mexico" policy on the part of the United States to

> inform the American workingmen that the workingmen of the Mexican Republic hereby protest against intervention by foreign governments in the affairs of the Mexican people. Inspired with the universal spirit of fraternity, union and justice, they call upon the workingmen of the American Union, protesting against the attitude of the government, the ambition of the capitalists and the predominance of the clergy of Mexico, as they want the brothers of both countries to enter into a strife so that they can satisfy their personal ambitions.

The telegram closed: "Lincoln freed four millions of slaves; Carranza gives liberty to ten millions of Mexicans."[26]

The telegram was brought to the *New York Call* by Edmund E. Martínez, who introduced himself as a special envoy of the Mexican labor movement to the United States. He said he had been sent by the Federation of Labor in Vera Cruz to offset the distortions about the Mexican Revolution in the commercial press, and to try to enlist Gompers' support in influencing Wilson to recognize the Carranza government.[27]

When Martínez met the AFL president, Gompers leaped to assist. He pleaded with Wilson to interrupt his vacation in New Hampshire to meet with Martínez and hear his analysis of the existing situation in Mexico. Wilson replied that while he could not grant Martínez an interview, he was interested in what he had to say and suggested that he put it in writing.[28]

Martínez then sent Wilson a long letter in which he revealed that he had been sent not only by the Mexican Federation of Labor but by the Mexican Masons as well, and had been "entreated by the Evangelical (Protestant) Mexicans to try to secure for Mexico the same rights other people have." He then asserted that "the Mexican people desire the leadership of Mr. Carranza, as he has put an end to the domination in Mexico of the church of Rome." He urged Wilson to support the Mexican people's desire to be free of Rome." As "a Christian gentleman and though in favor of the freedom of conscience," Wilson surely must be "opposed to the political domination of any church in the affairs of your or our nation."

"Another thing," Martínez continued, "we want Mr. Carranza because he has been to us what you have been to the American people. The big corporations have not been able to buy him and he has conducted the revolution without the help of them." He urged Wilson to remember that "the slave drivers of this country have attacked you because they could not rob your nation. They have done the same with Mr. Carranza because he does not let them do as they please."

Finally, Martínez reminded Wilson that Carranza had the full support of Samuel Gompers. "We think a great deal of him in Mexico, and trust that with his fatherly advice, we will settle many a rough path." With Gompers' assistance, he hoped that he would be able to obtain Wilson's approval of the Carranza government which, in turn, would enable the President to "avert the war which your millionaires and the Church of Rome are bringing on."[29]

Gompers received a copy of the letter to Wilson, and made no comment on the references to Rome. However, he did voice his approval of Martínez's high regard for the AFL president. At the same time, he urged Martínez to impress upon Carranza that it was the duty of the people of Mexico "to bring their numberless revolutions to an end," and he again voiced his support of the Monroe Doctrine, writing: "upon the United States rests a sort of responsibility to help maintain the integrity of the Pan American countries independent from interference, intrusion or invasion from other countries." But this did not include intervention by the United States, and Gompers gave a veiled threat that unless the Mexicans stabilized their country, the United States would very likely intervene, but he expressed the hope "that the President will not feel obliged to in any way interfere with the internal affairs of Mexico except in an advisory and friendly capacity."[30]

On September 22, 1915, after obtaining authorization from the AFL Executive Council, Gompers wrote Wilson asking him to recognize the Carranza government as the de facto government of Mexico. The conflict in Mexico, Gompers argued, was part "of the world-old struggle for freedom." If not entirely, "in accord with our ideals," nevertheless, the Mexicans should be allowed to proceed "without unwarranted outside interference even from those who seek their welfare." The AFL president closed with high praise for Carranza's attitude toward and relationship with the Mexican working class:

> General Carranza is recognized as the friend of the working people and the real leader of the people generally of Mexico. He has granted to the wage classes the right of organization and has secured them opportunities for carrying out the legitimate purposes of organization. He has been thoroughly in sympathy with the ideals of greater opportunity and freedom of the masses of the people. The working people have been supporting him. They have adjourned their trade unions to enlist in the Carranza army with their union officials serving as the officers of their regiments.[31]

In reply Wilson told Gompers that the Mexican crisis was "near a solution," and that the Gompers' letter "will form a valuable part of my thought" regarding the nature of the final outcome.[32]

On October 19, 1915, less than a month later, Carranza received *de facto* U.S. recognition, with most other countries following the U.S. lead. Along with recognition came a list of demands concerning protection of foreign (primarily U.S.) economic interests. Carranza promised to honor these grants, but with the important proviso that foreign holdings would be regulated by Mexican laws. He promised no land "confiscations," but declared that he would "unrelentingly assail those privileges which tend to produce unearned wealth on the one hand and undeserved pverty on the other." When the U.S. State Department expressed annoyance at these conditions, Carranza informed his representative in Washington to advise the United States not to meddle in internal Mexican affairs and "to leave us in peace. . . ."[33]

Martínez also informed Gompers that the Mexican labor movement was having a medal struck of the President of the AFL, and would have it presented at a public ceremony. Gompers replied, taking credit for the fact that Wilson had not intervened, and did "not send the troops into Mexico" to eliminate Carranza, but rather "to give General Carranza further time and opportunity as the leader whom the white Mexican organized workers volunteered to serve in the cause of freedom." (One can only assume that in Gompers' way of thinking, the supporters of Zapata were non-white, and since most of them were mainly Indians, this probably explains the comment.) Gompers then urged Martínez to make sure to let the Mexican authorities know that it was only a few days after he had sent his letter to Wilson, that General Carranza was recognized, "and that from that moment practically the revolutionary or rebellious effort against the Carranza government dwindled and died." He then added:

> Whether the action of the American Federation of Labor and myself may be counted as cause and effect with the action of the President and Government of the United States, is not a question with which we can concern ourselves. The facts are as they are, and each must draw his own reference as his judgment and conscience may direct.[34]

The Martínez-Gompers correspondence is a curious phase of the relationship of the U.S. labor movement to the Mexican Revolution. Martínez is a strange and contradictory character. In a statement to the *New York Call*, he urged American workers not to be "fooled by the Wall Street crowd," and informed them he represented the radical wing of the Mexican labor movement. Yet he attacked the Casa del Obrero Mundial as "anarchists, impossibilists and the I.W.W. of Mexico."[35] He certainly knew that socialist opposition to military intervention played an important role in keeping the U.S. president from putting his choice in the presidential chair of Mexico. Yet Martínez was willing to accept, without the slightest disagreement, Gompers' claim that he—Gompers—was mainly responsible.

When Gompers wrote to President Wilson that "General Carranza is recognized as the friend of the working people," and had "granted to the wage classes the right of organization and has secured them opportunities for carrying out the legitimate purposes of organization," he was probably not aware that the Mexican President was already rapidly retreating from this position. To cary its program into effect, the Casa del Obrero Mundial began organizing new unions in various industrial centers. In addition strikes closed down the Mexico City rail system, the Electric Power Company, and the Telephone Company.

Unwilling as yet to provoke a direct confrontation with the unions, the Carranza government found a solution to the power company strikes. In order to restore service, it gave the union a partial management role. The government then handpicked a trade union leader, Luis N. Morones, to administer the union's functions in the company. Morones resigned his labor post, and suddenly emerged with enormous influence. The leaders of the Casa at first applauded these developments, since it appeared to represent workers' control of industry.

But they soon learned to regret their action. Morones quickly proved that he was a very adroit opportunist. He established close friendships with many high-ranking government officials, and laid the foundation for his future rise to power as leader of the Department of Labor and the government-sponsored *Confederación Regional de Obreros Mexicanos (CROM)* that, to the great relief of Mexican, U.S. and other foreign capitalists, replaced the Casa del Obrero Mundial.

Meanwhile, Carranza and his top administrators were taking an increasingly dim view of the Casa. The director of Carranza's security apparatus urged the government to tell the Casa leaders that "the liberty they still want is premature," and that even when it did come, it would not be "in the form they propose." Carranza was also told that a baker's strike fomented by the Casa was simply a matter of the workers "wanting more wages without working much." "The roots of this evil must be cut out in order to avoid future examples," the report concluded. Carranza's security officers threatened to crush the Casa with an iron heel if the organization "introduced disorder among the working people."

Never one to tolerate opposition, Carranza cut off aid to the Casa newspaper, began harrassing its organizers, and followed that up with jailing some members. On January 30, 1916, he ordered his governors carefully to check the credentials of traveling Casa delegates and arrest those who "upset public order."

As these develpments took place, and as their economic situation deteriorated steadily, workers' enthusiasm for Carranza began to fade. Faced with increasing trade union unrest, Carranza ordered the Red Battalions dissolved. But impoverished veterans held violent street demonstrations in protest. They demanded jobs and government compensation for their service in the Red Battalions.

This time the Carranza government responded by raiding the Casa headquarters and arresting its leaders. A number of Casa leaders remained jailed at military headquarters in Mexico City for nearly four months.

The infuriated workers responded with a general strike that paralyzed Mexico City on May 22, 1916. Called by the Federation of Federal District Syndicates, an amalgam of Casa unions with 9,000 members, it protested the arrests and the seizure of the House of Tiles—the prestigious Casa headquarters. It raised demands for economic improvement of declining workers' living standards. (The key demand was that workers be paid in bullion or its equivalent in paper money, with an eight-hour working day and a minimum wage of one peso a day.) When employers did not respond to the 72-hour deadline, the Casa approved the general strike.

Thousands of workers marched in Mexico City to support the strike demands. Faced with the tremendous uprising and caught by surprise, the government capitulated and forced the employers to make certain concessions, including agreement to pay the workers in a currency that had real value. The government itself, while acknowledging no wrongdoing, agreed to examine the question of veterans' unemployment and the complaints regarding the arrest of Casa leaders, as well as the seizure of Casa's headquarters.

Believing they had won the general strike, the workers agreed to return to work. But the government was merely playing for time. Nothing was done to alleviate the grievances which had provoked the general strike, and agitation for a new general strike started. It began when the electricians shut off Mexico City's electricity at dawn on July 31, 1916.* By the following day, the city had no electricity, public transportation, or newspapers. Carranza bitterly told the strike committee that they were threatening the nation's very life and security and were traitors to the revolution.

This time the government was prepared. Carranza decreed the death penalty for any worker "threatening public order." Loyal troops occupied Casa headquarters, power plants and nearly every street corner, while other soldiers operated the public services. Working class leaders all over Mexico were arrested, and regional offices and armories of the Casa in the provinces were closed down. On August 2, 1916, martial law was declared in Mexico, and the strike was broken. The Casa del Obrero Mundial was declared subversive and outlawed.

New labor leaders, in the mold of Luis N. Morones—pragmatic, career-oriented, bureaucratic, staunch believers in working with the government and enjoying its patronage, and equally firm believers in class collaboration with the employers— emerge to take over the leadership of the Mexican labor movement. Slowly but surely this ambitious labor leadership established itself, over the bitter opposition of the other militants.[36]

Less than six months after the recognition of Carranza by the United States government, the U.S. labor movement was shocked to learn that Carranza had broken a strike with troops, re-enacted an old law from the days of Benito Juarez (often used by Porfirio Díaz) making it treason to strike, arrested and imprisoned the strike leaders and officials of the Casa del Obrero Mundial, and raided and demolished Casa headquarters all over Mexico. John Murray was among those shocked, and he urged Gompers to write for a full report on what had occurred.

Gompers did make the necessary inquiry, and he, too, was shocked to learn that the reports of Carranza's anti-union activities, including "a rescusitation of the decree under Juarez promulgated in 1862," were all too true. Upon raising the issue with Carranza's representatives in the United States, Gompers was informed

> that Mr. Carranza and his government still are in entire sympathy with the working people and want to keep faith with the labor unions; that he had been accused by the enemies of Mexico within and without of leaning too much toward the working people; that he and the government were charged with catering to the I.W.W. and the anarchists and encouraging socialism; that was one reason why the credit of the country had been somewhat impaired . . . that the general strike was not a real strike for better conditions; it was not intended to accomplish that purpose but that it was a political act to overthrow and destroy the government and that it was not intended to be in the interests of the working people.

Gompers had been around too long to be taken in so easily, and he indicated he was not satisfied with the explanation. He reported, in a private memorandum,

*The strike movement had been temporarily postponed by a border meeting of Mexican labor leaders with Samuel Gompers about strategy to stop a threatening war between Mexico and the United States, which we will discuss in the next chapter.

that he told the representatives of Carranza "that a government which found it necessary to resort to the extremes as indicated in the decree—the denial of the rights of the working people—did not deserve to be maintained or deserve the sympathy of the American working people."[37]

But as in so many cases with Samuel Gompers, militant deeds rarely followed militant words. This was no exception. When the United States grudgingly recognized Carranza as *de jure* (not simply *de facto*) president in August 1917, one of those who hailed the action was the same man who had written in a private memorandum that the anti-labor actions of the Carranza government should render it unworthy of "the sympathy of the American working people."

· XI ·

THE "PUNITIVE EXPEDITION" OF 1916

I n 1915 General Alvaro Obregón had won major victories for the Constitution-alists over Francisco "Pancho" Villa. But Villa was not completely defeated, and he continued to operate in the northwest of Mexico. On January 8, 1916, at San Geronimo, Villa wrote a letter to Emiliano Zapata, leader of revolutionary forces in southern Mexico. He began by blaming his defeat on actions by the United States in not only recognizing Carranza, but also permitting thousands of Carranza's soldiers to move back and forth across the Mexican-U.S. border, strengthening the forces against Villa. He charged that Carranza had betrayed his country by offering the United States valuable economic privileges in Mexico—but presented no evidence for his charge. The North Americans, he insisted, were Mexico's real enemies, and Villa hoped Zapata and his army would join him in Chihuahua so that together they could attack the United States, the common foe of all Mexicans, and maintain the sovereignty of the republic.[1]

Zapata never replied but two days later, on January 10, 1916, Villa's forces, under the command of Páblo López, stopped a train of the Mexican North Western Railway Company near Santa Ysabel, Chihuahua. The passenger car carried American engineers returning to work in Mexico under safe conduct issued by the Carranza government. Lopez marched sixteen Americans off the train and had them murdered.

The massacre at Santa Ysabel has generally been regarded as retaliation against the United States for the *de facto* recognition of Carranza. The Mexican president immediately responded by declaring Villa and López outlaws, and by ordering increased Constitutionalist military activity in Chihuahua.

Two months later, Villa struck again. On the night of March 9, 1916, a Mexican raiding force of 500 men attacked the town of Columbus, New Mexico to cries of

"Viva Villa!" and "Viva Mexico!" According to all available evidence, the leader of the attack was Villa himself. The raiders were repulsed by units of the 13th U.S. Cavalry garrisoned in Columbus, after a six-hour battle. More than 100 Mexicans and 17 Americans died in the fighting.

The response of the United States came quickly. Within a week a punitive expedition initially composed of 1,000 men and later increased to 10,000, under the command of General John J. Pershing, invaded the Mexican state of Chihuahua under orders from President Wilson to capture Villa and destroy his forces.[2]

A considerable scholarly debate has emerged in the United States and Mexico over Villa's motives for these acts, but most scholars agree that conflicts along the U.S.-Mexican border were by 1916 almost an every-day feature of life, especially as discontent among Mexican-American communities in the United States grew.[3] An outstanding example of this dicontent was the Plan de San Diego. Named after a small town in Texas, the plan called for an uprising of Mexican-Americans and Mexican nationals with the objective of creating an independent Social Republic of Texas to be carved out of the states of Texas, New Mexico, Arizona, Colorado, Nevada, Utah, and California—territory lost by Mexico to the United States following the 1846–48 Mexican War. The plan also called upon blacks and Native Americans to join Mexican-Americans and Mexicans in seizing these parts of the Southwest and West, killing many of the Anglo majority and expelling the others, after which the blacks would establish their own Republic in six adjoining states, and all lands stolen from the Indians of the Territory of Arizona would be returned to them.

A "Manifesto to the Oppressed Peoples of America," issued by the organizers of the plan, listed the grievances of Mexican, Latin and black workers in Texas. It made special note of agricultural workers in the cotton fields who were particularly exploited, discrimination and segregation in education, transportation and public and recreational facilities, and the abuses of the Texas Rangers. The new Social Republic of Texas would be a socialist state in which all rural lands and all transportation systems would be owned communally, and "all forms of physical and moral exploitation of the proletariat would be abolished." The Plan of San Diego had as its symbol a red banner with a white stripe, bearing the inscription, *"LI-BERTAD, IGUALDAD, INDEPENDENCIA."*[4]

The plan of San Diego attracted followers of Ricardo Flores Magón, and Mexican-Americans and others along the Texas border who were looking for a way to stop the abuses of the Rangers, long notorious for their anti-Mexican prejudice, their strikebreaking and other anti-working-class activities. The Plan was printed in Mexico with the consent of both Carranza and Villa, and the former has been accused of masterminding the entire venture.[5] In the end nothing came of the venture except some bloody skirmishes between Mexican bands and Rangers in which several were killed on both sides. But the Plan of San Diego did arouse a great deal of alarm in Texas and resulted in vigilante attacks on Mexican-Americans with a fairly large number of deaths and casualties.[6]

Some idea of the fear and hatred of Mexicans among Anglo-Americans on the border is reflected in an hysterical letter sent from San Antonio, Texas to New Mexico's Senator Albert S. Fall, a top spokesperson for U.S. capitalists seeking to overthrow the Mexican Revolution and return Mexico to the era of Porfirio Díaz. Signed "American Refugees in Texas," the letter went in part:

> We would like very much for President Wilson, and Sec. Bryan, to define the difference, in the loss of American lives on the "Lusitania"* and the loss of the lives of hundreds in Mexico.
>
> Americans have been murdered by the wholesale in Mexico, many because they were Americans, our women have been outraged, our flag desecrated thousands of times, our Consuls put in the Penitentiary, on bread and water, and one kicked out of a Bandit headquarters by a bandit chief, our property has been destroyed thereby making paupers out of thousands of good red blooded Americans, we have been ran out of Mexico by bands of Bandits, and are today on actual starvation many of us, without any hope for the future, too old to begin life again, and with no prospect of ever being allowed to return to our homes in Mexico. Traces of the same blood that flows through the veins of Crocket [sic], Bowie, Houston, Travis, and other Patriots flow through our veins, and we are just as ready to defend our rights as they were. . . .[7]

After Villa's attack on Columbus, the United States sent a note to Carranza on March 13, 1916, requesting permission for an American expedition to pursue Villa on Mexican territory. Although the Mexican president granted no such permission, the expeditionary force headed by Pershing crossed the border and penetrated deep into the state of Chihuahua. At a meeting in the White House, with Senator Robert M. La Follette of Wisconsin, Wilson told the progressive Republican that Carranza supported the expedition. As a result, La Follette himself endorsed Wilson's response.[8] Later, however, when the "Punitive Expedition" threatened to become a war between the United States and Mexico, La Follete spoke out vigorously against the forces seeking war, and placed the blame on American capitalists who wanted Mexico's ruin. "It is FINANCIAL IMPERIALISM," he charged. An invasion of Mexico leading to war would come only "because American capital has gone down there and invested. They who own Mexico are the ones who want war."[9]

The "Punitve Expedition" turned "Pancho" Villa into a symbol of national resistance against foreign invaders, and his popularity in Mexico soared. The ranks of his army also soared in numbers as thousands of workers volunteered to fight the Americans, shouting "Death to the gringoes!" Carranza at first held back from protesting sharply against Pershing's invasion of Mexico. (He was not averse to having Villa crushed.) But as the expedition penetrated deeply into northern Mexico supposedly "for the single purpose of capturing the bandit Villa," Carranza recognized that it threatened the very existence of his government as well as any reforms

---

*On May 7, 1915, a German submarine sank the British liner *Lusitania*, with the loss of 1,198 passengers, 128 of them Americans. Although the ship was not a military vessel, it carried rifles and other contraband and thus invited attack.

directed against U.S. financial and industrial interests in Mexico. He then sent a sharp protest against the U.S. military presence in Mexico. At the same time, dozens of Mexican working class organizations offered armed support to Carranza. They ranged from such clubs as Mexico City's "Glories of the Red Battalion" to Treasury printers, railroad workers, and workers in the national arms factory.[10]

On June 16, 1916, upon instructions from Carranza, General Jacinto Trevino telegraphed General Pershing: "I have orders from my government to prevent, by use of arms . . . the American forces that are in this State [Chihuahua] from moving to the south, east or west of the places they now occupy." Pershing responded that Washington had placed no restrictions upon the movement of American forces.

When, five days later, a force dispatched by Pershing moved east to Carrizal and refused to halt, a clash occurred. Twelve Americans (including the commander) were killed, ten wounded. Mexican casualties were even higher. Twenty-four American soldiers were captured by the Mexican army and held as prisoners of war.[11]

At this point it appeared that the interventionists in the United States had a free hand to achieve all they had been seeking since the overthrow of Porfirio Díaz. Indeed, Albert S. Fall, the arch-interventionist, launched a vigorous campaign calling for sending an army of 500,000 men into Mexico. His call, in the form of a Senate resolution, was endorsed by former President Theodore Roosevelt and publisher William Randolph Hearst as well as all others who, like Hearst, had substantial investments in Mexico. The Catholic press joined the campaign, and Father Francis Clement Kelly,[12] the veteran anti-Mexican propagandist, loudly demanded that the AFL show its patriotism by supporting Fall's call.[13]

But the socialists and organized labor (with the exception of the Railroad Brotherhoods) acted swiftly to prevent war between the United States and Mexico.

"This is Just not the Time Not to Intervene," cried the *New York Call* on January 10, 1916 when it received the news of the massacre of Americans at Santa Ysabel. "Twenty [sic] Americans killed!" Was that not enough justification? "What of it?" the *Call* replied to its own question. "Are not eight thousand murdered each year in America?" Thousands were slaughtered wantonly year in and year out in the nation's industries, and nothing was done. "If the United States should intervene [in Mexico], it would mean that we have succumbed to sinister forces of loot and graft, and that we have besmirched ourselves for all time, as being untrue to our own profession."[14]

Other socialists reminded the nation that Americans had been warned to keep out of territory in which "Villista bandits" were operating. They had failed to heed this warning. "Now the lives of thousands of other Americans and of innocent Mexicans will be sacrificed if the jingoes and militants can have their way." The answer was clear: "Socialists should uphold this slogan, 'Keep Hands off Mexico!' "[15]

But would socialists continue to raise the slogan once news broke in March, 1916 that Villa's troops had raided Colombus, New Mexico, killing civilians as well as soldiers, and that Wilson had dispatched the "Punitive Expedition" to capture Villa? The official answer came almost immediately from the Socialist Party. The National Executive Committee issued a firm protest against the Pershing Expedition.

The Committee held that the murder of American citizens was "doubtless inspired by the same American capitalist interests who have so freely hired gunmen to kill to break strikes in the past." Further, it asserted that Villa was an agent of Wall Street, that Wilson would now push for a Mexican war to ensure his re-election and "the complete overthrow of the progressive Mexican workers," and that this policy would receive Congessional support. There was only one force in the country that could prevent this outcome—the working class. The statement closed with a terse anti-war appeal:

> Workers, you have the power to prevent all wars. You have no enemy but the same enemy which the Mexican workers seek to overthrow. Use your power to prevent not only war with Mexico, but to prevent that preparation for war which leads to war.[16]

With one exception, the socialist press joined the National Executive Committee in opposing the Pershing expedition and calling for workers and their allies to act at once to prevent war. The exception was the *Milwaukee Leader*, edited by Victor Berger. Under the heading, "No Alternative," Berger wrote: "The invasion of the United States by Mexican bandits under the leadership of Francisco Villa with the subsequent massacre of American citizens, left no alternative to the government at Washingtion except to use the military forces of the United States to pursue the murderers with a view to their capture or destruction." President Wilson could not have avoided a "punitive expedition. The patience of Congress has reached an end." In fact, a "government that should refuse to resent invasion of its territory by an armed force sent on murder and pillage could not long endure."[17]

But just as Jack London was virtually alone among Socialists to defend the invasion of Mexico and the occupation of Vera Cruz in 1914,* so now Berger was alone in publicly supporting the "Punitive Expedition."[18]

The socialists had not been able to prevent the invasion of Mexico. But they now raised the demand, "Withdraw From Mexico!" The National Executive Committee coupled this call with a proposal aimed at preventing border conflicts in the future. In a statement issued in June 1916, it asserted that American interests sought annexation of a part of Mexico for the exploitation of its great wealth, and that to achieve this conquest, the "interests" were seeking to embroil Mexico and the United States in war. Therefore, the Villa raids were launched by American "capitalist interests." To prevent these "interests" from repeatedly provoking conflicts, it was wise to cope with the border situation. The "frontier should be protected, but we believe it should be protected by troops stationed upon our side of the Río Grande," and "we also demand the capture of the Americans who have inspired Mexican raids across our border."[19]

---

*Jack London remained quiet this time on events in Mexico. For one thing, he was in Honolulu. For another, he resigned from the Socialist Party. Ironically, in a letter sent from Honolulu on March 7, 1916, he gave as his reason for resigning—"its [the Socialist Party's] lack of fire and fight, and its loss of emphasis upon the class struggle." Foner, *Jack London: American Rebel*, p. 123.

It was common in socialist circles to couple the demand for withdrawal form Mexico with one calling upon the government to investigate the Wall Street connections to Villa[20] and the "reliable information that Mexican raids upon American interests," interests which hoped to force the annexation of Mexico. Kate Richards O'Hare, "the first lady of American Socialism," also called for an investigation of William Randolph Hearst, Rockefeller, and Morgan and other capitalists who "could throw some light upon this subject."

> The arch-criminals in this case are the capitalists, promoters and other thieves who have stolen valuable properties in Mexico and want the United States flag raised above their booty to protect it against the people from whom it is stolen. . . .
> Here is a conspiracy that cries aloud for investigation. Let the searchlight be turned in the right direction and it will not be necessary to pursue Villa, a lone bandit, with an entire army. Instead of invading Mexico . . . let us invade the lairs of the pirates in the financial centers and their clerical allies and bring them to swift justice for their crimes.[21]

The socialist press, including left-wing journals like the *International Socialist Review* and the *New Review*, treated Villa as only a mercenary bandit, and practically every socialist followed suit. John Reed stood alone when he told John Kenneth Turner who had published a bitter indictment of Villa: "I don't care if he is only a bandit. I like him just the same."[22] *The Blast*, an anarchist journal published by Alexander Berkman in San Francisco, asked the following question: "Villa or Wilson—Which Is the Bandit?" It argued that Villa "has kept up the fight against tremendous odds. Nor has Wall Street been able to corrupt and buy him off as they did with Carranza." It was Wilson and not Villa who was the bandit.[23]*

On June 24, 1916, the *New York Call's* special "Anti-War-With-Mexico" edition was hawked by a volunteer squad all over New York City. Young socialist women selling the edition wore belts made of streamers bearing the message, "Keep Out of Mexico," and they distributed leaflets urging all to attend the anti-Mexican War mass meeting that evening at Carnegie Hall, sponsored by the New York Local of the Socialist Party.[24]

A widely-reported feature of the meeting was the reading of an appeal from Mexican trade unions.[25] The appeal had been brought by two delegates from the labor movement in Yucatán, who were seated on the platform at Carnegie Hall throughout the proceedings. One of two was Carlos Loveira y Chirinos, the Cuban novelist and revolutionist who had become chief of the Yucatán Department of Labor. The other was Baltasar Pages, a Spaniard of anarchist tendencies and editor of *La Voz de la Revolución*, published in Merida, Yucatán, which was the semi-official organ of the Constitutionalists and also the organ of the *Partido Socialista de Yucatán*. founded by the socialist governor of Yucatán.[26] The two men had arrived in Washington a week before the Carnegie Hall meeting as emissaries of Governor

---

*In recent years Francisco "Pancho" Villa has been rehabilitated in Mexican scholarship. Instead of being considered a mere bandit, he is viewed as one of the heroes of the Revolution.

Alvarado, they had conferred with Samuel Gompers in Washington, then left for New York where they visited the office of the *Call*. They were then invited to be honored guests at the anti-war-with-Mexico meeting. They brought to the meeting an appeal for peace signed by representatives of twelve unions of Yucatán.

"On the Border, which politically, separates our land from yours," the appeal began, "there are at this very moment two armies, face to face, waiting for the opportunity of throwing themselves into a war that, no matter which side might win, would nevertheless cause great evils, both moral and material to both our countries." Behind the war frenzy mounting in the United States, the appeal continued, were the "purse-proud pusillanimous pirates of Wall Street" who had been intriguing since the overthrow of Díaz to get the people of the United States to spill their blood "in rescuing the loot which the bloody Díaz had allowed them to sweat out of the flesh and blood of the Mexican workers."

> What did it matter to these murderers and thieves in Wall Street if some scores of Americans were killed on the border line in Texas and other States? What did it matter if scores of others, soldiers of this country, lost their lives in the pursuit of the bandits whom the Wall Street bankers financed to raid the border areas, even penetrating into the United States? Did not they kill hundreds and maim thousands every day in their industrial hells, in their coal mines and on their railroads? . . . Had they ever stayed their bloody hands when loot was in sight? Had they not slaughtered innocent women and children at Ludlow for a much smaller gain than the looting of Mexico?

The appeal indicated that the Mexicans would have no objection to soldiers being stationed by the United States at the border "to protect the lives of those dwell in the border States." But when the soldiers were ordered to cross the border "to risk their lives to protect the loot of the murderous, thieving industrial and financial bandits" of the country, then it was the duty of the working class of that country to

> give notice that they will yield up not one drop of blood, not one ounce of gold, in the service of those who have robbed them of the fruits of their toil; who have driven their children from schoolhouses and play into the prisons of toil.

Invoking the memory of the Haymarket martyrs, the appeal urged:

> Be on watch, North American comrades. Do not allow any one to fool you with the lies of those who, as long as they can make money, do not care very much about the killing of thousands of laborers. Do not be fooled by the false laments of the Mexican Catholic Church.
>
> Workers of the United States, you have been food for plunder these many years. Have you so little manhood that you are now willing to be food for powder to protect the loot of those who have plundered you? We hope that you will answer this with a gigantic No; that the Rockefellers, the Morgans, the Hearsts and the whole thievish crew will seek refuge from your wrath

and the infamous conspiracy to bring on a war with Mexico come to naught! Help us to secure that, once and forever. Help us by demanding that the United States Army be recalled, thereby avoiding the great danger there and must be while a khaki uniform remains in Mexican territory.

And if, even by this means, it is impossible to avoid a bloody struggle, then, Workers of the United States, do as we would fain to do with our reactionaries—put at the head of your army all those who are responsible for the tragedy, the magnates of the Standard Oil Company and of the International Harvester Company, William R. Hearst, Harrison Gray Otis of the *Los Angeles Times*, professional soldiers and others who in any form and by any means are looking for intervention in Mexico.

Workers of the United States, solidarity![27]

The speeches and resolutions at the packed meeting in Carnegie Hall endorsed the appeal for peace,[28] and charged that American owners of property in Mexico were conspiring "to involve the two republics in war, and every day that American troops remain on Mexican soil increases the danger that this malign attempt will succeed." Therefore, the way to prevent this tragedy was immediately to withdraw the troops from Mexico and bring an end to the "Punitive Expedition." The continued presence of United States troops was an "invasion of the rights of the Mexican people and unworthy of the American nation."[29]

On May 25, 1916 the *New York Call* featured an article by John Murray headed: "INTERNATIONAL LABOR CONFERENCE IS CALLED TO MEET AT EL PASO." The sub-headings read: "Official Request Sent by President Gompers to Mexican Secretary, Labor Movements of Two Republics to meet to Insure Peace· and Beget Mutual Understanding, According to Plan Set forth by Head of A.F. of L. in Invitation to Powerful Casa del Obrero Mundial." The meeting of trade union representatives from both countries had been proposed by Gompers following a conference with Murray and "Judge" Charles Douglas, Carranza's legal representative in the United States.[30] On May 23, 1916, with Pershing's troops deep inside Mexico and with tensions mounting, Gompers sent an invitation to the Secretary of Casa del Obrero Mundial for an international trade union conference of representatives of the AFL, the Casa, and as many other Mexican labor organizations as possible at El Paso, Texas, at a date to be agreed upon. In his letter, Gompers reviewed the progress of organized labor in Mexico, praised the "historic agreement between the Casa del Obrero Mundial and the Constitutionalist government," praised the "bravery and determination of the Mexican miners in the State of Arizona," who, "with their brother Americans of the North," had just won a stunning victory in their strike, gaining not only improvements in their conditions but striking a blow for "the cause of international solidarity."[31] Gompers then urged the sending representatives to meet with those from the AFL in El Paso, Texas, where "the mutual welfare of the sister republic could . . . be discussed and a future co-operative policy outlined." He closed:

With you I agree that the future peace of the world rests in the hands of the wage-earners and this is most urgently expressed by the organized labor movement of each and all countries.[32]

Copies of the letter of invitation to the conference were also sent to President Carranza, governors of the various districts of Mexico, Dr. Atl (editor of *Acción Mundial* in Mexico City), and other trade unions in Mexico. In his letter to Carranza, Gompers wrote: "I think it is needless for me to say how thoroughly interested and concerned are my associates in the American Federation of Labor as am I, in all that may make for the advancement and protection of the rights and interests of the masses of the workers of Mexico, and that we are hoping and will be glad to aid as far as our ability and opportunities go in establishing higher and better standards of higher justice, right, freedom and the concepts of humanity."[33]

In presenting Gompers' two letters to the readers of the *New York Call*, John Murray went to great lengths to caution against their reading a "political significance" in Gompers' call for the conference. It was "entirely international in its aims," whatever that might mean. Its significance in bringing a peaceful solution to the Mexican-American crisis was enormous, Murray insisted. "Military conferences, commercial conferences, all may stage themselves along the border and all be regarded by the Mexican worker as a mere turn of the wheel, which brings no change in his age-long servitude. But a meeting of wage-workers, hands clasped across the border by Mexican and American toilers, will stand the test of the peon's closest scrutiny. Only by such means can fraternity become an actuality between the two republics." Peace between Mexico and the United States hung on a thread. Nothing yet proposed in the United States had the potential of preventing war to the gegree represented by "this call for a conference of labor representatives." Indeed, this was "the first time in the history of the world that it was proposed that the workers themselves hold conferences at the border when armies were actually in the field."[34]

How it could be that such a unique, historic, and overwhelmingly significant a conference would have "no political significance" can only be explained by Murray's awareness of Gompers' sensitivity to anything that smacked of reducing the significance of the economic power of labor. Florence C. Thorne, Gompers' secretary, informed him that Murray had told her that he was "so glad to find out his [Gompers'] real attitude of mind during the time he had been associated with him in this work for Mexico," and that "he agreed fully with Mr. Gompers in that the labor movement was the thing to be fostered—the labor movement was the power to which all would look."[35] Although a socialist, Murray had little respect for the power of the Socialist Party.

After sending copies of his letter to the Casa del Obrero Mundial to President Wilson, Secretary of State Lansing, and other members of the administration, Gompers departed for the mid-west on trade union matters, leaving Mexican-American affairs in the hands of John Murray, his chief adviser on matters south of the border.[36] Florence Thorne kept him aware of Murray's progress. She reported that Judge Douglas had informed Murray that "in his opinion the labor movement of the two countries was the only thing that could have any influence now in moving the Carranza government"; that Murray had obtained endorsement for the proposed conference from United Mine Workers Vice President Frank Hayes, and James Lord, president of the AFL's mining department—each of whom had long concerned himself with Mexican affairs. Lord had told Murray "that Mr. Gompers' course had won for him an immense number of friends particularly among Socialists and those who have looked upon him as a conservative."[37]

Thorne also reported that Murray had met with enthusiastic response to the proposed conference from Chester M. Wright, "who has controlling power in directing the editorial policy of the Call," and that Wright told Murray "he was so glad that the control over the conference and the relations between the labor movement of the United States and the Mexico was in Mr. Gompers' hands and not in those of any other man or organization." Thorne added: "A careful reading of the editorials and an understanding of the way the Call news has been edited, will show that Mr. Wright is using his influence for constructive reform." Murray, however, had told Thorne that Wright "was having a hard fight to maintain his course in New York."[38]

Wright had an important ally. Mother Jones, who had earned the respect and admiration of all socialists for her militant role in the miners' strikes in West Virginia, Colorado, and Michigan, and for her contributions to the Mexican Revolution, wrote to John Murray:

> I have noticed that President Gompers was calling for a conference in El Paso, the representatives of Labor in both nations. I thought it was a remarkable move and sincerely [hope] it will be carried to its end and if it can be, it will have a strong tendency to stop this war which these pirates are trying to force.
>
> You have done some very good work in Mexico and there is a good deal more to be done yet John. . . .[39]

Murray used this letter to support the position Chester M. Wright was taking in the *New York Call*.[40]

The response to the proposed conference from Mexico was gratifying. In a joint telegram to Gompers, the Casa del Obrero Mundial and the Confederación de Sindicatos Obreros accepted the invitation. (In addition, as we noted above, the Casa postponed a general strike in Mexico City to allow for the proposed conference to take place.) The federation of trade unions of Orizaba, Río Blanco, Certitos, Miera Fuentes, San Carexo, the unions of bank employees, carpenters, and jute workers, and one thousand working men of Orizaba telegraphed Gompers endorsing the conference. They urged the AFL to join them in opposing "interventionist forces." Dr. Atl wired Gompers that his letter had been published in *Acción Mundial*, and that the response of the Mexican workers to the proposed conference was enthusiastic, and strengthened their hope of preventing war between the United States and Mexico.[41]

The Casa del Obrero Mundial and the Confederación de Sindicatos Obreros took the next step. They proposed that the conference be held in Eagle Pass, Texas. Gompers wired back asking for a suggested date. The response from Mexico was that June 25, would be suitable.[42]

The decision to switch to Eagle Pass from El Paso was made because of the fear that anti-Mexican feeling was so intense in the latter city that it was not safe for the delegates from Mexico to meet there. The fear was justified. During this period, David Starr Jordan, president of Stanford University, was in El Paso for the American Union Against Militarism, which was pursuing another peace initative. Hostility from the El Paso authorities was so intense that Jordan was forced to withdraw to Albuquerque.[43]

The Mexican delegates proceeded to Eagle Pass, Texas, where they expected the Conference would be held. The skirmish between members of Pershing's expedition and Mexican troops had occurred at Carrizal only a few days before, and the Mexican labor delegates informed Gompers they were anxious to begin the conference immediately so as to do what they could to avert the war which seemed to be coming closer and closer. To their disappointment, Gompers wired the Mexicans that a meeting of the AFL Executive Council would make it impossible for him to come to Eagle Pass. He suggested that if the Mexicans agreed, the conference could be transferred to Washington. Gompers proposed they arrive no later than July 1 while the Executive Council was still in session. Thereupon the Mexican delegates appointed a subdelegation consistying of Luis N. Morones and Salvador Gonzalez García, which set out to Washington. They brought with them a program for peace which they planned to present to the AFL Executive Council.[44]

While the telegrams had been flying back and forth between the United States and Mexico City in relation to the labor conference, official relations between the United States and Mexico were deteriorating. In an effort to prevent still further disintegration, Gompers and Sercretary of Labor William B. Wilson met with the President on June 22. Gompers rehearsed for the President the history of events in Mexico since the rule of Díaz, and pointed out that "the efforts of the workers of Mexico were making to organize and their movement had not yet taken form and shape; that it was crude, but it represented their opportunities and their efforts to take advantage of them." He pointed out, too, as "Judge" Douglas had urged him to, that Secretary of State Lansing (who was paranoid in his hatred of the Mexican labor movement) in replying to Carranza's latest note demanding Pershing's withdrawal, had deliberately made an important omission which made Carranza appear more adamant than he really was. In reproducing Carranza's notes in his answer, Lansing had ommitted entirely the portion in which Carranza referred to Section 21 of the Treaty of Guadalupe Hidalgo of 1848 (ending the war of aggression by the United States against Mexico), in which provision was made for the mediation of disputes between two countries. When Gompers brought this up in his meeting with President Wilson, "the President seemed intensely interested in this." Recommending that he do everything that was possible "to avoid a break" between the two countries, Gompers urged the President to consider the possibility of arbitration.

In her memorandum of the meeting, Florence C. Thorne recorded: "Mr. Gompers said the conference with the President was one of the most impressive in which he had ever been present, and he felt that it was momentous."[45]

Later that day, "Judge" Douglas, after consulting with Gompers, wired Carranza asking him if he would look with favor on arbitration. The following morning, Douglas received a reply from Carranza "that every offer to adjust matters would be looked upon with favor by the people of Mexico."[46]

Two days later, the four-column headline on the first page of the *New York Call* reported: 'LABOR WILL HAVE NO WAR,' SAYS GOMPERS." Under the byline of Julian Pierce, formerly an AFL organizer, appeared an account of the Gompers-Wilson meeting at the White House. In a lead editorial, Chester M. Wright wrote breathlessly: "Samuel Gompers is Doing Great and Good Work for Peace. Whether it is war with Mexico or not, the eforts of President Samuel Gompers in behalf of peace must command the attention and admiration of workers everywhere."[47]

The workers meanwhile were doing what they could to prevent the full military intervention of the United States, should Carranza not immediately release the Carrizal prisoners as President Wilson demanded. To be sure, the Railroad Brotherhoods, as in the Vera Cruz episode, were eager for war, and also ready to send "Railroad men into Mexico for the transportation of troops and supplies."[48] But trade union groups all over the country adopted resolutions against intervention. "Keep Us Out of War In Mexico," the central labor unions of Chicago, Detroit, New York City, and Brooklyn as well as those in other cities and other labor bodies wired President Wilson. The International Brotherhood Welfare Association (the Hoboes' Brotherhood) stood ready "to go down to the Mexican border in a body, without shot or steel and entreat our fellow working people in Mexico to lay down their arms."[49]

On June 28, with the Carrizal prisoners not released, and Wilson ready to act, John Murray called Gompers away from a session of the AFL Executive Council, to explain that "Judge" Douglas was "extremely anxious about the situation and thought that the only thing that should be done, and the best thing that could be done, was to ask Mr. Gompers to send a telegram direct to General Carranza asking him to release the American soldiers detained as prisoners by the Mexican soldiers." Gompers immediately dictated the following telegram to General Venustiano Carranza, First Chief, Constitutionalist Government, Mexico City, Mexico:

> In the name of common justice and humanity, in the interest of a better understanding between the peoples and the government of the United States and Mexico, for the purpose of giving the opportunity to maintain people and avoid the horrors of war, upon the grounds of highest patriotism and love, I appeal to you to release the American soldiers held by your officers in Chihuahua.
>
> Samuel Gompers, President,
> American Federation of Labor.

Murray carried copies of the telegram to "Judge" Douglas and to the Mexican Embassy, while a third copy was sent to Secretary of Labor Wilson. Within hours, an Extra announced the prisoners would be released. Gompers called Murray to a meeting where the "whole situation was discussed with gratification and a feeling of the utmost relief." Murray left to send a telegram to the *New York Call* giving the text of Gompers' wire to Caranza.[50]

In the evening of June 29, Gompers received the following telegram from Carranza: "In replying to your message dated yesterday I would state that the government in my charge has ordered the liberty of the American soldiers whom the Mexican forces took as prisoners in Carrizal. Salute very affectionately. V. Carranza."[51]

The telegram was read to the AFL Executive Council on the morning of June 30, and the Council authorized Gompers to express by wire "our appreciation of your order releasing the American soldiers and thus helping to clear the way for a mutually honorable settlement of any differences existing between the Governments of the United States and Mexico."[52]

On July 4, 1916, the Department of State received the official notice of the release of the American prisoners.[53] Soon the war crisis with Mexico faded in inportance as most Americans turned their attention to the war in Europe and the increasing danger of American involvment.

On July 28, 1916, the *New York Times* carried the following headline: "GOMPERS WANTS CREDIT. SAYS IT WAS FEDERATION INFLUENCE THAT AVERTED WAR WITH MEXICO." The story that followed reported that Gompers had made public telegrams and letters exchanged with First Chief Venustiano Carranza of Mexico and President Woodrow Wilson which, Gompers claimed, showed that AFL (and he himself particularly) was instrumental in persuading President Wilson to recognize the Carranza Government, in convincing Wilson "of the folly of intervention, and in procuring the release of United States soldiers held by Carranza at Chihuahua." Gompers also made public a letter by Edmundo E. Martínez in which the Mexican representative congratulated the AFL on the part it played in the crisis surrounding the "Punitive Expedition."

The *New York Times* brusquely dismissed Gompers' claim with the observation that Carranza had initially ordered the prisoners released on June 24, four days before he repeated the order on June 28, and that Wilson had decided against war before he actually heard of the prisoner release.[54]

Actually, neither Gompers nor the *Times* was entirely correct. Although there is no doubt that Gompers carried on effective informal diplomatic manuevers to avert war, it is quite typical of the AFL president that in his statement he mentioned no other group as also deserving credit. Yet historians of the peace movement have demonstrated that the American Union Against Militarism played a crucial role in turning public opinion in favor of a negotiated settlement in late June 1916, thereby bringing pressure on Wilson to avoid war. It was the AUAM which persuaded Captain Lewis C. Morey, the senior survivor of Carrizal, to disclose the fact that the United States had been the aggressor against Mexico, and had inserted his statement as a full-page advertisement in the *New York Times* and other major dailies. In so doing, the AUAM prevented Wilson (who had seen an official Army report which described the United States as the aggressor at Carrizal) from delivering a warlike message in which he planned to tell Congress the Mexican forces had attacked first.[55]

It was also the AUAM which met with Mexican peace groups in formal meetings.

The informal commission included Geraldo Murrillo, better known as Dr. Atl (who was also part of the Mexcian labor group which went to Eagle Pass), David Start Jordan, Moorfield Storey, and Paul Kellogg. Lincoln Steffens acted as the group's link with the White House.[56]

All this does not mean that Gompers did not help lay the groundwork for peaceful negotiations. But to claim all the credit, as Gompers did in 1916, and as several historians have since done for him, is to mix fact with fantasy. William G. Whittaker is one of these historians,[57] and he quotes extensively from memoranda of Florence C. Thorne. He omits her report dealing with the efforts of the American Union Against Militarism to cooperate with the AFL in the effort to prevent war developing fron the Carrizal episode, and their appeal to Gompers that he join with them to "bring all of the anti-war forces in the country in a concentrated effort to prevent war." Gompers bluntly refused, making it plain "that he was not going to have the labor movement used by any outside organization to further their purposes and schemes. All fanatics would have to keep their hands off."[58] Since Gompers was determined to lay the foundation for the claim that the AFL alone was responsible for having averted the war, he was in no mood to consider unity with any other group, even though the Mexicans were ready for joint activity for peace.

Whatever criticism Gompers received from the press for his claim relating to the peaceful settlement of the Mexican-U.S. crisis was more than compensated for by a letter that came from Frank Duffy of the Carpenters' Union, spokesperson for the Catholic Church on the AFL Executive Council. For over a year Duffy had protested Gompers'. Mexican policies,[59] and he had opposed the call to the Mexican labor movement for a joint trade union conference. But now Duffy praised Gompers for his role in maintaining the peace, and even chided him for being "entirely too modest" in congratulating the AFL Executive Council and the American labor movement "on the happy consummation of the present situation and upon the fact that we have helped to avert war with Mexico." Duffy wrote: "You did not give yourself the degree of credit which is due you for bringing about this state of affairs." He closed his letter on an even higher note of praise:

> The great service which you personally performed is not and it never can be known to the general public, for the reason that the press as a general rule is not inclined to give Labor credit for its achievements. Allow me to take this opportunity to congradulate you for the personal interest you have taken in the Mexican situation.

And Duffy added in a postscript: "Sam, you've changed me on this question."[60]

In reply Gompers quoted the remark of Admiral Schley after his victory in the naval battle at Santiago de Cuba during the war against Spain:

> It was something like this: There is enough glory for all of us in it. I know that we have all of us just cause to feel proud of the fact that we have helped to avert a bloody long drawn-out war with Mexico and one which could not have accomplished such just, humane, and far-reaching liberty-guaranteeing results as will be accomplished by the methods of peace, and in addition we

have already made toward the establishment of better relations with the organized labor movement of Mexico, and what is still greater gratification we have sown the seed by which better relations will be established between the organized labor movement as represented by the American Federation of Labor and organized labor movements of all the Pan American countries through the Pan-American Federation of Labor.[61]

The reference to the Pan-American Federation of Labor concerned a conference just concluded in Washington, D.C. On July 1, 1916, the representatives of the Casa, Luis Morones and Salvador Gonzáles García, had arived in Washington from Eagle Pass, Texas. They were joined by Edmundo E. Martínez, Carlos Loveira, and Baltasar Pages who were already in Washington. For the next several days, these delegates conferred with Gompers, John Murray, and the entire AFL Executive Council. On July 31 a joint declaration of principles was issued. Drafted by Gompers and signed by the entire AFL Executive Council as well as by the Mexican delegates, it outlined a plan for the establishment of international relations between the workers of the two adjoining republics, as well as for the labor unity of the entire western hemisphere:

> We are confident that personal conference of the workers of the United States and Mexico will be a constructive force in bringing about understanding necessary for better relations between our countries and for maintaining peace founded upon a proper regard for the rights of all. It is our opinion that this conference should be followed by another more generally represented, for the purpose of agreeing upon plans for maintaining permanent relations and for the federation of the labor movements of all countries of the two Americas.[62]

The declaration was described as "the first joint appeal and proclamation of principles ever issued on this continent by an international labor conference called in the face of war between two nations."[63] Signed by labor representatives from the United States and Mexico, it laid the foundation for the Pan-American Federation of Labor.

· XII ·

FOUNDING OF THE PAN-AMERICAN FEDERATION OF LABOR

On June 12, 1915 *Solidarity* featured an "Appeal" from Covington Hall, the New Orleans Wobbly poet and editor, for the IWW to sponsor an "American Labor Congress" which would "devise ways and means to unite the North and South American workers in a great offensive and defensive union." The purpose of the union would be "not only the protection of the pressing, immediate interests of the workers, but the alignment of the forces struggling for industrial democracy on an inter-continental basis." Hall noted that the capitalist class was "making every effort to unite its North and South American interests." It was essential, therefore, for the workers to act immediately, and establish an "Inter-American Labor Congress." Hall concluded his "Appeal":

> Let's try to bring it to fruition. For too long the American workers have not known each other well enough. Let's not lag behind the capitalist class in protection of class interests. Let's get busy.[1]

Covington Hall's proposal is hardly surprising. From the time of its founding the IWW considered itself a worldwide organization. IWW membership cards were transferrable from one nation to another. As part of its ideology, the IWW espoused the organization of a worldwide general strike which necessitated the international cooperation and solidarity of labor.

Sailors of the Marine Transport Workers Industrial Union (MTWIU) were mainly responsible for the diffusion of IWW ideas around the world, serving as missionaries in the cause of industrial unionism. Language proved to be no handicap for many IWW sailors in Latin America; by 1915, 50 percent of all firemen shipping out of United States Atlantic ports were Spanish-speaking. Originally from Spain and different Latin American countries, these firemen had been snubbed by the AFL-affiliated International Seamen's Union, and in 1913 they joined the IWW *en masse*. In 1917, one-half of the New York MTWIU local was Spanish-speaking, some 2,500 sailors in all. IWW seamen from both the East and West Coasts of the United States also distributed IWW material throughout Latin America, including two Spanish newspapers, *El Rebelde* of Los Angeles, which was first published in 1916, and *Solidaridad*, the Spanish-language organ of the IWW, established in 1918.

In our next volume we will deal at some length with the establishment of the IWW in Latin America. But here we may note that it was firmly established in Chile by 1918. Indeed, the official organ of the IWW announced in its June 18, 1918 issue:"The latest addition to our international union is the Chilean (South American) administration." The IWW expanded steadily between 1918 and its first national convention in Chile, December 24–27, 1919. The initials IWW were adopted by the Chileans to identify their organization, although the words them-selves were translated into Spanish—*"los Trabajadores Industrial del Mundo."*[2]

Covington Hall's proposal for the IWW to sponsor an "American Labor Congress" which would "devise ways and means to unite the North and South American workers in a great offensive and defensive union" was never actually carried into effect by an IWW weakened and almost totally destroyed by the vicious government offensive against the organization during World War I. But Hall's appeal may have influenced Gompers to recommend in 1915 that the AFL authorize its Executive Council to enter into correspondence with organized labor in Latin America with the aim of concerted action. The AFL approved the suggestion. But it was not until July 1916, immediately following the AFL-Mexican labor conference in Washing-ton, D.C., that the first steps were taken to realize this goal.

When Carlos Loveira and Baltasar Pages came to the United States from Mexico and met with the AFL in Washington, they brought with them authorization from the labor movement of Yucatán to help achieve the federation of the workers of both continents. They had been authorized by their state government to visit all Latin American countries to urge that a Congress be held to establish a Pan-American Federation of Labor.[3] Gompers expressed approval and support of the Loveira-Pages mission, in an open letter addressed "To the Workers of All American Countries," and noted that "the effort to establish a Pan-American Federation of Labor . . . was not a new thought for the American Federation of Labor."

But Gompers also commented that "the necessity for such a labor federation" had been made increasingly important because of "efforts to establish closer relations between the countries included in the Pan-American Union." He pointed specifically to the trip made in the spring of 1916 by the High Commission of the Pan-American Union "for the purpose of promoting better commercial and industrial relations," and he noted that there was no one on that Commission who distinctively represented "human interests and the rights and welfare of the masses of the people." Gompers said he had urged the government of the United States to rectify this "serious omission," and urged the labor movements of all Pan-American countries to do the same with their governments. Nevertheless, he was convinced that even such representation was "not sufficient to protect and promote the rights and welfare of the workers of all countries."

A Pan-American Federation of Labor is not only possible but it is necessary. It will constitute a ready and fit agency for injecting into international deliberations at opportune and critical times consideration of human rights, interests and welfare. . . .[4]

Gompers' reference to the High Commission of the Pan-American Union reflected his understanding that both businessmen and government officials in the United States viewed World War I as a golden opportunity for economic penetration of Latin America. As Willard Straight of J.P. Morgan and Company pointed out, (before the U.S. entered the conflict), the war "left the United States as the only country not engaged in hostilities with the banking facilities and financial resources necessary for foreign trade development." Gompers was concerned that the labor movement would be left out in this "development," and he acted to prevent it through the Pan-American Federation of Labor.[5]

At the AFL convention of November 1916, Gompers asked for authority to create the Pan-American Federation of Labor Conference Committee, the body which would lay the groundwork for the Pan-American Federation of Labor. His request was granted, and a committee was named consisting of Gompers as chairman; John Murray, secretary; and Santiago Iglesias, "representing the organized workers of Porto Rico," and Carlos Loveira, "representing the organized workers of Yucatán, Mexico," as committeemen. The purpose of the Conference Committee was to organize "the projected conference of bonafide labor representatives from all Pan-American countries."[6]

On February 9, 1917, the Conference Committee issued a "Manifesto" to the workers of Latin America in both English and Spanish. It requested that the labor movements of Latin America select representatives to join the Conference Committee in Washington. The need for such joint activity was urgent:

As is well known, the capitalists of North America and some of European countries are scattering millions of dollars through Latin America, acquiring concessions and business properties which are disposed of to the masses of the people. . . .[7] If the employers, the capitalists of Pan-America thus unite for the protection of their common advantage, it becomes all the more evident that the wage-earners of these countries must also unite for their common protection and benefit. . . .

The purpose of the Pan-American Federation of Labor, the "Manifesto" continued, would be to permeate the Western Hemisphere "with a humane influence," and this would more truly represent the sentiments of the American people "than the influence of all the corporations in the United States, and is in strong contrast with those capitalists who are eternally crying 'Business, business,' and 'Dollars, dollars.' "[8]

One sentence in the "Manifesto," which at first reading seemed to be out of context, stated: "Above all things the Pan-American Federation of Labor should stand as a guard on watch to protect the Western Hemisphere from being overrun by military domination from any quarter."[9] Although the meaning was not spelled out, these words clearly referred to the alleged designs of Germany on Latin America. In fact, in a note appended to the "Manifesto," the Conference Committee stated that the document was drafted before the severing of diplomatic relations between the United States and Germany, and that when this occurred, the printing was delayed in order to incorporate that paragraph. Moreover, now that the break had come, there was a greater need than ever "for a Pan-American Federation of Labor and a spirit of Pan-Americanism."[10]

It would thus appear that, from the viewpoint of the AFL leadership, a major purpose for the formation of the Pan-American Federation of Labor was to secure the support of Latin American workers for the Allies. The *Los Angeles Citizen*, which published the "Manifesto" in English and Spanish, emphasized this point. The *Citizen* went on to add, however, that at the end of the war, "the unions will gain tremendously in the countries now at war, and with the growth of wage-earners' organizations throughout Latin America, it well may be said that the Labor Movement will assume world-wide importance."[11]

Soon after the publication of the Conference Committee's "Manifesto," the United States declared war on Germany. Gompers soon saw the value of using the Conference Committee to counter support for Germany in Latin America. In May 1918, he sent John Murray, Santiago Iglesias, and James Lord of the AFL's Mining Department to Mexico. Ostensibly the purpose of the mission was to continue the work that had already been done toward the formation of the Pan-American Federation of Labor. But the real objective was to persuade President Carranza of Mexico to abandon his neutral position on the war.

In a lengthy memorandum to Gompers, Judge Douglas described an interview he had with Carranza in Mexico City. The Mexican president had just cabled birthday greetings to Kaiser Wilhelm of Germany, and Douglas told Carranza that this action had been a terrible mistake. Carranza replied that the message was "done merely in the course of social intercourse," and that he sent similar messages of congratulations to President Wilson and Secretary of State Lansing. Douglas then told Carranza that "Mexico must come out for the Allies. Not to do so gave every opportunity for attack from Mexico's enemies from without and within." Carranza answered that he was "not unfriendly to the United States," but he thought Mexico's best interests "lay in her being a neutral country." Douglas scoffed at the idea of neutrality, calling it a "hollow phrase." He warned that after the war, if Mexico had not supported the allies, it "would take but a spark, but a ghost of an excuse, to drive the whole military machine of the United States through Mexico." On the other hand, through an alliance with the Allies, Mexico would get needed protection for her oil fields, and money to develop the country.[12]

Douglas informed Gompers that he had not been able to persuade Carranza. But he felt that a commission from the AFL would be welcomed by Carranza, and would be welcomed by the Mexican trade unions. Murray, Iglesias, and Lord did meet with Mexican trade unions. They learned that the Mexicans were anxious to promote the interchange of trade union delegations and to protect workers emigrating from one country to another. As for supporting the Allied cause in the war, said the Mexicans, it would be very premature and inconvenient at this moment "to form a labor program which might compromise our efforts and action in the matter relating to international policies."

Nevertheless, the Mexican trade unions agreed to send representatives to the 1918 AFL convention in St. Paul, Minnesota. The two were Salvador Alvarez, representing the *Federación de Sindicatos Obrero del Distrito Federal*, and Luis N. Morones, head of the newly-formed *Confederacion Regional Obrero Mexicana (CROM)*. It was with the CROM, which had broken with the pro-IWW trade unionists of Mexico and was to espouse a conservative business unionism, that the AFL would cooperate in the formation of the Pan-American Federation of Labor.

By the time Alvarez and Morones arrived in Laredo, Texas it was clear that they could not reach St. Paul before the AFL convention ended. So Gompers wired them to proceed to Washington where a series of conferences was held with Gompers, Murray, Iglesias, and several members of the AFL Executive Council. Out of them came a call for an international labor conference to be held at Laredo, Texas on November 13, 1918. The questions to be considered would include the formation of the Pan-American Federation of Labor; the establishment of better conditions for international migratory workers; the improvement of relations between the United States and Mexico; the promotion and protection of the interests and well-being of the people in the two countries; and the cultivation of friendly relations between the labor movements, peoples, and the governments of the United States and Mexico.[13]

To further the aims of the conference, a bilingual paper (in English and Spanish) was launched. Called the *Pan-American Labor Press: El Obrero Pan-Americano*, it was designed to carry items of interest to workers of the Southwestern United States and Mexico. It was to be published in Texas, and from there distributed throughout Mexico and the border areas of the United States.[14]

The problem of financing the newspaper arose immediately. No help could be expected from the Mexican labor movement, and Gompers would have found it difficult to raise funds for the project through the usual AFL channels. The AFL leaders turned to the United States government. On July 17, 1918, the AFL representatives to Mexico reported to a gathering which included Secretary of Labor William B. Wilson, War Labor Policies Board Chairman Felix Frankfurter, Edgar Sisson (representing George Creel, head of the wartime Committee on Public Information), and Chester Wright, serving both as the director of the news department of the AFL's American Alliance for Labor and Democracy,[15] and labor publications director of the government's Committee on Public Information. The Wilson Administration was convinced that the Pan-American labor press would play an important role in the war effort by helping to convince Mexican workers to support the Allied cause and the United States' war effort.[16]

The project was approved and funds were allocated in a surreptitious manner to avoid publicity either in the United States or in Latin America, where it was felt that government subsidy would be resented and exploited by opponents of the United States.* $50,000 was transferred by the U.S. government through the Committee on Public Information, which turned the money over to the American Alliance for Labor and Democracy which, in turn, gave it to the officers of the *Pan-American Labor Press*. The $50,000 was recorded as "for the use of the American Federation of Labor on the Mexican border."[17]

Beginning on August 28, 1918, ten issues of the *Pan-American Labor Press: El Obrero Panamericana* were published. John Murray, the chief editor, set the tone of the journal when he wrote in that first issue: "Mexico will either open the door for the United States to all Latin America or close it. . . . All Latin America knows that as the United States does to Mexico so it will to all Latin America."[18] In view of two recent invasions of Mexico by U.S. troops, this was hardly a comforting thought for Latin Americans.

The last issue of the *Pan-American Labor Press* contained the proceedings of what became known as the First Congress of the Pan-American Federation of Labor, held as scheduled on November 13 in Laredo. Two days before the delegates convened, the Armistice ending World War I was signed.

Gompers and the mayor of Nuevo Laredo, Mexico welcomed the delegates to the Congress at the Mexican-United States boundary on the International Bridge. Secretary of Labor William B. Wilson, representing President Wilson, and General Barza, representing President Carranza, also welcomed the 72 delegates from six countries. (All but four of these delegates were from the United States and Mexico.) The Congress opened with addresses by Ricardo de Leon, representing the workers of Central America, Luis Morones of CROM, and Samuel Gompers. Gompers was elected chairman of the convention, and Morones vice-chairman.[19]

Several Mexican proposals were then discussed. One related to the discrimination against Mexican workers by the trade unions of the United States and the abuse of Mexican workers in cities north of the border, by U.S. authorities. William Green, chairman of the resolutions committee, made an effort to shut off discussion on the subject by referring the matter to the AFL Executive Council. But he was not successful. Instead, heated debate broke out in which U.S. representatives complained that Mexican workers in the southwestern states were indifferent to appeals to join American unions, and Mexican replies that if the Mexicans were dealt with fairly and sincerely, they would respond to appeals for organization. Finally, it was agreed that the AFL Executive Council, in cooperation with the Mexican labor organizations, should investigate the matter. It was also agreed that the CROM should have a resident organizer in the United States to cooperate with the AFL in organizing Mexican workers and to watch over their interests.[20]

---

*"Such publicity," notes Sinclair Snow, "would have been disastrous, for it would have borne out the charge of the pro-Germans in Mexico that the movement was backed by the United States government." "Samuel Gompers and the Pan-American Federation of Labor" (Ph.D. diss., University of Virginia, 1960), p. 70.

Since the AFL had not displayed much interest in fighting for the rights of Mexican workers in the Southwest of the United States, it is not clear what was expected from this proposal.

Three other Mexican proposals were unanimously approved. These stated that the AFL and the CROM were to appoint permanent representatives in the border cities to see that workers going from one country to the other received fair treatment; that Mexican workers be allowed to join American trade unions without discrimination, and that the CROM be given a larger voice in the preparations for a Pan-American labor congress.[21]

Another Mexican proposal sparked a discussion that lasted nearly all of the third day. It urged that labor exert itself to secure justice for the IWWs who were imprisoned under the Espionage Act on the charge of distributing antiwar propaganda and obstructing the recruitment of soldiers. Green again tried to cut off consideration by recommending that the matter be referred to the Executive Council. But once again he failed.

The Mexican representatives pointed out that the war was now over and that the spirit of international labor solidarity demanded that all labor organizations have the right to the form of organization and to the principles which they preferred, whether in accord with the AFL or not. But the AFL delegates would have none of this. Daniel Tobin of the Teamsters denied that the IWW was a bona fide labor organization and, in any case, the Wobblies had received a fair trial. Gompers insisted that the only labor organization in the United States was the AFL:

> It is all very good for anyone to say, "why not give these people, the I.W.W.'s, the opportunity to live and work out their own propaganda as they want to! But I want to say this to you, my friends, that we have one labor movement, cohesive, militant and determined, in the United States of America, and because we have one labor movement in America we occupy a position of power and influence to bring a better time into the lives of the working people of our country.

As for the IWW, Gompers continued:

> The I.W.W.'s in the United States are exactly what the Bolsheviki are in Russia, and we have seen what the I.W.W. Bolsheviki in Russia have done for the working people of Russia, where the people have no peace, no security, no land and no bread. . . .[22]

No one challenged this blatant distortion of the facts, and Gompers swept ahead. The AFL, he emphasized, had already helped the workers of Puerto Rico and Mexico, and was prepared to continue to do the same for workers all over Latin America. But only if it was welcomed:

> If you place us in the position, as this discussion has developed, of defense, if you in this discussion endeavor to make it appear that you resent our advances, our efforts—well, that is for you to decide . . . if you will accept our assistance . . . we will gladly do our level best to help you. If, on the

other hand, you resent it, cast aspersions on our motives and our purposes, if you look upon us with suspicion, why, I suppose we shall have to accept the situation. . . .[23]

Faced with this sweeping ultimatum, the Mexican representatives retreated. They made it clear they did not seek to defend the IWW or attack the AFL, "but in a fraternal spirit to state how the Mexican workers felt and thought. . . ." In the end, Green's motion to refer the matter to the AFL Executive Council was adopted.[24]

An even more bitter struggle emerged over the Mexican resolution calling upon the convention to exclude all subjects which might infringe upon Mexican neutrality in the European war. Green was successful at first in having the resolution tabled on the ground that it dealt not with labor problems but with political issues, and was therefore extraneous to the objectives of the convention. But the issue emerged again when Gompers demanded an endorsement of the peace terms and the labor charter already adopted by the AFL for submission to the Commission on International Labor Legislation at the peace congress to be held in Europe. This, in Gompers' opinion, was the most important action the convention could take. But the Mexican delegates insisted that consideration of peace terms should be ruled out for the same reason that the Mexican resolution was tabled. They warned that if they supported Gompers' proposal, the Mexican people would view their action as yielding to a violation of Mexican neutrality.

This stand infuriated Gompers. He shouted, "I challenge the delegates from Mexico to vote against the declarations made in this resolution and then defend their position before the Mexican people. . . . I am going to ask this Conference to give our friends and fellow workers of Mexico the chance to vote on these propositions separate from the others, so that they may vote against them if they choose to do so. I shall not make any arguments."[25]

Morones tried to mollify Gompers by urging him not to demand too much of the Mexicans. It would take time to overcome the prevailing attitude in Latin America toward the AFL and the people of the United States. "All the knowledge they have of the people of the United States is through the soldiers' bayonets." The Mexican labor movement wanted to develop a different attitude toward the United States, but it could not be done in a day. But Gompers refused to yield, and insisted that the resolution be adopted. After further discussion, the Mexican delegates agreed to vote for the resolution subject to the ratification of the Mexican labor movement, and it was unanimously adopted.[26]

It was thus clear that it was the viewpoint of the American Federation of Labor, and especially that of its president, that would determine the policies of the Pan-American Federation of Labor. The Latin Americans could object, advise caution and other proposals, but in the end, they would yield to the demands of the AFL spokespersons. When Luis Morones said that he could not agree with Gompers' proposal to vote separately on his resolutions dealing with the peace terms, Gompers burst out, "Yes sir; you will."[27] This was the way in which Gompers viewed the role that Latin American trade unionists should play in the Pan-American Federation of Labor. Unanimously elected president of the new federation, Gompers was in the position to attempt to carry out his approach.

Thus the Pan-American Federation of Labor came into existence, created with the assistance of the United States Government and dominated by the American Federation of Labor."[28] It was, as Santiago Iglesias later emphasized, "the child of the American Federation of Labor, "the instrumentality" through which the influence of radical labor unions in Latin America, inspired by the example of the Bolshevik Revolution of 1917 in Russia*, would be checked. It was fundamentally the product of such factors as Samuel Gompers's vanity and desire to seal off Latin America and thus the United States from revolutionary unionism. Thus the Pan-American Federation of Labor set out to create a labor movement in Latin America that would work "in harmony with the policies of the American Federation of Labor."[29]

---

*The impact of the Bolshevik Revolution on Latin America will be discussed in Volume 2 of this work. But those who wish to examine this subject will find the following useful: B. Kaval, *La Gran Revolución de Octubre y America Latina* (Moscow: 1978); and Erasmo Dumpierre, *La Revolución de Octubre y Su Repercusion en Cuba* (La Habana: 1967). For a brief discussion in English, see Hobart A. Spalding, Jr., *Organized Labor in Latin America: Historical Case Studies of Workers in Dependent Societies* (New York: 1977), pp. 54–57.

REFERENCES

Preface

1. See, for example, Henry Berger, "Union Diplomacy: American Labor's Foreign Policy in Latin America, 1932–1955" (Ph.D. diss., University of Wisconsin, 1966), and Ronald Radosh, *American Labor and United States Foreign Policy: The Cold War in the Unions from Gompers to Loveston* (New York: 1969).

2. See Diana K. Christopulos, "American Radicals and the Mexican Revolution, 1900–1925" (Ph.D. diss., State University of New York at Binghamton, 1980), and Harold A. Levenstein, *Labor Organizations in the United States and Mexico: A History of Their Relations* (Westport, Conn.: 1971).

3. Jack Scott discusses earlier relations between U.S. trade unions and Latin America in *Yankee Unions Go Home: How the AFL Helped the U.S. Build an Empire in Latin America* (Vancouver: 1978). But it is mainly confined to Cuba and Puerto Rico and omits Mexico entirely.

Chapter I

1. Eugene C. Barker, *The Life of Stephen F. Austin Founder of Texas, 1793–1836* (Dallas: 1923), pp. 147, 237–42, 254–56, 324; Eugene C. Barker, ed., *The Austin Papers*, (Washington, D.C., and Austin, Texas: 1919–1926) 3: 101–2; James G. Greer, "The Texas Declaration of Independence," in Eugene C. Barker, ed., *Readings in Texas History* (Dallas: 1929), pp. 234–45.

2. *Working Man's Advocate*, May 11, 1844.

3. Reprinted in ibid., Aug. 10, 1844.

4. Philip S. Foner, *History of the Labor Movement in the United States* (New York: 1947), pp. 277–78.

5. *Liberator*, June 27, 1845; Philip S. Foner, *History of Black Americans: From the Emergence of the Cotton Kingdom to the Eve of the Compromise of 1850* (Westport, Conn: 1983), p. 543.

6. Glenn W. Price, *Origins of War with Mexico: The Polk-Stockton Intrigue* (Austin and London: 1967), pp. 13–26.

7. Irving McCormack, *James K. Polk: A Political Biography* (Berkeley: 1922), pp. 77–82; J.D. Fuller, *The Movement for the Acquisition of All Mexico, 1846–1848* (Baltimore: 1936), pp. 126–34.

8. Alfred Hoyt Bill, *Rehearsal for Conflict: The Story of Our War with Mexico, 1846–1948* (Indianapolis: 1950), pp. 86–90.

9. John Edward Weems, *To Conquer a Peace: The War Between the United States and Mexico* (New York: 1974), pp. 76–80.

10. Ibid., pp. 126–30.

11. John H. Schroeder, *Mr. Polk's War: American Opposition and Dissent, 1846–1848* (Madison, Wis.: 1973), pp. 84–86.

12. Bill, *Rehearsal for Conflict*, pp. 134–38.

13. Frank Friedel, *Dissent in Three American Wars* (Cambridge, Mass.: 1976), pp. 12–23; Schroeder, *Mr. Polk's War*, pp. 194–99; Philip S. Foner, ed., *Life and Writings of Frederick Douglass*, vol. 1. (New York: 1950) 182–83, 187–88, 291–96.

14. Foner, *History of Black Americans*, p. 543.

15. Foner, *History of Labor Movement in U.S.*, p. 278.

16. Philip S. Foner, ed., *The Factory Girls* (Urbana, Ill.: 1977), p. 142.

17. *Voice of Industry*, June 12, 1846.

18. Ibid., Dec. 11, 18, 1846.

19. Ibid., Dec. 18, 1846; Schroeder, *Mr. Polks' War*, p. 182.

20. Foner, *History of Black Americans*, p. 545.

21. Grant came to regard the war as a conspiracy of slaveholders and the U.S. Army as simply an instrument for achieving the Slave Power's objectives. "We [the military] were employed to provoke the war," he wrote, "but it was essential that Mexico begin it; then the army could announce, the war exists by the acts of Mexico. . . . " Grant wrote that he regarded the war as "one of the most unjust ever waged by a stronger against a weaker nation."

22. Albert C. Ramsey, *The Other Side of the Mexican War* (New York: 1850), pp. 88–92.

23. David Lockhart, *The United States and Mexico, 1821–1848*, vol. 1 (New York: 1931), pp. 122–26.

24. *Niles Register*, Oct. 16, 1847, pp. 103–4; John R. Kenly, *Memoirs of a Maryland Volunteer* (Philadelphia: 1873), pp. 39–41.

25. *House Executive Document No. 60*, 30 Congress, 1st Session, pp. 303–4; Thomas Riley, Case 3, U.S. Archives, AUS, J.A.G.O., EE531, National Archives.

26. See U.S. Archives, AUS, Office of the ADJ. Gen., 2793–1985, National Archives.

27. Frederick Merk, *Manifest Destiny and Mission in American History* (New York: 1963), pp. 89–93.

28. Winfield Scott, *Memoirs of Lieutenant General Scott, Written by Himself*, vol. 1 (New York: 1964), 322–26; Robert Louis Bodson, "A Description of the United States Occupation of Mexico as Reported by American Newspapers Published in Vera Cruz, Puebla, and Mexico City, September 14, 1847, to July 31, 1848" (Ph.D. diss., Ball State University, 1971), pp. 34–35, 86–88, 132–36.

29. Edward S. Wallace, "The Battalion of Saint Patrick in the Mexican War," *Military Affairs* 14(1950): 87.

30. G.T. Hopkins, "The San Patricio Battalion in the Mexican War," *Journal of the U.S. Calvary Association* 24(Sept. 1913): 281–82.

31. *Sketches of the Campaign in Northern Mexico, by an Officer of the First Regular Ohio Volunteers* (New York: 1853), pp. 220–28.

32. Manuel Babonlin, *La Invasion Americana* (Mexico: 1883), pp. 60–62.

33. James Henry Carleton, *The Battle of Buena Vista* (New York: 1840), pp. 80–83.

34. N.C Brooks, *A Complete History of the Mexican War* (Philadelphia: 1849), pp. 217–18; Richard Blaine McCormack, "The San Patricio Deserters in the Mexican War," *Americas* 8(1951): 133.

35. *House Executive Document No. 60*, 30 Congress, 1st Session, pp. 303–4.

36. Tom Malone, "30 Hanged and all 11 Branded; The Story of the San Patricio Battalion,"*Southwest Review* 32 (Autumn 1947): 373–75.

37. It is interesting to compare the treatment of the San Patricios and that of John Charles Frémont, who, though found guilty of mutiny by a general court martial, had his sentence remitted by President Polk.

38. Lt. Henry A. Wise, *Los Gringos* (New York: 1850), pp. 246–47; *The American Star*, Sept. 23, 1847.

39. *New Era of Industry*, June 15, 1848.

40. Philip S. Foner, *Life and Writings of Frederick Douglass*, 1: 295–96.

41. McCormack, *James K. Polk*, p. 232.

42. Jacob Oseandel, *Notes on the Mexican War* (Philadelphia: 1885), p. 427.

43. See especially Sister Blanche Marie McEniry, *American Catholics in the War with Mexico* (Washington, D.C.: 1937); Thomas F. Meehan, "Catholics in the War with Mexico," *Catholic Historical Review* 12(1918): 39–65; G.T. Hopkins, "The San Patricio Battalion in the Mexican War," *Journal of the U.S. Cavalry Association* 24(Sept. 1913): 279–84; William M. Sweeny, "Irish in the War with Mexico," *American Irish Historical Society Journal* 26(1927): 255–59; Edward S. Wallace, "Deserters in the Mexican War," *Hispanic American Historical Review* 15(1935): 374–83; Wallace, "The Battalion of Saint Patrick in the Mexican War," pp. 84–90; McCormack, "The San Patricio Deserters" p. 131–42. An important though biased source is *The American Star*, edited and printed by U.S. soldiers during their occupation of Mexico City from Oct. 1847 to April 1848.

44. See especially McCormack, *"San Patricio Deserters,"* p. 137.

45. José Maria Roa Barcena, *Recuerdos de la Invasion Norteamericana, 1846–1848*, vol. 4 (Mexico City: 1947), 232–33.

Chapter II

1. Philip Pines, "Organized Labor Views Latin America, 1891–1898," (M.A. thesis, Columbia University, 1947), pp. 8–9; Lewis Hanke, "The First Lecturer in Hispanic American Diplomatic History in the United States," *Hispanic American Historical Review* 16(Aug. 1936): 399–400; C. Glen Seretan, *Daniel De Leon: The Odyssey of an American Marxist,*(Cambridge, Mass.: 1979), pp. 10–11.

2. Samuel Flagg Bemis, *The United States and Latin America,* (New York: 1935), pp. 112–16.

3. Delber Lee McKee, "The American Federation of Labor and Foreign Policy, 1886–1912" (Ph.D. diss., Stanford University, 1952), p. 39.

4. *American Federationist* 2(Dec. 1895): 220–21.

5. George A. Fowles to Gompers, Dec. 30, 1895, *American Federation of Labor Correspondence* (hereinafter cited as *AFL Corr.*); *The People*, Dec. 22, 29, 1895; Pines, "Organized Labor," pp. 22–26; *American Federationist* 3(Feb. 1896): 22.

6. *Century Magazine*, Aug. 1896, pp. 634–35.

7. The first war for independence was the Ten Years' War of 1868 to 1878 which ended in defeat for the Cuban independence fighters. For the story of that war and for the role of

José Martí in organizing the second war for independence, see Philip S. Foner, *History of Cuba and its Relations with the United States*, vol. 2, (New York: 1963) and Philip S. Foner, ed., *Our America: Writings of José Martí on Latin America and the Struggle for Cuban Independence*, trans. by Elinor Randall (New York: 1977).

8. *Journal of the Knights of Labor*, Oct. 31, 1895; *American Federationist* 2(Nov. 1895): 168; *Painters' Journal*, Oct. 1895, p. 9; George Stevens, *New York Typographical Union No.6* (New York: 1913), p. 605; United Brotherhood of Carpenters and Joiners, *Convention Proceedings*, 1896, p. 245.

9. *Journal of the Knights of Labor*, July 11, 18, Nov. 28, 1895; *Proceedings*, General Assembly, Knights of Labor, 1895, pp. 73–74; *Proceedings*, AFL Convention, 1895, pp. 63, 102; John S. Appel, "The Relation of American Labor to United States Imperialism, 1895–1905" (Ph.D. diss., University of Wisconsin, 1950), p. 31.

10. McKee, "American Federation of Labor," pp. 38–40.

11. Harry C. Walker to Gompers, Oct. 28, 1897, *AFL Corr.*; *Congressional Record*, 55th Congress, 2nd Session, Part 7, pp. 6341, 6553. This feeling was further reinforced by the Arago decision of the Supreme Court, Jan. 25, 1897, in which case (Robertson *v.*Baldwin), the majority ruled that courts could compel seamen to fulfill their contracts, and pointed out that "the contract of a sailor has always been treated as an exceptional one, and involving to a certain extent the surrender of his personal liberty during the life of the contract." However, Justice John M. Harlan, protesting that there was nothing to prevent succeeding courts from including other occupations in the "exceptional category," predicted that eventually all workers would be compelled to work under the contract labor system. *U.S. Reports*, vol. 165, pp. 282–83.

12. *Proceedings*, AFL Convention, 1897, pp. 56. 89–91; *San Francisco Voice of Labor*, Jan. 1, 1898.

13. Gompers to Frank Morrison, June 2, 1897; Frank Morrison to Gompers, May 28, Aug. 11, 1897, *AFL Corr.*

14. Cf. Sylvester K. Stevens, *American Expansion in Hawaii, 1842–1898* (Harrisburg, Pa.: 1945), Chapter XI.

15. Richard Carlyle Winchester, "James G. Blaine and the Ideology of American Expansionism" (Ph.D. diss., University of Rochester, 1966), pp. 30–42; James G. Blaine to James Comly, Nov. 19, Dec. 1, 1881, in James G. Blaine, *Political Discussions, Legislative, Diplomatic and Popular, 1856–1876* (Norwich, Conn.: 1887), p. 395; *Foreign Relations of the United States, 1881* (Washington, D.C.: 1882), p. 637.

16. Alfred T. Mahan, "The United States Looking Outward," *Atlantic Monthly* 56(Dec. 1890): 800–2.

17. E. Sherman Gould, "Commercial Relations Between the United States and Cuba," *Engineering Magazine* 7(July 1894): 500–4; *Detroit Free Press*, May 16, 1891; Philip S. Foner, *History of Cuba*, 2: 341–46.

18. Victor Perlo, *American Imperialism* (New York: 1951), pp. 9–10.

19. Ibid., pp. 15–16.

20. *Third Annual Convention of New York State Bankers Association*, 1896, p. 81; *American Banker* 64(1898): 9.

21. 55th Congress, 2nd Session, *House of Representatives Report No. 1355*, p. 62.

22. John A. Garraty, *Henry Cabot Lodge: A Biography* (New York: 1955), pp. 88.

23. Marcus M. Wilkerson, *Public Opinion and the Spanish-American War: A Study in War Propaganda* (Baton Rouge: 1932); Joseph E. Wisan, *The Cuban Crisis as Reflected in the New York Press* (New York: 1934).

24. Philip S. Foner, *The Spanish-Cuban-American War and the Birth of American Imperialism* (New York: 1977)1: 232–34. To this day it is not known who blew up the battleship *Maine*.

See Donald A. Holman, "The Destruction of the *Maine,* Feb. 15, 1898," *Michigan Alumnus* 15 (Winter 1954): 112–39.

25. *Monthly Journal of the International Association of Machinists,* April 1898, pp. 191–92.

26. *The Craftsman,* April 1898, p. 87.

27. *Coast Seamen's Journal,* Feb. 23, March 2, April 6, 1898; H. Bates to Gompers, April 5, 1898, *AFL Corr.*

28. *Railroad Trainmen's Journal,* Jan. 1898.

29. *United Mine Workers' Journal,* March 17, 1898.

30. *Journal of the Brotherhood of Boilermakers and Iron Shipbuilders,* April 1898.

31. Gompers to Henry Demarest Lloyd, March 1898; Gompers to P.J. McGuire, March 28, 1898, Samuel Gompers Letterbooks, Library of Congress, Manuscripts Division. Hereinafter cited as GLB.

32. The Appeal was endorsed by Bishop Potter, William Dean Howells, Charles Frederick Adams, Ernest Crosby, and John S. Crosby.

33. It is doubtful that even Bolton Hall could have foreseen the extent of corrupton in the furnishing of supplies for the American army during the war against Spain in which "leaky boats, shoddy clothes, and pasteboard shoes" were supplemented by canned beef which poisoned whole regiments. For the whole sordid story, see Walter Millis, *The Martial Spirit,* (New York: 1931).

34. Copy in *AFL Corr.*

35. *The People,* April 17, May 1, 1898.

36. *Appeal to Reason,* March 26, April 16, 1898.

37. *The Coming Nation,* March 12, 1898.

38. *San Francisco Voice of Labor,* April 16, May 21, 1898; *The People,* April 10, 24, 1898.

39. Julius W. Pratt, *America's Colonial Expansion* (New York: 1950), p. 61.

40. *The Nation,* April 21, 1898.

41. *New York Times,* April 12, 1898.

42. The Homestead strike occurred in 1892 and involved steel workers; Pullman, in 1894, involved railroad workers; Brooklyn, in 1895, involved trolley car drivers. All of these strikes were crushed by the militia and, in the case of Pullman, the U.S. Army as well. Lattimer refers to the "Lattimer Massacre" which occurred on September 10, 1897 during the great coal strike, when deputy sheriffs in Luzerne County, Pennsylvania fired at unarmed miners, killing 19 and wounding 35 others. For a discussion of these episodes, see Philip S. Foner, *History of the Labor Movement in the United States,* vol. 2 (New York: 1955).

43. *San Francisco Voice of Labor,* June 11, 1898.

44. *Monthly Journal of the International Association of Machinists,* Oct. 1898; Foner, *Spanish-American War,* 1: 270.

45. *Coast Seamen's Journal,* April 1898; *Railroad Trainmen's Journal,* May 1898; *New York Tribune,* Aug. 1, 1898; *Proceedings,* AFL Convention, 1898, pp. 19–20.

46. *American Federationist,* July 1898, p. 92.

47. P.J. McGuire to Gompers, April 28, 1898, *AFL Corr.*

48. *Railroad Trainmen's Journal,* June 1898, pp. 516–17; *The Woodworker,* May, 1898; Appel, "The Relation of American Labor to United States Imperialism," pp. 137–40; *United Mine Workers' Journal,* July 14, 1898.

49. *The Bakers' Journal,* June 15, 1898, p. 358; *Monthly Journal* of the International Association of Machinists, May 1898, pp. 255–56.

50. *Weekly People,* May 8, 1898; Morris U. Schappes, "Jewish Labor in the Nineties," *Jewish Life,* June 1950, p. 16.

51. *Minnesota Union Advocate,* June 17, 1898; Ray Ginger, *The Bending Cross: A Biography of Eugene Victor Debs,* (New Brunswick, N.J.: 1949), p. 203.

52. *Railroad Trainmen's Journal*, July 1898, clipping in *AFL Corr.*; Appel, "The Relation of American Labor to United States Imperialism", p. 113; *Troy Advocate*, reprinted in *New York Evening Journal*, July 14, 1898.

53. The Western Labor Union was founded at a convention held at Salt Lake City on May 10, 1898. The delegates, representing the Western Federation of Miners and various trades around the mining camps and towns, emphasized their dissatisfaction with the failure of the AFL to meet the needs of the western workers, particularly the unskilled, and pointed to the importance of bringing together all workers "irrespective of occupation, nationality, creed or color." *Pueblo Courier*, May 25, June 3, 1898; *San Francisco Voice of Labor*, May 28, 1898.

54. *Pueblo Courier*, June 24, 1898; *Chicago Labor World*, July 1898; A. Furuseth to Gompers, Aug. 23, 1898; John B. Lennon to Gompers, Aug. 26, 1898, *AFL Corr.*; Gompers to John B. Lennon, Aug. 16, 24, 1898, GLB.

Chapter III

1. Richard F. Pettigrew, *The Course of Empire* (New York: 1920), pp. 268–72.

2. *United States Investor*, vol. X (Feb. 1899): 60–61.

3. *Typographical Union*, May 1, 1899, p. 383; *The Commoner and Glassworker*, Sept. 1898; *Railroad Trainmen's Journal*, Sept. 1898, pp. 763–64.

4. Appel, "The Relation of American Labor to United States Imperialism," p. 155.

5. *Leather Workers' Journal*, 3(Nov. 1900): 65; *The Carpenter*, Nov. 1898, p. 3; *Cigar Makers' Journal*, December 1898, p. 8; Gompers to F.B. Thurber, Nov. 25, 1898, *AFL Corr.*; *American Federationist*, Dec. 1898, pp. 205–7.

6. Undated clipping from *Railroad Trainmen's Journal* in *AFL Corr.*; *The Carpenter*, Aug. 1898; *Cigar Makers' Journal*, Feb. 1898, p. 8; *Pueblo Courier*, May 19, 1899.

7. Quoted in *American Pressman*, Oct. 1899, p. 269.

8. *Proceedings*, AFL Convention, 1898, pp. 18–20, 90.

9. Ibid., p. 92.

10. *New York Journal*, Dec. 14, 1898.

11. *Kansas City {Mo.} Times*, Dec. 17, 1898; *National Labor Tribune*, Nov. 24, 1898; *Amalgamated Meat Cutters and Butcher Workmen Journal*, Aug. 1900, pp. 12–13; Erving Winslow to Gompers, Dec. 21, 1898, *AFL Corr.*

12. Letters to Gompers from Edwin Buritt Smith, June 24, Aug. 22, 1899; Edward Atkinson, June 30, July 3, Aug. 23, 1899; Erving Winslow, Aug. 22, Sept. 23, 1899; Bolton Hall, Sept. 14, 1899; Gompers to Frank Morrison, June 16, 1899, *AFL Corr.*; Gompers to Erving Winslow, July 13, 1899, GLB.

13. Maria C. Lanza, "The Anti-Imperialist League," *Philippine Social Science Review* 3(Aug. 1930): 7–13; David G. Haskins, Jr., to Gompers, Nov. 22, 1898, *AFL Corr.* The degree of Gompers' activity in the American Anti-Imperialist League is a matter of dispute. According to Igor Dementyev, the Soviet scholar of U.S. imperialism, "Gompers only created the outward impression of activity." *USA: Imperialists and Anti-Imperialists* Moscow: 1979, p. 269. For an opposite view, see William G. Whittaker, "Samuel Gompers, Anti-Imperialist," *Pacific Historical Review* 28 Nov. 1969: 29–55.

14. Appel, "The Relation of American Labor to United States Imperialism," pp. 178–79; Erving Winslow to Gompers, July 11, 1899, *AFL Corr.*

15. *Boston Globe*, March 20, 1899.

16. Walter Millis, *The Martial Spirit* (New York: 1931), p. 392, 402–3; Pettigrew, *The Course of Empire*, p. 271.

17. John A. Garraty, *Henry Cabot Lodge*, p. 121.

18. Leon Wolff, *Little Brown Brother: How the United States Purchased and Pacified the Philippine Islands at the Century's Turn* (New York: 1961), pp. 162–65.

19. *National Labor Standard*, Sept. 27, 1900.

20. Gompers had led the movement to influence Congress to pass the Exclusion Act of 1882, which suspended the immigration of Chinese workers for ten years. In 1902, partly as a result of his influence, the exclusion was made permanent.

21. *American Federationist*, Dec. 18, 1898, pp. 205–7; Samuel Gompers to James Duncan, May 14, 1898, GLB.

22. *New York Tribune*, Aug. 1, 1898.

23. *Proceedings*, AFL Convention, 1898, p. 27.

24. *Proceedings*, AFL Convention, 1899, p. 16.

25. *American Federationist* 4(Nov. 1897): 215–16; John C. Appel, "American Labor and the Annexation of Hawaii: A Study in Logic and Economic Interests," *Pacific Historical Review* 23(Feb. 1954): 17–18.

26. *American Federationist*, Sept. 1898, p. 138, Dec. 1898, pp. 205, 207; *Proceedings*, AFL Convention, 1898, p. 218.

27. Testimony of Samuel Gompers, U.S. House Committee on Labor, Hearings, "Hours of Labor for Workmen, Mechanics, etc., Employed upon Public Works of the United States," 56th Congress, 2nd Session, 1900, p. 429.

28. *Report of the United States Industrial Commission on the Relations and Conditions of Capital and Labor* (Washington, D.C.: 1901) 7: 267.

29. Henry W. Berger, "Unions and Empire: Labor and American Corporations Abroad," *Peace and Change* 3(Spring 1976): 36.

30. One who did was the editor of the *International WoodWorker*. "Who," he asked, "would not prefer to see the millions expended on the building of a useless navy go toward the construction of thousands of homes for the homeless?" Dec. 1898, p. 237.

31. *American Federationist* 5(Dec. 1898): 203–4.

32. *Journal of Boilermakers and Iron Shipbuilders*, Aug. 1, 1898.

33. Richard E. Welch, Jr., *Response to Imperialism: The United States and the Philippine-American War, 1899–1902*, (Chapel Hill, N. C.: 1979), pp. 84–85.

34. Philip S. Foner, *History of the Labor Movement in the United States* (New York: 1955), 2: 433; Bernard Mandel, *Samuel Gompers, A Biography* (Yellow Springs, Ohio: 1963), p. 206.

35. *Journal of the Knights of Labor*, Feb. 1899.

36. Ibid., March 1901.

37. *National Labor Standard*, Nov. 29, 1900; Foner, *History of the Labor Movement in the United States*, 2: 437.

38. *The Garment Worker*, Jan. 1900. For a study of the attitude of British workers and trade unions towards the Boer War, see Richard Price, *An Imperial War and the British Working Class: Working-Class Attitudes and Reactions to the Boer War, 1899–1902* (London: 1972).

39. *Cleveland Citizen*, Jan. 18, 1900.

40. *International Woodworker*, Jan. 1900.

41. *Proceedings*, AFL Convention, 1901, p. 118.

42. Welch, *Response to Imperialism*, pp. 120, 152.

43. *National Labor Standard*, May 23, 1901.

44. Wolff, *Little Brown Brother*, p. 356–57.

45. *Journal of the Knights of Labor*, April 1902, p. 4.

46. Welch, *Response to Imperialism*, p. 88.

47. *Proceedings*, AFL Convention, 1899, p. 128.

48. *National Labor Standard*, Nov. 9, 1900; Guy Kendall and A. Grove Day, *Hawaii, A History* (New York: 1948), p. 196; Charles Masayoshi Najua, "A Short History of Labor in Hawaii" (M.A. thesis, University of Iowa, 1956), pp. 23–26.

49. *Boot and Shoe Worker*, Nov. 1900; Appel, "Relationship of American Labor to United States Imperialism," p. 249.

50. *Boot and Shoe Worker*, March 1901.

51. Appel, *"Relationship of American Labor to United States Imperialism,"* pp. 264–66.

52. *Proceedings*, AFL Convention, 1902, pp. 72, 147.

53. *Proceedings*, AFL Convention, 1909, p. 40.

54. Ed Rosenberg to Samuel Gompers, May 22, 1904, *AFL Corr.*; *Proceedings*, AFL Convention, 1905, p. 17.

55. Gerald Melvin Torkelson, "Attitudes of American Labor on Expansion: 1896–1903," (M.A. thesis, University of Wisconsin, 1945), p. 134.

56. Appel, "The Relationship of American Labor to U.S. Imperialism," pp. 318–20; *Proceedings*, AFL Convention, 1905, p. 17.

57. For these developments, see Gordon M. Jensen, "The National Civic Federation: American Business in an Age of Social Change and Social Reform, 1900–1910" (Ph.D. diss., Princeton University), 1956; Marguerite Green, *The National Civic Federation and the American Labor Movement, 1900–1925,* (Washington D.C.: 1956); Philip S. Foner, *History of the Labor Movement in the United States* vol. 3 (New York: 1964), pp. 65–110; Berger, "Unions and Empire," p. 37.

58. V.I. Lenin, *Imperialism* (New York: 1935), p. 110.

59. For a discussion of labor's attitude towards Independence Day, see Philip S. Foner, ed., *We, the Other people: Alternative Declarations of Independence by Labor Groups, Farmers, Woman's Rights Advocates, Socialists, and Blacks, 1825–1875* (Urbana, Ill.: 1976.)

60. *Railroad Trainmen's Journal*, Aug. 1905, p. 612.

61. *Miners' Magazine*, July 1902.

62. Robert Randall, "The Fourth of July," *Miners' Magazine*, June 22, 1905.

63. John Laslett, *Labor and the Left: A Study of Socialist and Radical Influences in the American Labor Movement, 1881–1924* (New York: 1970), pp. 251, 258–59, 260, 267–68, 270–71, 273.

64. *Compte Rendu Sténographique non officiel de la Version Français du Cinquième Congress Socialiste International tenu à Paris du 24 au 27 Sept. 1900* (Paris: 1901), p. 175; Josef Lenz, *The Rise and Fall of the Second International* (New York: 1932), pp. 110–11.

65. Igor Dementyev, *USA: Imperialists and anti-Imperialists* (Moscow: 1979), p. 282; *Social Democratic Herald*, Nov. 19, 1898; Ginger, *The Bending Cross*, p. 203; Foner, *History of the Labor Movement in the United States*, vol. 2 (New York: 1955): 417.

66. *Social Democratic Herald,* June 16, 1900.

67. *Workers' Call*, May 13, 1899, Oct. 3, 1900; Dementyev, *USA: Imperialists,* p. 297.

68. H.L. Boothman, "Philosophy of Imperialism," *International Socialist Review* 1(1900): 303.

69. Kirk H. Porter, comp., *National Party Platforms* (New York: 1924), pp. 239–42.

70. *Workers' Call*, Sept. 22, 1900.

71. *International Socialist Review* 1 (Sept. 1900): 132–33.

72. Eugene V. Debs, "The Socialist Party and the Working Class," ibid. 5(1904–05): 130.

73. Some scholars argue that this position was influenced by the fact that Marx, in discussing British conquest of India while aware of the "barbaric" treatment of the Indians and the havoc that ensued from British colonial policies, also thought that this was necessary in their development to a higher state. See *Karl Marx on Colonialism and Modernization,* ed., with an introduction by, Shlomo Avineri (Garden City: 1969), pp. 132–36; Horace B. Davis, *Nationalism and Socialism: Marxist and Labor Theories of Nationalism to 1917* (New York: 1967), pp. 14, 175–76; and Ian Cummins, *Marx, Engels and National Movements* (London: 1980), pp. 46–52.

Marx did not develop a theory of imperialism. Although he planned to write a book about capitalism and world markets, he did not live to do so. However, it is clear from what Marx did write that he thought that capitalism was an inherently expansionary system. Capitalism, according to Marx, has an inherent necesary tendancy to expand abroad for its own development and the accumulation of capital. It can obtain a higher rate of profit in foreign lands by using forced labor, i.e., "coolies and slaves," from whom absolute surplus-value can be extracted more easily than from labor in the more developed countries where it has become more organized and resistant. See *Karl Marx, Capital* (New York: 1935) 3: 237–39, 450–51.

As capitalism expands, Marx pointed out, it transforms the non-capitalist world "in its own image," creating capitalist relations of production everywhere. "It compels all nations, on pain of extinction, to adopt the bourgeois mode of production; it compels them to introduce what it calls civilization into their midst, i.e., to become bourgeois to themselves. In a word, it creates a world after its own image." Karl Marx and Frederick Engels, *The Communist Manifesto* (New York: 1948), pp. 12–13.

74. Debs, "The Socialist Party and the Working Class," pp. 13, 15.

75. Wilfred H. Peterson, "The Foreign Policy and Foreign Policy Theory of the American Socialist Party, 1901–1920" (Ph.D. diss., University of Minnesota, 1957), pp. 67–74; Wilfred H. Peterson, "The Foreign Policy of the Socialist Party of America Before World War I," *Pacific Northwest Quarterly* 63(Oct. 1974): 177–80.

Chapter IV

1. Jack C. Lane, "Instrument for Empire: The American Military Government in Cuba, 1899–1902," *Science and Society* 36(Fall 1972): 312; Foner, *The Spanish-Cuban-American War* 2: 466.

2. *New York World*, July 20, 1898.

3. Charles Morris, *Our Island Empire* (Philadelphia: 1899), pp. 162–64.

4. *National Business League, Opinions of United States Consuls, Prominent Business Men and Educators on the Establishment of Permanent International Expositions and Trade Courts in the Great Commercial Centers of the World in Reply to Letters Suggested by Volney W. Foster* (Chicago: 1902), p. 12.

5. *Lumbermen's Review,* reprinted in *The State* (Columbia, S. C.), July 4, 1898.

6. *Washington Evening Star*, Feb. 10, 1898, reprinted in *Congressional Record,* 55th Cong., 3rd sess., vol. XXXIII, p. 2807.

7. Foraker to James H. Wilson, July 24, 1899, James H. Wilson Papers, Library of Congress; *Congressional Record*, 55th Cong., 3rd Sess., vol. XXXII, p. 2572; David F. Healy, *The United States in Cuba, 1898–1902* (Madison, Wis.: 1963), pp. 82–84.

8. *Congressional Record,* 55th Cong., 3rd Sess., vol. XXXII, p. 2812.

9. Leland H. Jenks, *Our Cuban Colony* (New York: 1928), p. 162.

10. Ibid., pp. 130–31.

11. Ibid., p. 134.

12. Ibid., p. 130.

13. Ibid., pp. 156–58; *Daily People*, Jan. 29, 1902

14. *New York Evening Post*, May 23, 1901.

15. Quoted in Foner, *Spanish-Cuban-American War*, p. 471.

16. *Foreign Policy Reports,* Nov. 18, 1935, p. 250.

17. Samuel Gompers, "Imperialism, Its Dangers and Wrongs," *American Federationist* 5(1898): 179–80.

18. *The People,* June 26, 1898.

19. *The Railroad Trainman's Journal,* March 1900.

20. *The Carpenter,* June 1899.

21. James Campbell, president of the Glass Workers' Union, was also proud of the fact that an increasing number of glass bottles was being exported to the Philippines now that

they were an American possession. Appel, "The Relationship of American Labor to United States Imperialism," p. 185.

22. *The Woodworker,* May 1898.

23. *The Carpenter,* June 1899, p. 9.

24. *United Mine Workers Journal,* July 21, 1899, p. 9.

25. Also quoted in Jack Scott, *Yankee Unions, Go Home: How the AFL Helped the U.S. Build in Latin America* (Vancouver, B.C.: 1978), p. 109.

26. José Rivero Muñiz, *El Movimiento Obrero durante la primera Intervención: Apuntes par la historia de proletariado en Cuba* (Las Villas, Cuba: 1961), p. 41.

27. These figures are based on the estimate of the census made by Victor S. Clark in his study, "Labor Conditions in Cuba," *Bulletin of the Department of Labor, No. 41* (Washington, D.C.: July 1902), p. 689.

28. Rivero, *El Movimiento Obrero,* pp. 11–12.

29. Ibid., p. 21.

30. Clark, "Labor Conditions in Cuba," pp. 677–78.

31. Ibid., p. 748.

32. Rivero, *El Movimiento Obrero,* p. 11.

33. Clark, "Labor Conditions in Cuba," p. 655.

34. Rivero, *El Movimiento Obrero,* pp. 84.

35. Ibid., p. 114.

36. José Rivero Muñiz, *El Primer Partido Socialista Cubano,* (Las Villas, Cuba: 1962), pp. 99–104; Joaquin Ordoqui, *Elementos Para la Historia del Movimiento Obero en Cuba* (La Habana: 1961), p. 15.

37. Rivero, *El Movimiento Obrero,* pp. 92–108.

38. Bliss to Chafee, Aug. 26, 1899, "Strikes in Cuba," Records of the United States Military Government of Cuba, Selected Documents Concerning Strikes in Cuba, 1899–1908, National Archives. Hereinafter cited as "Strikes in Cuba."

39. There does not appear to be in existence a copy of the original leaflet in Spanish, and even Cuban historians have had to use the English translation appearing in the report on the strike submitted to Washington by General Ludlow, military governor of Havana.

40. See Foner, *History of the Labor Movement in the United States* 2: 105–15.

41. Rivero, *El Movimiento Obrero,* pp. 109–16; *Annual Report of Brigadier-General William S. Ludlow, United States Army, Military Governor Havana,* "Strikes," Oct. 4, 1899, pp. 184–85.

42. Rivero, *El Movimiento Obrero,* pp. 116–20, 123–25.

43. Ibid., pp. 126, 133.

44. Ibid., pp. 129–32; *The People,* Oct. 8, 1899.

45. Rivero, *El Movimiento Obrero,* p. 147.

46. Ibid., pp. 147–48.

47. The *Guardia Rural,* or Rural Guard, made up of veterans of the Cuban Liberating Army and established during the American Occupation, was created to help assure American control of the island. "The Guard," Louis A. Pérez points out, "came to consist largely of Cubans sympathetic to the occupation effort; members were required to be in Wood's terms, 'obedient and faithful' to the Provisional Government." Louis A. Pérez, "Supervision of a Protectorate: The United States and the Cuban Army, 1898–1908," *Hispanic American Historical Review* 52(May 1972): 258–59.

48. Rivero, *El Movimiento Obrero,* pp. 134–35

49. Ibid., p. 160; Charles Albert Page, "The Development of Organized Labor in Cuba" (Ph.D. diss., University of California, Berkeley, 1952), p. 39.

50. Ibid.

51. Foner, *Spanish-Cuban-American War,* p. 503.

52. *Annual Report of Brigadier-General William S. Ludlow*, pp. 186–87.

53. *The Carpenter*, Oct. 1899; *Coast Seamen's Journal*, Dec. 27, 1899, p. 4; *Labor Advocate*, Sept. 30, 1899.

54. *The People*, Oct. 1, 1899.

55. *Proceedings*, General Assembly of the Knights of Labor, Nov. 14–23, 1899, p. 79.

56. *Proceedings*, AFL Convention, 1899, p. 16.

57. Foner, *History of the Labor Movement in the United States*, 2: 379–80.

58. Samuel Gompers, "A Trip to Cuba," *American Federationist*, March 1900, p. 61–62. What really happened, too, was that the arrested strike leaders were brought before General Ludlow, who offered them the opportunity to go free as soon as each signed two joint letters: one repenting for their actions, and the other urging the workers to end the strike. Faced with indefinite imprisonment, the strike leaders complied and issued the manifestoes written for them by General Ludlow. Foner, *The Spanish-Cuban-American War*,) 2: 500–1.

59. *Proceedings*, AFL Convention, 1900, p. 30.

60. Hermann Hagedorn, *Leonard Wood*, vol. 1 (New York: 1931), p. 275.

61. Gompers, "A Trip to Cuba," pp. 59–60.

62. In his study of the history of the Cuban labor movement, Charles Page reports that he interviewed Manual Muñiz Rivero and Antonio Pechet, active labor leaders of the time, and that neither recalled any such action by Gompers. Page, "The Development of Organized Labor in Cuba," p. 46.

63. Rito Estaban, *Sobre el Movimiento Obrero de America y Europa* (La Habana: 1946), p. 87.

64. Gompers, "A Trip to Cuba," p. 62.

65. Ibid.

66. Durward Long, "La Resistencia: Tampa's Immigrant Labor Union," *Labor History* 6 (Fall 1965): 193–213; Foner, *History of the Labor Movement in the United States*, 3: 260–62.

67. Lt. Stokes to Adj. General, Havana, Jan. 1, 2, 3, 4, 1901; Wood to Lt. Stokes, Jan. 2, 1901; Capt. Foltz to Adjutant General, Jan. 4, 1901; "Strikes in Cuba."

68. *The People*, Jan. 13, 1901.

69. *National Labor Standard*, Jan. 10, 1901.

70. During the meetings of the AFL Executive Council, Feb. 17–20, 1901, nothing was said about events in Cuba. See *American Federationist* 7(March 1901): 112–20.

71. Foner, *History of the Labor Movement in the United States*, 3: 61–110.

72. "They complain that they are compelled to work overtime, often thirteen hours, and they are not paid for their work," reported an American investigator. Lt. W.W. Wallace to Adjutant General, Matanzas, Feb. 14, 1901; "Strikes in Cuba."

73. Lt. W.W. Wallace to Adjutant General, Matanzas, Feb. 14, 1901; Hickey, by command of Major General Wood, to Col. Noyes, Feb. 8, 1901; Noyes to Adjutant General Department, Matanzas, Feb. 9, 11, 12, 1901, "Strikes in Cuba."

74. *Daily People*, Feb. 19, 1901; Commanding Acting Chief Rasco, Rural Guard, to General Wood, March 14, 1901; Capt. Walter B. Barker, to Lt. Frank McCoy, March 20, 1901; "Strikes in Cuba."

75. R.G. Ward to Col. H.L. Scott, Aug. 11, 1901; Scott to Adjutant General, Sept. 5, 1901; "Strikes in Cuba."

76. Louis V. Cavaiarc to General Wood, Departmento de Policía de la Ciudad de la Habana, Sección Secreta, Feb. 15, 19, 1901; Juan Rios to Leonard Wood, May 14, 1901; Unsigned letter to the chief of the Detective Bureau, Havana, Feb. 19, 1901; "Strikes in Cuba."

77. Rivero, *El Movimiento Obrero*, p. 168.

78. *Daily People*, Feb. 19, 1901.

79. W.M. Malloy, ed., *Treaties, Concessions, International Acts, Protocols and Agreements between the United States of America and other Powers*, vol. 2 (Washington, D.C.: 1910), pp. 1690–95.

80. Leonard Wood to Theodore Roosevelt, Oct. 28, 1901, copy in Leonard Wood Papers,

Library of Congress. Wood added: "The people ask me what we mean by a stable government in Cuba? I tell them that when money can be borrowed at a reasonable rate of interest and when capital is willing to invest in the Island, a condition of stability will have been reached."

81. Máximo Gómez to Sotero Figueroa, 8 de majo de 1902, in Emilio Rodrígúez Demouzi, *Papeles dominicanos de Máximo Gómez* (Ciudad Trujillo: 1954), pp. 396–97; Máximo Gómez,*Horas de trequa* (La Habana: 1916), pp. 38–40.

82. *Railway Conductor*, May 1, 1901, p. 409.

83. *National Labor Standard*, May 23, 1901.

84. Howard C. Hill, *Roosevelt and the Caribbean* (Chicago: 1927), p. 93.

85. Charles E. Chapman, *A History of the Cuban Republic: A Study in Hispanic American Politics* (New York: 1927), p. 208; Russell H. Fitzgibbon, *Cuba and the United States, 1900–1935*(Menasha, Wis.: 1935), p. 119.

86. Ralph Eldin Minger, "William H. Taft and the United States Intervention in Cuba in 1906," *Hispanic American Historical Review* 41(Feb. 1965): 87; Ralph Eldin Minger, *William Howard Taft and the United States Foreign Policy: The Apprenticship Years, 1900–1908* (Urbana, Ill.: 1975), pp. 118–38.

87. There are two studies of the Magoon administration in Cuba: David A. Lockmiller, *Magoon in Cuba: A History of the Second Intervention* (Chapel Hill: 1938), and Allen Reed Millett, *The Politics of Intervention: The Military Occupation of Cuba* (Columbus, Ohio: 1968).

88. Gompers to Daniel J. Keefe, Jan. 22, 1907, *AFL Corr.*

89. "Talks on Labor," *American Federationist* 13(1906): 545.

90. *The Worker*, April 21, 1907.

91. George Whitfield, "Present Conditions in Cuba and the Outlook," *International Socialist Review* 9 (Aug. 1908): 138–39. The *Review* appeared to think that this was the first Socialist political party organized in Cuba. But as we have seen, the *Partido Socialistic Cubano* (Cuban Socialist Party) was organized in 1899. However, it ceased to exist a few months after it was founded.

92. The letter was signed by J.A. Cruz, A. Castells González. It was originally published in Spanish in *La Voz Obrera*, Havana, 15 de Julio de 1907, and reprinted in Mario Antoniata Julia, ed., *El Movimiento Obrero Cubano Documentos Y Articulos Tomo 1 1865–1925*, Instituto de Historia del Movimiento Comunista y la Revolución Socialista de Cuba, La Habana (n.d.), pp. 265–71.

93. Lockmiller, *Magoon in Cuba*, pp. 91–92; Charles Albert Page, "The Development of Organized Labor in Cuba," pp. 46–47.

94. Antoniata Julia, *El Movimiento Obrero*, p. 263; Juan Ramirez, "La Huelga de La Moneda, 22 de febrero–15 julio de 1907," *Hoy* (Havana), Feb. 22, 1964.

95. Millett, *The Politics of Intervention*, pp. 200–4.

96. Charles E. Magoon to Secretary of War, Havana, July 5, 1907; "Strikes in Cuba."

97. J.W. Staples, Jr., to Charles E. Magoon, July 25, 1907; "Strikes in Cuba."

98. Charles E. Magoon to Secretary of War, July 25, 1907; "Strikes in Cuba."

99. Whitfield, "Present Conditions in Cuba,", pp. 138–39.

100. Millett, *The Politics of Intervention*, pp. 168–70.

101. Whitfield, "Present Conditions in Cuba," pp. 138–39.

102. It is interesting in this connection that the Brotherhood of Locomotive Engineers, eager to enlarge its membership, considered extending its jurisdiction to Cuba but, after investigation, abandoned the plan. In May 1910, at the ninth convention of the engineers, F.A. Burgess, grand chief, explained why: "We did not organize any of the engineers in Cuba for what we consider the most excellent of reasons; that we were unable to distinguish the nigger from the white man. Our color conception is not sensitive enough to draw a line. I do not believe the condition will improve in a year from now or in 10 years from now or

in any other time, unless you stock the island of Cuba with a new race, entirely getting rid of the old. . . . I hope the time will never come when the organization will have to join hands with the negro or a man with a fractional part of a negro in him." George James Stevenson, "The Brotherhood of Locomotive Engineers and Its Leaders" (Ph.D. diss., Vanderbilt University, 1954), p. 232.

103. Frank Morrison to Executive Council, American Federation of Labor, Aug. 2, 1910, including attached copies of translations of correspondence between Santiago Iglesias and José J. Corratge, Havana, Cuba, *AFL Corr.*

Chapter V

1. Whitney Perkins, *Denial of Empire: The United States and Its Dependencies* (Leyden: 1962), p. 112.

2. Bailey W. Diffie and Justine Whitfield Diffie, *Porto Rico: A Broken Pledge* (New York: 1931), pp. 188–89.

3. J.A. Corretjer, *La Lucha Por La Independencia de Puerto Rico* (Río Piedras, Puerto Rico: 1949), pp. 20–39.

4. Betances, however, was not to be at Lares on the day of the insurrection. His ship, *El Telegrafo,* which he had bought in St. Thomas to take him and some 500 rifles to Puerto Rico, was confiscated by the Dominican government.

5. Gordon K. Lewis, *Puerto Rico: Freedom and Power in the Caribbean* (New York: 1963), p. 56; Miles F. Gavin, *The Organized Labor Movement in Puerto Rico* (Rutherford, N.J.: 1979), p. 34.

6. Foner, *The Spanish-Cuban-American War*, 1: 285; 2: 302, 342, 343.

7. Diffie and Diffie, *Porto Rico,* p. 189.

8. Rafael Ruiz, "The Independence Movement of Puerto Rico" (M.A. thesis, Georgetown University, 1965), pp. 12–22.

9. Eugenio Maria de Hostos, *Obras Completas*, vol. 9 (Habana: 1939), pp. 10–15.

10. Geigel Polanco, "Hostos y la Independencia," *Puerto Rico Illustrado,* Jan. 14, 1939, p. 15.

11. "Even the strongly anti-imperialist editor of the *Advocate of Peace,* like many others in the anti-imperialist movement," observes C. Roland Marchand, "made little complaint about retention of Puerto Rico. . . ." *The American Peace Movement and Social Reform, 1898–1918* (Princeton, N.J.: 1972), p. 27.

12. *Proceedings,* AFL Convention, 1898, p. 19.

13. *Cigar Makers' Journal,* July 1900, p. 13.

14. *Journal of the Knights of Labor,* April 1901.

15. *National Labor Standard,* May 23, 1901.

16. S.L. Descarter, *Basic Statistics in Puerto Rico* (Washington, D.C.: 1946), p. 62.

17. Ibid.

18. In 1901 Azel Ames noted that "all amounts of wages have been reduced to United States currency," and that "prices of nearly all commodities involved in the cost of living have been much increased (temporarily) and some have been doubled." ("Labor Unions in Puerto Rico," *Bulletin No. 61*, U.S. Department of Labor [Washington, D.C.: 1905], p. 806.) Since the change in currency was already two years old when Ames made his study, the use of the word "temporarily" is rather strange.

19. T.D. Elito, ed., *American Standards and Planes of Living* (New York: 1931), pp. 331, 347.

20. Harry K. Carroll, *Report on the Industrial and Commercial Conditions of Porto Rico*, U.S. Treasury Department Document No. 2118. (Washington, D.C.: 1899), pp. 48–52, 75.

21. The *National Labor Standard* charged that food that had been sent to the island to relieve the hurricane sufferers was unfairly distributed by those in authority. "The needy workingmen received very little as a result of profiteering." ("Labor in Porto Rico," *National Labor Standard*, April 1900.)

22. Diffie and Diffie, *Porto Rico,*, p. 35.

23. *Journal of the Knights of Labor*, April 1901. See also *Literary Digest* 19(Aug. 19, 1899): 211.

24. Truman R. Clark, "Educating the Natives in Self-Determination: Puerto Rico and the United States, 1900–1933," *Pacific Historical Review* 42(May 1973): 220.

25. U.S. Department of War, *Annual Reports of the Secretary of War, 1899–1903* (Washington, D.C.: 1904), p. 34.

26. "Porto Rican Franchises," *The Public*, April 21, 1900.

27. Earl King Senff, "Puerto Rico Under American Rule" (Ph.D. diss., University of Kentucky, 1948), p. 15.

28. Ibid., pp. 20–21.

29. William H. Hunt, *Inaugural Address of William H. Hunt, Governor of Porto Rico* (San Juan: 1901), p. 13.

30. Angel Quintero Rivera, *Workers' Struggle in Puerto Rico: A Documentary History*, Cedric Belfrage, trans. (New York and London: 1976), pp. 17–19.

31. Ibid., pp. 20–21.

32. Gavin, *Organized Labor Movement in Puerto Rico*, p. 37.

33. Santiago Iglesias Pantín, *Luchas Emancipadores*, vol. 1 (San Juan: 1958), pp. 417–55; Juan Carerras, *Santiago Iglesias Pantín* (San Juan: 1965), pp. 32–35.

34. Iglesias, *Luchas Emancipadores*, 1: 94; Gavin, *Organized Labor Movement in Puerto Rico*, pp. 45–46.

35. Rafael Alsono Torres, *Cuarenta Anos de Lucha Proletaria* (San Juan: 1939), pp. 30–31.

36. Jesus Colon, "Puerto Rico's First May Day," *The Worker*, May 1, 1960, p. 8.

37. The headline in *The People* read: "IN PUERTO RICO. The Socialist Labor Party is Solemnly Organized." (Aug. 27, 1899.) It is interesting that Daniel De Leon, its editor, who came originally from Curaçao, and was interested in the problems of Latin America, spelled the name of the island correctly.

38. The letter noted that "it is now three years since we have been constantly struggling to wean our fellow wage slaves of Puerto Rico from the bourgeois-political tendencies that had so completely captivated them, due to the errors and prejudices we had been living in." Ibid.

39. *Proceedings of the Tenth Convention of the Socialist Labor Party, Held in New York City, June 2 to June 8, 1900* (New York: 1901), p. 56.

40. "In Puerto Rico," *The People*, Aug. 27, 1899. For a discussion of Daniel De Leon and the forces that opposed him and his views, especially his dual unionism, see Foner, *History of the Labor Movement in the United States*, 2: 388–401.

41. Iglesias, *Luchas Emancipadores*, 1: 64–66.

42. *The Carpenter*, March 1900, p. 15.

43. Appel, "Relation of American Labor to U.S. Imperialism," pp. 199–200.

44. *National Labor Standard*, April 1900; *Bricklayer and Mason*, March 23, 1900.

45. *Bricklayer and Mason*, April 1, 1900; Philip S. Foner, *Organized Labor and the Black Worker, 1619–1981* (New York: 1981), pp. 94–95; Paul B. Worthman, ed., "A Black Worker and the Bricklayers and Masons Union, 1903," *Journal of Negro History* 55(Oct. 1969): 398–404.

46. Walter E. Weyl, "Labor Conditions in Porto Rico," *Bulletin No. 61*, U.S. Department of Labor, Washington, D.C., Nov. 1905, p. 806; Iglesias, *Luchas Emancipadores*, 1: 171–96; Gavin, *Organized Labor Movement in Puerto Rico*, p. 44.

47. *New York Times,* April 7, 1900.

48. Interestingly, the *Journal of the Knights of Labor* justified the "unpatriotic expressions" of Puerto Rican workers. How could they have the same attachment for the United States as American workers when "the constitution of the United States has not been extended to the island and . . . the privileges of American citizenship have been denied them." Aug. 1900, p. 4.

49. *Bricklayer and Mason,* Oct. 1, 1900.

50. *Typographical Journal,* Nov. 15, 1900; *National Labor Standard, Oct. 22, 1900.*

51. *Bricklayer and Mason,* Oct. 1, 1900.

52. Iglesias, *Luchas Emancipadores,* 1: 144–51.

53. Ibid., pp. 152–54.

54. *Proceedings,* AFL Convention, 1900, pp. 63–65.

55. Ibid., pp. 65, 116–19; Gompers to Theodore F. Cuno, Dec. 16, 1900, GLB; Samuel Gompers, *Seventy Years of Life and Labor,* vol. 2 (New York: 1924), pp. 69–70.

56. Gompers to Iglesias, Dec. 26, 1900, GLB; Iglesias, *Luchas Emancipadores,* 1: 203.

57. Iglesias, *Luchas Emancipadores,* 1: 210; Bolivar Pagán, *Historia de los Partidos Puertor-riqueños,* vol. 1 (San Juan: 1959), pp. 52–60.

58. William G. Whittaker, "The Santiago Iglesias Case, 1901–1902: Origins of American Trade Union Involvement in Puerto Rico," *The Americas* 25(April 1968): 379.

59. *American Federationist,* Oct. 1901, p. 445.

60. Gompers to Iglesias, Oct. 1, 1901, GLB.

61. Iglesias, *Luchas Emancipadores,* 1: 216–17.

62. Gompers to William H. Hunt, Oct. 14, 1901, GLB.

63. Gompers to Iglesias, Oct. 14, 1901, GLB; Whittaker, *"Santiago Iglesias Case,"* pp. 380–81.

64. *Washington Evening Star,* Nov. 17, 1901.

65. Ibid., Nov. 11, 13, 1901; Gompers to Iglesias, Nov. 10, 11, 12, 1901, GLB; Iglesias, *Luchas Emancipadores,* 1: 217–18; Whittaker, *"Santiago Iglesias Case,"* p. 381.

66. Whittaker, *"Santiago Iglesias Case,"* p. 382.

67. *San Juan News,* Nov. 13, 1901, quoted in ibid., p. 382.

68. *San Juan News,* Nov. 15, 1901, reprinted in ibid., p. 383.

69. *San Juan News,* Nov. 15–16, 1901, quoted in ibid., p. 383.

70. *San Juan News,* Nov. 15, 1901, quoted in ibid., p. 383.

71. Gompers to AFL Executive Council, Nov. 20, 1901, GLB.

72. Whittaker, *"Santiago Iglesias Case,"* p. 384.

73. Iglesias, *Luchas Emancipadores,* 1: 220–22; Gompers to Iglesias, Nov. 10, 1901, GLB. Part of the money was paid back in 1905. *Proceedings,* AFL Convention, 1905, p. 112.

74. Leo S. Rowe, *The United States and Porto Rico* (New York: 1904), p. 259.

75. *Proceedings,* AFL Convention, 1901, pp. 122–25.

76. "Proceedings of Socialist Party Convention, held at Indianapolis, Indiana," July 19, 1901, p. 11. Typewritten copy in Tamiment Institute Library, New York University.

77. *Proceedings,* AFL Convention, 1901, pp. 160, 230.

78. *Washington Evening Star,* Dec. 17, 18, 1901; Whittaker, "Santiago Iglesias Case," p. 382.

79. Quoted in Samuel Gompers, "The Conspiracy to Raise the Price of Labor," *"American Federationist* 9(Jan. 1902): 27–28.

80. Gompers to William H. Hunt, Dec. 30, 1901, GLB. See also Gompers to Iglesias, Nov. 12, 20, 1901, ibid.

81. *American Federationist* 9(Feb. 1902): 75.

82. U.S. War Department, Bureau of Insular Affairs, *Compilation of the Revised Statutes and Codes of Puerto Rico* (Washington, D.C.: 1913), pp. 1653–54.

83. Iglesias, *Luchas Emancipadores,* 1: 214.

84. *Proceedings,* AFL Convention, 1902, p. 151.

85. Whittaker, "Santiago Iglesias Case," p. 392.

86. *Proceedings,* AFL Convention, 1902, p. 15.

87. Ibid., p. 78.

88. *The Worker,* July 13, 1902.

89. Iglesias, *Luchas Emancipadores,,* 1: 222–25.

90. Ibid., pp. 227–29.

91. *American Federationist* 11(April 1904): 297, (May 1904): 412–13.

92. *Washington Evening Star,* May 7, 1905.

93. *American Federationist* 12(June 1905): 380–81.

94. *Washington Evening Star,* May 7, 1905.

95. Ibid.

96. Ibid.

97. Ibid.; Samuel Gompers to Santiago Iglesias, May 12, 1905, Gompers Papers, State Historical Society of Wisconsin.

98. *American Federationist* 12(June 1905): 380–81.

99. Ibid., 11(June 1904): 521.

100. Mandel, *Samuel Gompers,* p. 210.

101. Gompers to Iglesias, July 22, Dec. 30, 1904, GLB; Mandel, *Samuel Gompers,* p. 211.

102. *American Federationist* 10(Dec. 1903): 1300.

103. Gavin, *Organized Labor Movement in Puerto Rico,* p. 61; *New York Call,* Sept. 19, 1911.

104. Mandel, *Samuel Gompers,* p. 209.

105. Ibid., p. 210.

106. *American Federationist* 11(May 1904): 412–16; *Proceedings,* AFL Convention, 1904, pp. 188–90; McKee, "American Federation of Labor," pp. 138–39.

107. José Soto García, Manuel Valdes, and Juan Guerra Rivera, President, Secretary, and Treasurer, Carpenters' Union, Local 1456, San Juan, Puerto Rico, to Gompers, Nov. 26, 1910, *AFL Corr.*; *New York Call,* Aug. 5, 21, 1911.

108. *New York Call,* March 2, 1913. Among the signers of the statement were P. Rivera Martínez, Acting President; Joaquín A. Becerrill, Treasurer; Rafael Alonso, Secretary-General; Esteban Padilla, Manuel Alvareas, Julio Aybar, Alejandro Escales, José Ferrer y Ferrer, Vice Presidents; and representatives of the Central Labor Union of San Juan, of the Sailors' Union No. 300 of San Juan; of the Cigarmakers' Union No. 460, San Juan; representatives of the unions of Untuado, Gurabo, of the Carpenters' Union No. 1,450 of San Juan; of the Masons' Union No. 10,892, of San Juan; of the Painters' Union No. 550 of San Juan; of the unions of Bayamón, of San Lorenzo Cedra, Cabo-Rojo, and San Germán, Caguas, and the District of Arecibo.

109. Arthur Yager, *Fourteenth Report of the Governor of Puerto Rico* (Washington, D.C.: 1914), pp. 52–58; *Proceedings,* AFL Convention, 1914, pp. 52, 377–89.

110. P. Rivera Martínez to F.C. Roberts, Jan. 13, 1916, copy in Samuel Gompers Papers, State Historical Society of Wisconsin.

111. Mandel, *Samuel Gompers,* p. 212; Iglesias, *Luchas Emancipadores,* 1: 276; Gavin, *Organized Labor Movement in Puerto Rico,* p. 64.

112. *The Public,* March 24, 1916.

113. Santiago Iglesias to Samuel Gompers, July 1, 1914, Gompers Papers, State Historical Society of Wisconsin.

114. Samuel Gompers to Joseph Tumulty, June 11, 1915, Gompers Papers, State Historical Society of Wisconsin.

115. *New York Call,* June 8, 1915. Gompers was furious when the *New York Call* reported

that the delegation had not even seen Tumulty, indicating the indifference of the Wilson Administration to the plight of the Puerto Rican workers (June 7, 1915). The error was corrected the following day, and an "editor's note" explained that the New York Socialist daily had been in error in its earlier report, and that the new article was intended to "correct facts in the case" (June 8, 1915). Gompers, however, refused to be mollified, and in an angry letter to Chester M. Wright, the *Call's* managing editor, he made the silly statement: "In the fifteen years that the American Federation of Labor has been giving very possible assistance and has been of tangible advantage to the Porto Rican working people, during which I have been a close observer of every event effecting the rights, interests and welfare of the Porto Rican workers, I know of no occurrence so calculated to play into the hands of the enemies of the Porto Rican working people as the miserable, willful misrepresentation published in the Call." (Samuel Gompers to Chester M. Wright, June 11, 1915, Samuel Gompers Papers, State Historical Society of Wisconsin.) Perhaps the only surprising thing about this letter is that Gompers did not blame the socialists for the terrible plight of the Puerto Rican workers.

116. Gompers to Santiago Iglesias and Prudencio Rivera Martínez, June 10, 1915, Gompers Papers, State Historical Society of Wisconsin.

117. Samuel Gompers to Woodrow Wilson, June 29, 1915, Gompers Papers, State Historical Society of Wisconsin.

Chapter VI

1. McKee, "American Federation of Labor," p. 140.

2. *Proceedings*, AFL Convention, 1898, pp. 128, 145.

3. *Locomotive Firemen's Journal*, Jan. 1899, p. 32; *Cleveland Citizen*, Jan. 25, 1899; *Coast Seamen's Journal*, April 18, 1900. See also *Journal of the Knights of Labor*, Aug. 1899, p. 4.

4. *New York Times*, June 29, 1902.

5. *Proceedings*, AFL Convention, 1898, pp. 128, 145.

6. Raul Perez, "The Treacherous Treaty: A Colombian Peace," *North American Review* 177(Dec. 1903): 939; *New York Times*, Dec. 9, 1903.

7. Bemis, *The Latin American Policy of the United States*, p. 15.

8. Tómas Herrán, "The Isthmian Question," *The Independent* 56(Jan. 1904): 65; Abelardo Aldana et al., *The Panama Canal Question: A Plea for Colombia* (New York: 1904), p. 48; Joseph C. Abena, "Colombian Reactions to the Independence of Panama, 1903–1904," *The Americas* 33(July 1976): 143–46.

9. *Proceedings*, AFL Convention, 1903, p. 147.

10. Ibid., p. 205.

11. *Boston Evening Transcript,* Nov. 19, 1903.

12. *Proceedings,* AFL Convention, 1903, p. 205.

13. McKee, "American Federation of Labor," pp. 162–64.

14. "Eight Hour Law and the Panama Canal," *American Federationist* 13(1906): 163–64.

15. *International Socialist Review* 11(July 1910): 15.

16. Ibid., pp. 13–15.

17. "On the Canal Zone," *Industrial Union Bulletin*, March 9, 1907.

18. Bernard Diederich, *Somoza and the Legacy of U.S. Involvement in Central America* (New York: 1981), pp. 82–84; Dana G. Munro, *Intervention and Dollar Diplomacy in the Caribbean, 1900–1921* (Princeton, N.J.: 1964), pp. 388–90.

19. *Literary Digest*, Oct. 24, 1909.

20. Ibid., Dec. 14, 18, 1909.

21. *Independent* Oct. 19, 1911, p. 841; *New York Times*, Jan. 12, 1911.

22. *Literary Digest*, Aug. 24, Sept. 28, Oct. 19, 1912; *New York Times*, Oct. 12, 1914; Marine Corps Historical Reference Series, Number 21, *The United States Marines in Nicaragua* (Washington, D.C.: 1967), p. 7.

23. *New York Times*, July 20, 1913.

24. Ibid., July 21, 1913; *Literary Digest*, Aug. 2, 1913.

25. *New York Evening Post*, reprinted in ibid., Sept. 17, 1913.

26. *New York Times*, Dec. 2, 1913.

27. "La Protesta De Nicaragua," *Acción Mundial* 1 (19): 21–22. Copy in John Murray Papers, Bancroft Library, University of California, Berkeley.

28. Agüello and Lejarza were listed as lawyers, Martínez as a merchant.

29. *Public Appeal of Nicaragua to the Congress and People of the United States, by Doctors Rosendo Agüello, Salvador Lejarza, and Mr. Carlos Martínez, L.* (New Orleans, La.: June 1914), pp. 1–10.

30. Ibid., pp. 18–20.

31. Ibid., pp. 122–32.

32. Ibid., pp. 163–69.

33. For a discussion of John Kenneth Turner, see p. 105.

34. Agüello, Lejarda, and Martínez, *Public Appeal of Nicaragua*, pp. 170–77.

35. Ibid., pp. 178–85.

36. Woodrow Wilson to William Jennings Bryan, Jan. 20, 1914, Woodrow Wilson Papers, Library of Congress, Manuscripts Division. Luis Corea, former Nicaraguan minister to the United States and later a lawyer in New York, urged President Wilson not to go forward with the treaty. He assured Wilson that while the government in Nicaragua was for the treaty, it "has no other hold on office than United States Marines, and I feel no other purpose than to make sure their continuance in office, by placing themselves under the protection of this country and invoking its military aid to suppress any opposition. . . ." C. Peter Evans Brownback, "The Acquisition of the Nicaraguan Canal Route: The Bryan-Chamorro Treaty" (Ph.D. diss., University of Pennsylvania, 1952), p. 145.

37. *New York Call*, Aug. 24, 1910.

38. It is strange that the *Public Appeal* did not reprint the following from the *New York Times* of July 22, 1913: "Imperialism, Says Borah. Senator [William E.] Borah poured hot shot into the Bryan proposal. 'This means the going up of the American flag all the way to the Panama Canal, so surely as time goes on,' he said. 'It is the beginning of that policy whose irrefutable logic is complete dominance and control and ownership by the United States from here to the Panama Canal. . . . The Central American States are vastly wealthy in natural resources. They are an inviting field for exploitation, and the minute we began establishing protectorates American capital will flow in and take possession and we will have to protect those citizens and that capital in all the minutest detail of government.' " The *Public Appeal* did not prevent ratification by the Senate of the Bryan-Chamorro Treaty. But with the criticism of the press, as well as the warning by Borah, it did contribute to the abandonment of the Protectorate features. Nicaragua's three neighbors, Costa Rica, El Salvador, and Honduras, protested the treaty and successfully challenged the treaty before a Central American court that had been established under a 1907 convention promoted by Washington. It was this very convention Washington cited as legal authority when the Marines landed in 1912. Washington refused to comply with the court's decision that Nicaragua had infringed on its neighbors' rights by agreeing to the treaty and ignored the court's opinion. It also sharply criticized Nicaragua's neighbors and eventually nullified the convention. Meanwhile, the Bryan-Chamorro Treaty remained in effect.

39. Richard Hofstadter, William Miller, and Daniel Aaron, *The United States* (Englewood Cliffs, N.J.: 1967), p. 640.

Chapter VII

1. John Kenneth Turner, *Barbarous Mexico* (Austin, Texas: 1969), pp. 100, 169, 176.

2. Marvin D. Bernstein, *Foreign Investments in Latin America* (New York: 1972), pp. 7–8, 10–11.

3. Turner, *Barbarous Mexico*, p. 219.

4. Ibid., p. 221; Bernstein, *Foreign Investments.*, pp. 7–8.

5. David M. Walker, "Porfirian Labor Politics: Working Class Organizations in Mexico City and Porfirio Díaz, 18761902," *The Americas* 3(Jan. 1981): 284; Turner, *Barbarous Mexico*, p. 217.

6. Theodore Roosevelt to James Creelman, March 7, 1908, in Elting E. Morison, ed., *The Letters of Theodore Roosevelt*, vol. 6 (Cambridge, Mass.: 1948–54) pp. 963–64.

7. Robert Freeman Smith, *The United States and Revolutionary Nationalism in Mexico 1916–1932* (Chicago: 1972), pp. 29–30.

8. William Dirk Raat, "The Diplomacy of Suppression: *Los Revoltosos*, Mexico, and the United States, 1906–1911," *Hispanic American Historical Review* 56(Nov. 1976): 530.

9. James Creelman, "President Díaz, Hero of the Americas," *Pearson's Magazine* 19(March 1908): 231–48; *El Imparcial*, March 3, 1908.

10. *El Socialista*, Jan. 23, 1873, quoted in John M. Hart, "Nineteenth Century Urban Labor Precursors of the Mexican Revolution: The Development of an Ideology," *The Americas* 30 (Jan. 1974): 297.

11. *La Convención Radical*, Nov. 24, 1901, quoted in Walker, *"Porfirian Labor Politics,"* p. 278.

12. Ramón Eduardo Ruiz, *Labor and the Ambivalent Revolution: Mexico, 1911–1923* (Baltimore and London: 1976), p. 7.

13. Ibid., pp. 8–9.

14. Ibid., p. 11.

15. Ibid., pp. 11–12.

16. Ibid., p. 13.

17. *Los Angeles Citizen*, July 21, 1916. The same situation prevailed, it should be noted, in the copper mines of Arizona. Regardless of whether they had recently arrived in the mining camps or had resided in the area a considerable number of years, the Mexican miners were paid "the same 'Mexican wage!' assigned menial tasks with little promise of upward mobility and treated in a distinct manner in comparison with their Anglo counterparts." A double standard of wages prevailed throughout the Southwest mining districts—a higher wage for Anglos and a lower wage for Mexicans. Moreover, Mexicans were paid by a system of "half-pay, half goods" under which a greater part of their wages went for goods at the company store. This resulted in a profit of 100 to 300 percent for the mine operators. (Victor S. Clark, "Mexican Labor in the United States," *Bulletin of the Bureau of Labor* 8[Sept. 1908]: 498; Michael E. Casillas, "Mexican Labor Militancy in the U.S.: 1896–1915," *Southwest Economy & Society* 4[Fall 1978]: 34; Philip S. Foner, *History of the Labor Movement in the United States* [New York: 1983], 6: 14).

18. John M. Hart, "Anarchist Thought in Nineteenth Century Mexico" (Ph.D. diss., University of California at Los Angeles, 1970), pp. 23–42; Walker, *"Porfirian Labor Politics,"* p. 258.

19. Diego G. Lopez Rosado, *Historia y pensamiento economico de Mexico*, vol. 3 (Mexico: 1968–72) pp. 349–68; Luis Araiza, *Historia del movimiento obrero mexicano*, vol. 2 (Mexico: 1964–65) pp. 12–94; Marjorie Ruth Clark, *Organized Labor in Mexico* (Chapel Hill, N.C.: 1967), pp. 2–14.

20. Ruiz, *Labor and the Ambivalent Revolution*, pp. 15–16.

21. Ibid., p. 16.

22. Herbert O. Buyer, "The Cananea Incident," *New Mexico Historical Review* 13(Oct. 1938): 387–415.

23. C.L. Sonnichsen, "Colonel William C. Greene and the Strike at Cananea Sonora, 1906," *Arizona and the West* 13(Winter 1971): 343–60; Moses Gonzalez Navarro, *El Profiriato: La Vida Social*, in Daniel Cosio Villegas, ed., *Historia Moderna de Mexico*, vol. 4 (Mexico: 1955–73), pp. 316–30.

24. Moises Gonzalez Navarro, "La huelga de Rio Blanco," *Historia Mexicana* 6(April-June 1957): 511–32.

25. Moises Gonzalez Navarro, *El Porfiriato* 4: 275–343; Robert D. Anderson, "The Mexican Textile Union Movement, 1906–1907: An Analysis of a Labor Crisis" (Ph.D. diss., American University, 1968), pp. 228–66.

26. See James D. Cockroft, *Intellectual Precursors of the Mexican Revolution, 1900–1913* (Austin, Texas: 1968), pp. 159–69; Lowell L. Blaisdell, *The Desert Revolution: Baja California, 1911* (Madison, Wis.: 1962), p. 8; Victor Alba, *Las ideas sociales contempraneas en Mexico* (Mexico: 1960), p. 124.

27. See especially Rodney D. Anderson, "Mexican Workers and the Politics of Revolution, 1906–1911," *Hispanic American Historical Review* 54(Feb. 1974): 96; Robert Anderson, "The Historiography of a Myth," in James C. Foster, ed., *American Labor in the Southwest: The First Hundred Years* (Tucson, Ariz.: 1982), pp. 172–84.

28. In an interview with Ralph Roeder in Mexico City, Jan. 25, 1963, I was informed by the distinguished historian of Mexico that Flores Magón's anarchism did not stem from theories of anarchists in Europe and the United States. Instead it originated with the Indians of Oaxaca, Mexico. Under the Indian village system, the emphasis was on economic holding of land and a total lack of interest in and distrust of central political authority outside the village tribe. Later, Roeder continued, Flores Magón read the writings of Kropotkin, the Russian anarchist, and made contact with Emma Goldman. But his anarchism derived basically from his Indian background in Mexico.

29. Charles C. Cumberland, "Precursors of the Mexican Revolution 1910," *Hispanic American Historical Review* 22(Aug. 1942): 344–56; Ethel Duffy Turner, *Ricardo Flores Magón y el Partido Liberal Mexicano* (Morelia: 1960), pp. 110–45; Lyle C. Brown, "The Mexican Liberals and Their Struggle Against the Díaz Dictatorship, 1900–1906," in *Antologia MCC* (Mexico City: 1956), pp. 22–38; Ellen Howell Myers, "The Mexican Liberal Party, 1903–1910" (Ph.D. diss., University of Mexico, 1970), pp. 192–218.

30. Cockroft, *Intellectual Precursors*, pp. 239–45.

31. Michael E. Casillas, "Mexicans, Labor, and Strife in Arizona, 1896–1917" (M.A. thesis, University of Mexico, 1979), p. 66.

32. "A Mexican Manifesto," *The Public*, May 21, 1909.

33. Ibid.

34. The most recent and best of these studies is William Dirk Raat, *Revoltosos: Mexico's Rebels in the United States, 1903–1923* (College Station, Texas: 1981). The study is based on extensive research in Mexican and U.S. archives, and private papers, published documents, memoirs, newspapers, and journals.

35. The volumes of intercepted PLM correspondence in the Mexican Foreign Ministry archives testify to the government's surveillance techniques. There are 37 volumes of *magonista* material in the Ministry's archives. The postal authorities and inspectors in Mexico and in the United States cooperated in the interception of the mails.

36. John Murray, "Behind the Drums of Revolution: The Labor Movement in Mexico as Seen by an American Trade Unionist," *Survey*, Dec. 2, 1916, p. 241.

37. Raat, *Revoltosos* pp. 119–20; Clark, *Organized Labor in Mexico*, p. 11; Mary Jones, *The Autobiography of Mother Jones*; U.S. Congress, House Committee on Rules, Proceeding of a

Joint Committee to Investigate Alleged Persecution of Mexican Citizens, by the Government of Mexico, *Hearings on H.J.R. 201,* 61st Cong., 2nd Sess., June 8–14, 1910, pp. 90–93. The most complete account of Mother Jones's varied activites in behalf of the Mexican Revolution and the revolutionists who were fighting the Díaz dictatorship in the United States is Philip S. Foner, ed., *Mother Jones Speaks: Collected Speeches and Writings* (New York: 1983), which includes Mother Jones's speeches, writings in journals, letters, and testimony before Congressional Committees on the subject.

38. Jones, *Autobiography,* p. 137; Christopulos, "American Radicals," pp. 80–86.

39. Foner, *Mother Jones Speaks,* pp. 122–34; Edward M. Steel, ed., *The Correspondence of Mother Jones* (Pittsburgh: 1985), pp. 65–77.

40. Ibid., pp. 142–43.

41. *Appeal to Reason,* Feb. 20, 1909; Mother Jones, "Oh! Ye Lovers of Liberty," copy in State Department Files, NF case 174/104, National Archives, reprinted in Foner, *Mother Jones Speaks* pp. 459–62.

42. Raat, *Revoltosos,* p. 48.

43. The letter is in the Mother Mary Jones Papers, Department of Archives and Manuscripts, Catholic University of America, reprinted in Foner, *Mother Jones Speaks,* pp. 135–36, and in Dale Featherling, *Mother Jones: The Miners' Angel* (Carbondale, Ill.: 1974), p. 81.

44. *Miners' Magazine,* Oct. 3, 1907.

45. *Industrial Union Bulletin,* Feb. 29, July 25, 1908.

46. *Appeal to Reason,* Jan. 16, 1909.

47. Raat, *Revoltosos,* p. 51; Eugene V. Debs, "This Plot Must Be Foiled," p. 4, copy in State Department Files, NF. case 174/100–4, National Archives; Ivan E. Cadenhead, Jr., "The American Socialists and the Mexican Revolution in 1910," *Southwestern Social Science Quarterly* 43 (Sept. 1962): 103–9.

48. Grace H. Stimson, *The Rise of the Labor Movement in Los Angeles* (Berkeley and Los Angeles: 1955), p. 322; Harvey A. Levenstein, *Labor Organizations in the United States and Mexico: A History of their Relations* (Westport, Conn.: 1971), p. 9.

49. *Proceedings,* AFL Convention, 1908, p. 122; United States Congress, Senate Committee on Foreign Relations, *Investigation of Mexican Affairs. Hearings on S. 106,* 66th Cong., 2nd sess., 1920, S. Doc. 285, vol. 2, p. 2642.

50. *Appeal to Reason,* April 20, May 22, 1909.

51. Ibid., June 13, 1909; Christopulos, *"American Radicals and the Mexican Revolution,"* p. 94.

52. Jones, *Autobiography,* pp. 141–42; *Alleged Persecution of Mexican Citizens by the Government of Mexico,* pp. 92–93.

53. Edward P. Holley, *Revolution and Intervention: The Diplomacy of Taft and Wilson with Mexico, 1909–1917* (Cambridge, Mass.: 1970), p. 14.

54. *New York Times,* June 11, 1910; Gompers, *Seventy Years of Life and Labor,* 2: 308–09; Raat, *Revoltosos,* p. 49; Christopulos, "American Radicals," p. 95.

55. *Alleged Persecutions of Mexican Citizens,* pp. 12–14.

56. Ibid., pp. 95–112.

57. *Chicago Daily Socialist,* June 10, 1910.

58. Ibid., July 22, 1910.

59. Sinclair Snow, Introduction to *Barbarous Mexico* (Austin, Texas: 1969), pp. xxii–xxiii; Christopulous, "American Radicals," p. 110.

60. Turner, *Barbarous Mexico,* p. 218.

61. Ibid., pp. 186, 221.

62. Mark Reisler, *By the Sweat of Their Brow: Mexican Immigrant Labor in the United States, 1900–1914* (Westport, Conn.: 1976), pp. 3–16; Victor S. Clark, "Mexican Labor in the

United States," 475–79; Carey McWilliams, *North from Mexico,* (Philadelphia: 1949), pp. 170–75.

63. *Proceedings,* AFL Convention, 1909, p. 105; 1910, p. 243.

64. *Proceedings of the Tenth Annual Convention of the California State Federation of Labor,* 1909, p. 34.

65. *New York Call,* April 16, 1910.

Chapter VIII

1. *La Regeneración,* reprinted in Blaisdell, *The Desert Revolution,* pp. 13–14. The English translation is by Blaisdell.

2. Stanley R. Ross, *Francisco I. Madero, Apostle of Mexican Democracy* (New York: 1955), pp. 34–43.

3. Stanley R. Ross and Charles Curtis Cumberland argue that Madero either opposed armed revolution or wanted "to have recourse to arms only as a last resort," while Robert E. Quirk insists that there is "no indication that he [Madero] planned or even favored a revolution." (Ross, *Francisco I. Madero,* p. 63; Charles Curtis Cumberland, *Mexican Revolution: Genesis under Madero* [Austin, Texas: 1952], p. 117; Robert E. Quirk, *The Mexican Revolution and the Catholic Church, 1910–1929* [Bloomington, Ind.; 196], p. 19.) However, for evidence that Madero favored armed revolution as early as 1910, see Jerry W. Knudson, "When Did Francisco I. Madero Decide on Revolution?" *The Americas* 30 (April 1974): 529–34.

4. Cumberland, *Mexican Revolution,* pp. 88–94; Howard F. Cline, *The United States and Mexico* (New York: 1963), pp. 120–21.

5. All students of this period of the Mexican Revolution agree that the U.S. government worked closely with Madero in harrassing and arresting the PLM leaders. W. Dirk Raat, who has made the most intensive study, notes that Madero developed an espionage operation and that his secret service agents worked closely with private detectives who were also working for the United States government. He also points out that "neutrality laws were not enforced against Madero with the degree of effectiveness that was used against the *magonistas.* . . ." ("The Diplomacy of Suppression," 548–49.) Raat develops this theme in greater detail in his *Revoltosos: Mexico's Rebels in the United States, 1903–1925.*

6. Ricardo Flores Magón's article is summarized in English in *Solidarity,* March 11, 1911, and *The Agitator,* March 15, 1911.

7. Blaisdell, *The Desert Revolution,* pp. 116–18.

8. *The Agitator,* April 15, 1911; *Mother Earth,* April 1911; *The Public,* March 24, 1911.

9. Frank Tannenbaum, *The Mexican Agrarian Revolution* (Washington, D.C.: 1930), pp. 157–58.

10. Ibid.

11. *The Agitator,* April 15, 1911; Tannenbaum, *Mexican Agrarian Revolution,* p. 158.

12. Ibid., pp. 159–61.

13. Raat, *Revoltosos,* pp. 128–29; *Mother Earth,* April 1911; Mandel, *Samuel Gompers,* pp. 336–37.

14. Christopulos, *"American Radicals,",* pp. 135–39.

15. John Murray, "Behind the Drums of Revolution: The Labor Movement in Mexico as Seen by an American Trade Unionist," *Survey,* Dec. 2, 1916, p. 242; *Autobiography of Mother Jones,* p. 143. Since Madero had applauded Díaz for his refusal to raise wages during the textile strike of 1907, and he himself was an industrialist and landowner who paid the low wages typical of the times, Mother Jones's report may seem strange. However, as Ramón Eduardo Ruiz points out, "Madero was a humanitarian and a progressive." He was shocked

by the terrible conditions he found among Mexican industrial workers, and he promised to improve wages if elected. Moreover, he acknowledged the right of workers to organize real labor unions, and he urged businessmen not to take reprisals against workers active in the trade union movement. (Ruiz, *Labor and the Ambivalent Revolutionaries*, p. 29.) See also Rodney D. Anderson, "Mexican Workers and the Politics of Revolution," pp. 94–95.

16. *New York Call*, April 12, 1911.

17. *Solidarity*, April 22, 1911.

18. John Kenneth Turner, "The Revolution in Mexico," *International Socialist Review* 11(Jan. 1911): 417–23; Christopulos, *"American Radicals,"* pp. 46–47.

19. Blaisdell, *The Desert Revolution*, p. 42; Gordon Mills, "Jack London's Quest for Salvation," *American Quarterly* 7(Spring 1955): 3–15.

20. Jack London, "The Mexican," in *The Bodley Head Jack London*, Arthur Calder-Marshall, ed. (London: 1963), pp. 296–322.

21. Christopulos, *"American Radicals,"*, p. 81.

22. *Solidarity*, Nov. 5, 1910.

23. *Industrial Worker*, March 14, May 25, 1911; *Solidarity*, March 18, 1911.

24. Blaisdell, *Desert Revolution*, Chapter 7.

25. James R. Green, "Socialism, Social Banditry, and the Mexican Revolution," in Thomas R. Frazier, ed., *The Underside of American History* (New York: 1982), p. 137.

26. Raat, *Revoltosos* pp. 55–58.

27. Blaisdell, *Desert Revolution*, pp. 112–15.

28. *Solidarity*, May 26, 1911.

29. Ibid., March 18, 1911.

30. S.G., in *Industrial Worker*, May 25, 1911. The discussion of the Baja California episode is based on Blaisdell, *Desert Revolution*, pp. 70–187; Peter Gerhard, "The Socialist Invasion of Baja California, 1911," *Pacific Historical Review* 15(Sept. 1936): 295–305; Raat, *Revoltos*, pp. 56–58; Pablo L. Martínez, *A History of Lower California*, Ethel Duffy Turner, trans. (Mexico City: 1960), pp. 462–502; Pablo L. Martínez, *El Magonismo in Baja California: Documentos* (Mexico City: 1958), pp. 18–89; Hyman Weintraub, "The I.W.W. in California, 1903–1931" (M.A. thesis , University of California at Los Angeles, 1947), pp. 73–76.

31. Blaisdell, *Desert Revolution*., p. 153–56.

32. *New York Times*, June 23, 1911.

33. Raat, *Revoltosos*, p. 58.

34. Blaisdell, *Desert Revolution*, pp. 170–72.

35. Raat, *Revoltosos*, pp. 242–43.

36. Ibid., p. 243.

37. Blaisdell, *Desert Revolution*, p. 204.

38. Ibid. pp. 202–04.

39. Carlton Beals, the distinguished progressive North American authority on Latin America, summed up these charges in his *Porfirio Díaz, Dictator of Mexico*, published in 1932. "Certain practical Americans in Los Angeles, owning vast stretches of land and properties, secretly backed various soldiers of fortune to engage in the Magon movement, the real purpose being to wrench the territory away from Mexico." (Philadelphia: 1932), p. 428.

40. Alfonso Taracena, *La Verdadera revolución Mexicana, 1909 a 1911* (Mexico City: 1965), pp. 187–89; Lowell L. Blaisdell, "Was it Revolution or Filibustering: The Mystery of the Flores Magón Revolt in Baja California," *Hispanic American Historical Review* 23(May 1954): 157–59.

41. Blaisdell,*Desert Revolution*, p. 152.

42. Mother Jones to Calero, Oct. 25, 1911, and Mother Jones to Ricardo Flores Magón, Nov. 4, 1911, in Isidro Fabela, ed., *Documentos Historicos de la Revolución Mexicans*, vol. 10

(Mexico City: 1966), pp. 371–73, 380–82, reprinted in Foner, *Mother Jones Speaks,* pp. 580–85.

43. Foner, *Mother Jones Speaks,* pp. 25–26, 499–500.

44. *Appeal to Reason,* June 17, July 8, 1911.

45. Ibid., Aug. 19, 1911.

46. *Ibid.:*, Cadenhead, "The American Socialists and the Mexican Revolution of 1910," p. 110.

47. Although Ricardo Flores Magón did not spell it out here, it was generally understood that he was referring to allegations published in the *London Star* in March 1911, charging that Standard Oil Company financed Madero's revolt in return for concessions which would enable the oil trust to eliminate British competitors in Mexico. W. Dirk Raat, who has investigated this charge in detail and is generally sympathetic to Ricardo Flores Magón, concludes that "it is unlikely that Standard Oil financed Madero's revolts," although he concedes that Standard Oil did benefit from Madero's revolt, and that Anglo-American international oil rivalries were "a part of the Mexican Revolution." (*Revoltosos,* pp. 56–58. Friedrich Katz takes a somewhat different position, writing: "There are also indications though it cannot clearly be demonstrated at present, that the Standard Oil Company provided the Madero movement with important aid." (*The Secret War in Mexico: Europe, The United States, and the Mexican Revolution* [Chicago: 1981], p. 39.)

48. *Solidarity,* July 8, 1911.

Chapter IX

1. Gonzalo G. Rivero, *Hacia la Verdad episodos de la Revolución* (México: 1911), pp. 60–62; Louis James Secrest, "The End of the Porfiriato: The Collapse of the Díaz Government, 1910–1911" (Ph.D. diss., University of New Mexico, 1965), pp. 86–95.

2. Tannenbaum, *The Mexican Agrarian Revolution,* pp. 157–58; *Proceedings,* AFL Convention, 1911, pp. 13–15.

3. *New York Call,* June 3, 1908.

4. Most of the troop movements between 1908 and 1910, referred to by Turner, were minor episodes, did not arouse much reaction at the time, and are not even mentioned in several studies of U.S.-Latin American relations. (See, for example, Samuel Flagg Bemis, *The Latin American Policy of the United States* [New York: 1954], pp. 170–71.)

5. John Kenneth Turner, "The American Partners of Díaz," *International Socialist Review* 10 (Dec. 1910): 328.

6. *Proceedings of the First National Congress of the Socialist Party,* p. 304.

7. Christopulos, "American Radicals," p. 154.

8. *International Socialist Review* 11(April 1911): 587; *Socialist Party Official Bulletin,* March 1911, p. 4.

9. Old Military Records, Division Record Group 94, Adjutant General's Office, 1747728, National Archives. Hereinafter cited as RG94, AGO, 1747728, National Archives.

10. Ibid.

11. Ibid.

12. Clipping in ibid.; Christopulos, "American Radicals," p. 159.

13. *Social Democratic Herald,* March 25, April 11, 1911; Peterson, "The Foreign Policy Theory of the American Socialist Party," pp. 52, 85.

14. *Socialist Party Official Bulletin,* March, Nov. 1911.

15. *Solidarity,* April 1, May 6, 1911.

16. *The Agitator,* May 15, 1911.

17. *Solidarity*, March 25, 1911.

18. *New York Call*, May 8, 1911.

19. Ibid. May 15, 22, 1911.

20. For a definition of "Dollar Diplomacy," see pp. 80.

21. Blaisdell, "Was it Revolution or Filibustering?" p. 152; Christopulos, "American Radicals," pp. 159–60.

22. Edward P. Haley, *Revolution and Intervention: The Diplomacy of Taft and Wilson with Mexico, 1910–1917* (Cambridge, Mass.: 1970), p. 14.

23. RG59, 812.000/747; 812.00/778; 812.00/800; RG 94, AGO, 181/492, National Archives.

24. Taft to Wood, March 12, 1911, in Gene Z. Hanrahan, *Documents on the Mexican Revolution* (Salisbury, N. C.: 1976), pp. 225–29.

25. Raat, *Revoltosos,* p. 238.

26. William Weber Johnson, *Heroic Mexico: The Violent Emergence of a Modern Nation* (Garden City, N.Y.: 1968), pp. 47–48.

27. Taft to Secretary of Treasury, May 12, 1911, RC165, WCD, 5761–222, National Archives; Raat, *Revoltosos*, p. 239.

28. In a letter to Senator Albert B. Fall, a follower of Ricardo Flores Magón informed him that the *magonistas* "understood that Pres. Taft in order to save Madero will force intervention by indirection. As he sees the triumph of the Real Revolution approaching, he has grown wonderfully anxious concerning the safety of Americans, when as a matter of fact, if Americans would remain strictly nuetral there would not have been, and would not be any danger. Pres. Taft has apparently arranged for Mex[ican] troops to pass through U.S. territory to crush the opposition to Madero, ostensibly to protect Americans." (José Salazar to Albert B. Fall, undated letter, Albert B. Fall Papers, University of New Mexico Library, Albuquerque, New Mexico.)

29. Berta Ulloa, *Las relaciones Mexicano-La Revolución intervenida: Relaciones diplomaticas entre Mexico y Estados 1910–1914* (Mexico City: 1971); Berta Ulloa, "Taft y los antimaderistas," in Bernardo García Martínez et al., *Historia y sociedad en el mundo de habla espanola* (Mexico City: 1970), pp. 319–28; Berta Ulloa, "Las relaciones Mexicano-Norteamericanas, 1910–1911," "*Historia Mexicana* 14(July-Sept. 1965): 25–46; Raat, *Revoltosos*, pp. 238–41.

30. Knox to Department of Commerce, Aug. 11, 1911, RG 85, 54108/71–A, National Archives; Raat, *Revoltosos*, p. 241.

31. Ulloa, "La relaciones Mexicano-Nortamericanas," pp. 43–45.

32. Luís Terrazas to Albert B. Fall, March 26, 1914; Albert B. Fall, to Charles F. Hunt, April 18, 1914, Albert B. Fall Papers, University of New Mexico Library.

33. Richard Ulric Miller, "American Railroad Unions and the National Railways of Mexico: An Exercise in Nineteenth Century Proletarian Manifest Destiny," *Labor History* 15(Spring 1970): 239.

34. McKee, "American Federation of Labor and American Foreign Policy," pp. 244–45.

35. Frederick C. Turner, "Anti-Americanism in Mexico, 1910–1913," *Hispanic American Historical Review* 47(1967): 502–18; Miller, "American Railroad Unions," pp. 254–55; McKee, "American Federation of Labor and American Foriegn Policy," p. 245.

36. Miller, "American Railroad Unions," pp. 256–60; Roberto de la Cerda Silva, *El Movimiento Obrero en Mexico* (México, D.F.: 1961), pp. 83–106; Sinclair Snow, *The Pan-American Federation of Labor* (Durham, N.C.: 1962), p. 5.

37. *Proceedings, AFL Convention, 1912*, p. 234.

38. *Socialist Party Official Bulletin*, Oct. 1911, p. 2; June 1912, p. 1, Oct. 1912, p. 2; "The National Socialist Convention," *International Socialist Review* 12 (June 1912): 327.

39. Peter Calvert, *The Mexican Revolution, 1910–1914* (New York: 1968) pp. 100–11.

40. Ross, *Francisco I. Madero*, p. 237; Katz, *The Secret War in Mexico*, p. 46; Arthur S. Link, *Wilson, the Diplomatist: A Look at His Major Policies* (Arlington Heights, Ill.: 1979), p. 108.

41. Link, *Wilson, the Diplomatist*, p. 108.

42. Arthur S. Link and associates, eds., *The Papers of Woodrow Wilson*, vol. 27 (Princeton, N.J.: 1978), pp. 18–19.

43. As is well-known, while re-elected in 1916 on the slogan, "He Kept Us Out of War," Wilson took the United States into the war against Germany and her allies less than a month after his second inaugural.

44. J. Fred Rippy, *Latin America in World Politics—An Outline Survey* (New York: 1928), p. 280.

45. Link, *Wilson, the Diplomatist*, pp. 132–33.

46. Hanrahan, *Documents on the Mexican Revolution*, pp. 325–33.

47. John Womack, Jr., *Zapata and the Mexican Revolution* (New York: 1968), chapters 4 and 5.

48. Arthur S. Link and associates, eds., *The Papers of Woodrow Wilson*, vol. 29 (Princeton, N.J.: 1979), pp. 188–90.

49. Raat, *Revoltosos*, pp. 259–60; Ralph Chaplin, *Wobbly: The Rough-and-Tumble Story of an American Radical* (Chicago: 1948), pp. 178–83; Ethel Duffy Turner, *Ricardo Flores Magón*, pp. 287–90; *The Toiler*, July 1914, p. 14.

50. *Los Angeles Citizen*, May 8, 15, 22, 1914.

51. *The Rebel*, May 30, 1914; *The Toiler*, July 1914, p. 14; Christopulos, "American Radicals," p. 306.

52. "Brothers and Comrades," undated letter issued by Rangel-Defense Committee, signed by Victor Crovello, copy in John Murray Papers, Bancroft Library, University of California, Berkeley.

53. *Los Angeles Citizen*, May 22, 1914.

54. Christopulos, "American Radicals," p. 306.

55. Katz, *Secret War in Mexico*, p. 167.

56. Link, *Wilson, the Diplomatist*, p. 122.

57. Secretary of the Navy Josephus Daniel to Woodrow Wilson (ca.), Aug. 8, 1913, enclosing memorandum from Assistant Secretary of War Henry S. Breckenridge, in Arthur S. Link and associates, ed., *The Papers of Woodrow Wilson*, vol. 28 (Princeton, N.J.: 1978), pp. 130–31.

58. *Foreign Relations, 1914*, pp. 448–49.

59. Ibid., pp. 459–65.

60. Link, *Wilson, the Diplomatist*, pp. 122–23.

61. *Foreign Relations, 1914*, pp. 482–83.

62. *New York Times*, April 21, 1914.

63. *Foreign Relations, 1914*, pp. 482–83.

64. Link, *Wilson, the Diplomatist*, pp. 124–25.

65. *Independent* 78 (April 1914): 195; Norval Neil Luxon, "The Periodical Press and Woodrow Wilson's Mexican Policy" (M.A. thesis, Ohio State University, 1931), p. 13; *New York Times*, April 21, 1914.

66. *New York Times*, April 23, 1914.

67. Ibid., April 27, 1914. For a disscussion of the months John Reed spent among the Mexican revolutionists in 1913–14, see Robert A. Rosenstone, *Romantic Revolutionary: A Biography of John Reed* (New York: 1975), pp. 149–69. John Reed's own writings on Mexico are included in his famous *Insurgent Mexico*. A convenient selection is in *The Education of John Reed*, ed. with a biographical essay by John Stuart (New York: 1955), pp. 47–73.

68. *Cleveland Citizen*, April 22, 1914; *New York Call*, April 22, 1914. "The number of fatalities at Ludlow may never be known for certain," concludes George P. McGovern in his study of the strike. But it is likely that thirty-two persons were either shot or burned to death in the "Ludlow Massacre." (See George P. McGovern, "The Colorado Strike, 1913–1914, [Ph.D. diss., University of Illinois, 1953, p. 282.]) For the story of the Colorado strike and the "Ludlow Massacre," see Philip S. Foner, *History of the Labor Movement in the United States* (New York: 1980), 5: 196–213.)

69. *New York Call*, April 23, 1924.

70. Ibid.

71. *Party Builder*, Extra Edition, April 25, 1914, p. 1.

72. *New York Call*, April 24, 1914.

73. *The Rebel*, May 16, 1914; Christopulos, "American Radicals," p. 235.

74. *New York Call*, April 25, 1914.

75. *International Socialist Review* 14(Jan. 1914): 122.

76. Peterson, "Foreign Policy and Foreign Policy Theory," p. 90; *The Party Builder*, April 25, 1914, p. 2; *New Review*, June 1914, p. 368; *International Socialist Review* 14(June 1914): 293.

77. Carolyn Johnston Willson, "Jack London's Socialism" (Ph.D. diss., University of California, Berkeley, 1976), p. 149.

78. Ibid., pp. 151–52.

79. Ibid., p. 153.

80. Ibid., p. 154.

81. Ibid., p. 155; see also Carolyn Johnston, *Jack London: An American Radical?* (Westport, Conn.: 1984), pp. 154–59.

82. Morris Hillquit, *United States Report of the Socialist Party* (Vienna: 1914[?]), Pamphlet, Box 441, Papers of the Socialist Party of America, Duke University Library; Christopulos, "American Radicals," p. 235.

83. *New York Call*, April 27, 1914.

84. Ibid., April 28, 1914.

85. *Cleveland Citizen*, April 27, 1914.

86. Ibid., May 4, 1914.

87. Harvey A. Levenstein, *Labor Organizations in the United States and Mexico: A History of their Relations* (Westport, Conn.: 1971), p. 15; Mandel, *Samuel Gompers*, pp. 338–39; McKee, "American Federation of Labor," p. 248; transcript of discussion by President Gompers, held Nov. 21, 1913, Gompers Papers, AFL Archives, State Historical Society of Wisconsin.

88. Gompers to R. Zuberan, July 25, 1914, Gompers Papers, AFL Archives, State Historical Society of Wisconsin; *New York Times*, April 21, 1914.

89. *New York Call* April 22, 28, 1914, *Cleveland Citizen*, July 9, 1914.

90. *New York Call*, April 22, 1914.

91. *New York Times*, April 20, 1914. Haywood is referring to the fact that delegates of the United Mining Congress at Stuttgart, Germany, in Sept. 1912, introduced a resolution stating that all miners in all countries represented in the Congress vow that no coal would be dug in the event of war. The resolution would thus initiate a general strike in one of the most vital parts of the war machine—fuel! The host delegation was so shocked at this proposal that they threatened to dissolve the Congress. The proposal was finally dropped, but not before the United Mine Workers warned that it would reintroduce the same resolution at the next convention in the fall of 1914. (*United Mine Workers' Journal* 23[Oct. 24, 1912]: 4.)

92. *New York Times*, April 21, 1914; *Philadelphia Public Ledger*, April 21, 1914.

93. *New York Times*, April 21, 1914.

94. Ibid.

95. Ibid., *Philadelphia Public Ledger*, April 21, 1914.

96. *New York Times*, April 21, 1914; *New York Call*, April 22, 1914.

97. *New York Call*, April 22, 1914.

98. Ibid.; *Philadelphia Public Ledger*, April 21, 1914.

99. *New York Times*, April 21, 1914; *New York Call*, April 22, 1914.

100. *New York Times*, April 23, 24, 25, 26, 27, 28, 1914.

101. *Philadelphia Public Ledger*, April 23, 24, 26, 27, 28, 1914.

102. *Los Angeles Citizen*, April 17, 24, May 8, 1914.

103. *New York Times*, April 24, 1914.

104. *Cleveland Plain Dealer*, June 29, July 2, 1914.

105. *Socialist News* (Cleveland), July 5, 1914.

106. Garraty, *Henry Cabot Lodge* pp. 303–5; *New York Times*, April 22, 1914, Link, *Wilson the Diplomatist*, pp. 124–125.

107. George L. Rausch, Jr., "The Exile and Death of Victoriano Huerta," *Hispanic American Historical Review* 42(1962): 133–34.

108. *New York Call*, Aug. 24, 1914; *American Socialist*, Sept. 5, 1914.

109. *Party Builder*, Nov. 30, 1914, p. 1.

110. Link, *The Papers of Woodrow Wilson*, 2: 404–6; Arthur S. Link, *Woodrow Wilson and the Progressive Era, 1910–1917* (New York: 1954), p. 125; Katz, *Secret War in Mexico*, p. 198. In her study, "American Radicals and the Mexican Revolution, 1900–1925," Diana K. Christopulos rejects this view (pp. 292–95). But her discussion contradicts her conclusion.

111. Among these studies are: Haley, *Revolution and Intervention*; Larry D. Hill, *Emissaries of a Revolution: Diplomacy and Revolution: U.S.-Mexican Relations under Wilson and Carranza* (Tucson: 1977); N. Gordon Levin, *Woodrow Wilson and World Politics: America's Response to War and Revolution* (New York: 1968); Arthur S. Link, *Wilson: The Struggle for Neutrality, 1914–1915* (Princeton, N.J.: 1961); Link, *Wilson, the Diplomatist*; Robert E. Quick, *An Affair of Honor: Woodrow Wilson and the Occupation of Vera Cruz* (New York: 1962); John Milton Cooper, "An 'Irony of Fate' Woodrow Wilson's Pre-World War I Diplomacy," *Diplomatic History* 3(Fall 1979): 425–37; Kendrick A. Clements, "Woodrow Wilson's Mexican Policy," ibid. 4(Spring 1980): 113–36. The most recent study, based on archives in Mexico, the United States, Germany, and Great Britain is Katz, *The Secret War in Mexico*. The Mexican crisis dominates three volumes (27, 28, and 29) in *The Papers of Woodrow Wilson*, edited by Arthur S. Link and associates. Among the many studies published in Mexico, a useful one is Ulloa, *La Revolución intervenida: replacione entre México y Estados Unidos, 1910–1914*.

Chapter X

1. John M. Hart, "The Urban Working Class and the Mexican Revolution, The Case of the Casa del Obrero Mundial," *Hispanic American Historical Review* 58(1978): 1–9.

2. While workers' May Day observances occurred even in the nineteenth century, and Barry Carr maintains that the first May Day in Mexican history occurred in 1912, most authorities agree that the first big and important May Day demonstration took place on May 1, 1913. On the other hand, Rosalinda Morizón lists 1914 as the first Mexican May Day. Barry Carr, *El Moviemiento obrero y la politica en México, 1910–1929*, vol. 1 (México: 1976), p. 111; Rosalinda Morizón, "Celebraciones de Primero de Mayo en México (1914–1941)," in *El Primero de l de Mayo en el Mundo* (México: 1982), p. 159; Philip S. Foner, *May Day: A Short History of the International Workers' Holiday, 1886–1986* (New York: 1986), pp. 80–81;

Camacho Esamilla, "Gotero histórico: La tragedia de Chicago y oruneras commemoraciones en México," *Gaceta Obrero* 5(May 1962): 20–29.)

3. Murray, "Behind the Drums of Revolution," p. 238.

4. Luis Ariza, *Historia del movimiento Mexicano*, vol. 3. (México: 1966), pp. 138–58.

5. An outstanding example was General Salvador Alvarado. After involvement in the Cananea strike of 1906, he joined Francisco Madero's *Partido Anti-reelectionista* and the uprising in 1912. During the course of the Mexican Revolution, Alvarado rose from captain to the rank of General. Appointed Governor and Military Commander in Yucatán by President Carranza, he became noted as a socialist and for reforms involving redistributing income, broadening educational reforms, and widening the political base to include labor, the peasants, the rural and proletariat, and women. During his governorship, Yucatán was the site of the first Feminist Congress in Mexico's history. (David Arthur Franz, "Bullets and Bolshevists: A History of the Mexican Revolution and Reform in Yucatán, 1910–1925," [Ph.D. diss., University of New Mexico, 1973], pp. 130–43.)

6. Jacinto Huitrón, *Origenes e historia del movimiento obrero en México* (México: 1975), pp. 134–45; Carr, *El movimiento obrero*, 1: 112–15.

7. Hart, "The Urban Working Class," pp. 13–16.

8. Ibid., pp. 17–18; Murray, "Behind the Drums of Revolution," pp. 41–42.

9. Ruiz, *Labor and the Ambivalent Revolutionaries*, pp. 50–55.

10. Hart, "The Urban Working Class," pp. 18–19.

11. The statement was caused by the report in the *Cleveland Leader* of July 6, 1914 which read: "Fifteen I.W.W. agitators, who have been trying to start a strike of Mexican miners in Chihuahua, Villa's own state, have been arrested by that fearsome bandit and notified that after their expulsion from Mexico they must never return, on pain of immediate execution. It is quite safe to say that they will heed the warning."

12. *Solidarity*, June 10, 1915.

13. Foner, *History of the Labor Movement in the United States* 2: 112.

14. Memorandum, July 7, 1917, in Gompers Papers, AFL Archives, State Historical Society of Wisconsin; Levenstein, "Samuel Gompers and the Mexican Labor Movement," p. 167.

15. Gompers to R. Zuberan, July 25, 1914, Gompers Papers, AFL Archives, State Historical Society of Wisconsin.

16. *Los Angeles Citizen*, Dec. 5, 1919.

17. Snow, *The Pan-American Federation of Labor*, p. 10.

18. Katz, *Secret War in Mexico*, pp. 151–52.

19. R.M. Easley to Gompers, June 25, 1915, Gompers Papers, AFL Archives, State Historical Society of Winconsin.

20. *Appeal to Reason*, May 21, 1915. See also Christopulos, "American Radicals," pp. 309–10; Cadenhead, "The American Socialists and the Mexican Revolution of 1910," p. 114.

21. Snow, *Pan-American Federation of Labor*, pp. 10–11.

22. *New York Times*, May 28–30, 1915.

23. *New York Call*, June 1, 1915.

24. Gompers to Woodrow Wilson, June 14, 1911; Gompers to Rafael Quintero, Secretary La Casa del Obrero Mundial, Vera Cruz, Mexico, June 18, 1915. Gompers Papers, State Historical Society of Wisconsin.

25. Gompers to Wilson, July 17, 1915, including copy of telegram of Joaquin Corra, July 9, 1915, Gompers Papers, State Historical Society of Wisconsin.

26. *New York Call*, Aug. 20, 1915.

27. Edmundo E. Martínez, to Gompers, Aug. 5, 1915, Gompers Papers, State Historical Society of Wisconsin.

28. Gompers to Wilson, Aug. 9, 1915; Wilson to Gompers, Aug. 11, 1915, Gompers

Papers, State Historical Society of Wisconsin, and State Department Archives, National Archives.

29. Edmundo E. Martínez to Woodrow Wilson, Aug. 12, 1915, Papers of Woodrow Wilson, Library of Congress; copy in Gompers Papers, State Historical Society of Wisconsin.

30. Gompers to Edmund E. Martínez, Aug. 23, 1915, Gompers Papers, State Historical Society of Wisconsin.

31. Gompers to Woodrow Wilson, Sept. 22, 1915, Gompers Papers, State Historical Society of Wisconsin; *New York Call*, Sept. 23, 24, 1915.

32. Wilson to Gompers, Sept. 24, 1915, State Department Archives, National Archives.

33. *New York Times*, Oct. 20, 1915.

34. Gompers to Edward E. Martínez, Dec. 30, 1915, Gompers Papers, State Historical Society of Wisconsin.

35. Katz, *Secret War in Mexico*, pp. 232–33; *New York Call*, July 22, Aug. 16, 1915. Harvey Levenstein believes that Martínez represented no important section of Mexican labor and was primarily an agent of Carranza. "Samuel Gompers and the Mexican Labor Movement," pp. 158–60.

36. Hart, "The Urban Working Class," pp. 16–20.

37. Gompers to John Murray, March 10, Oct. 16, 1916; Gompers to Luis Cabrera, Oct. 17, 1916; Memorandum dictated by Gompers to Miss Guard, Oct. 12, 1916, Gompers Papers, State Historical Society of Wisconsin.

Chapter XI

1. Villa to Zapata, San Geronimo, Jan. 8, 1916, Adjutant General File 2384602, RG94, National Archives; Thomas H. Naylor, "Massacre of San Pedro de la Cueva: The Significance of Pancho Villa's Disastrous Somora Campaign," *Western Historical Quarterly* 12(April 1977): 149.

2. Larry A. Harris, *Pancho Villa and the Columbus Raid* (El Paso: 1949); Katz, *Secret War in Mexico*, pp. 301–4.

3. For discussions of the raids by Villa and the "Punitive Expedition," see Clarence E. Clendenen, "The Punitive Expedition of 1916: A Re-Evaluation," *Arizona and the West* 3(Winter 1961): 311–20; James A. Sandos, "Pancho Villa and American Security: Wilson's Mexican Diplomacy Reconsidered," *Journal of Latin American Studies* 13(Nov. 1981): 293–311; Friedrich Katz, "Panch Villa and the Attack on Columbus, New Mexico," *American Historical Review* 83(Feb. 1978): 101–30, and the debate between Katz and James A. Sandos in ibid. 84(Feb. 1979): 304–7; Clarence E. Clendenen, *The United States and Pancho Villa* (Ithaca, N.Y.: 1961); Robert B. Johnson, "The Punitive Expedition: A Military, Diplomatic and Political History of Pershing's Chase After Pancho Villa, 1916–17," (Ph.D. diss., University of Southern California, 1964); Michael L. Tate, "Pershing's Punitive Expedition: Pursuer of Bandits or Presidential Panacea?" *The Americas* 32(1975): 46–72; Alberto Salinas Carranza, *La Expedición Punitiva* (México: 1936); Isidro Fabela and Josefina E. de Fabela, eds., *Documentos Historicos de la Revolución Mexicana. Expedición Punitiva* (México: 1967–68); Alberto Calzadiaz Barrera, *Purque Villa ataco a Columbus* (México: 1972); Douglas W. Richmond, "Mexican Immigration and Border Strategy During the Revolution, 1910–1920," *New Mexico Historical Review* 57(July 1982): 279–88.

4. William M. Hager, "The Plan of San Diego: Unrest on the Texas Border in 1915," *Arizona and the West* 5(Winter 1963): 327–36; Charles H. Harris and Louis R. Sadler, "The Plan of San Diego and the Mexican-United States War Crisis of 1916: A Reexamination," *Hispanic American Historical Review* 58(1918): 381–408.

5. Harris and Sadler contend that the Plan of San Diego was mainly a device by Carranza

to force recognition by the United States. ("The Plan of San Diego and the Mexican-United States War Crisis of 1916: A Reexamination.")

6. Raat, *Revoltosos*, pp. 262–64.

7. "American Refugees in Texas" to Senator Albert B. Fall, San Antonio, Texas, May 10–16, Albert B. Fall Papers, University of New Mexico Library, Albuquerque.

8. Robert Freeman Smith, *The United States and Revolutionary Nationalism in Mexico, 1916–1932* (Chicago: 1972), p. 137.

9. *New York Call*, July 21, Aug. 29, 1916.

10. Fabela and Fabela, *Documentos Historicos*, 1: 270–71; 2: 283–90, 298–305.

11. *New York Times*, June 22–23, 1916.

12. Father Kelly, who called himself spokesperson for "the exiled Mexican Bishops and other Mexican clergy who were either expelled or had to escape because of the cruelty of the Revolutionists," was the author of *The Book of Red and Yellow*, in which he charged that President Carranza and his supporters were "bandits" guilty of "tyrannizing Mexico, punishing priests and martyrizing the sisters and causing death everywhere." He was opposed, however, to the AFL's policy toward Carranza for reasons other than religion. As he pointed out in a letter to Frank Duffy, head of the Brotherhood of Carpenters and Joiners and leader of the Catholic forces in the AFL opposed to the Mexican Revolution: "With many others I deeply regretted the action of the American Federation of Labor in endorsing Carranza . . . also because I have watched with admiration the efforts of the American Federation of Labor to keep out of entangling alliances with Socialism and the I.W.W.; and I considered the endorsement of Carranza an endorsement of both Socialism and the I.W.W. in Mexico. What is not good for the laboring man in the United States, can scarcely be good for those or our sister-republic of Mexico." Kelly then cited articles in the American press that the Casa del Obrero Mundial, which had both endorsed and supported Carranza militarily, was dominated by the IWW, and that "the I.W.W. had received from Carranza governors, church buildings, including churches themselves, seminaries and bishop's residences for their meetings and as club houses." Duffy forwarded Kelly's letter to Gompers. (Frank Duffy to Gompers, May 2, 1916, Gompers Papers, AFL Archives, State Historical Society of Wisconsin.)

13. *New York Call*, June 8–9, 1916.

14. Ibid., Jan. 17, 1916.

15. Ibid., Jan. 24, 1916.

16. *American Socialist*, March 25, 1916. The appeal was drafted by Emil Seidel and signed by him, Adolph Germer, George H. Goebels, Arthur Le Seur, and James H. Maurer. For the preparedness movement referred to in the last part of the statement, see Philip S. Foner, *History of the Labor Movement in the United States* (New York: 1987), 7: 64–77.

17. *Milwaukee Leader*, March 13, 1916.

18. Christopulos, "American Radicals," p. 315.

19. *American Socialist,* July 10, 1916.

20. Allan M. Benson, the socialist candidate for president in the 1916 election, urged the National Executive Committee to demand that the United States government "with due formality" hang any American capitalist who funded Villa. (*America Socialist*, March 13, 1916. See also *Appeal to Reason*, July 8, 1916.)

21. *American Socialist*, June 19, 1916; *New Review* 4(April 1916): 97; *National Rip-Saw*, June 1916, p. 3.

22. Granville Hicks, *John Reed: The Making of a Revolutionary* (New York: 1936), pp. 209–10. For a discussion of the relations between Reed and Villa, see Jim Tuck, *Pancho Villa and John Reed: Two Faces of Romantic Revolution* (Tucson: 1984).

23. *The Blast*, March 15, 1916, p. 2.

24. *New York Call*, June 23, 24, 1916.

25. The appeal was signed by officers of twelve trade unions in Yucatán: Syndicate of Electricians; Seamen's Union; Dockers' Union; Bakers' Syndicate; Masons' Syndicate; Union of Clerks, Cooks, ect., and of Hotel Restaurants and Similars; Commercial Clerks' Club; Smelters' Syndicate; Hackmen's Syndicate; Yucatán Railroad Men's Union; Syndicate of Machinists, Blacksmiths and Boiler Makers. The appeal was dated Merida, México, May 29, 1916. ("Appeal to American Workers," *International Labor Forum*, copy in John Murray Papers, Bancroft Library, University of California, Berkeley.)

26. It was in the *La Voz de la Revolución* of Oct. 28, 1915 that General Alvardo announced that the First Feminist Congress in Mexico's history would convene for three days in Merida, Yucatán, beginning on Jan. 13, 1916. It was in that paper, too, that the Governor published the following statement: "I believe that if we do not improve the condition of women it will not be possible to build [our] nation. Our efforts ought to be directed to emancipate and dignify her. I found in Yucatán, with sorrow, that there were thousands in the fields as well as thousands of poor women in the cities, degraded in domestic servitude in such a way that, with the risk of being paternalistic [it] was in fact real slavery." "The best way to emancipate woman," he noted, "is to enable her to support herself so she will not be compelled by isolation or misery into forced marriages or illicit unions; and this is so much more urgent to accomplish . . . since until today she was considered an object of luxury and an article of social dissipation." In Dec. 1915, Governor Alvarado signed a labor law that greatly benefited working women. During his administration, moreover *Ligas Femeniles Socialistas*, special cooperatives for women, were started throughout Yucatán. Franz, "Bullets and Bolshevists," pp. 139–43.

27. *New York Call*, June 25, 1916.

28. There were actually two versions of the appeal published. One was the original, as read at the Carnegie Hall meeting, and published in full in the *New York Call*. The other was a toned-down version. At the advice of John Murray, the references to the Haymarket martyrs, the Catholic Church, and the role of Wall Street were deleted. Murray then transmitted the appeal to Secretary of Labor William B. Wilson who in turn promised to present it to President Wilson. (Whittaker, "Samuel Gompers, Labor, and the Mexican-American Crisis of 1916," pp. 558–59.) For the differences in the two versions, see *New York Call*, June 19, 25, 1916, and *Miners' Magazine*, July 3, 1916.

29. *New York Call*, June 19, 25, 1916.

30. According to John Murray, Douglas had never been sympathetic to organized labor until he became acquainted with the situation facing the workers in Mexico under Díaz. He had gradually become convinced that the labor movements in the two countries could play a vital role in maintaining peace between Mexico and the United States. (Memorandum of John Murray, June 13, 1916, original in John Murray Papers, Bancroft Library, University of California, Berkeley; copy in Gompers Papers, State Historical Society of Wisconsin.)

31. Gompers is referring to the strike of the miners, mainly Mexican-Americans in the copper mines operated by the Arizona Copper Company, the Shannon Copper Company, and the Detroit Copper Company. The three companies employed about five thousand miner, over two-thirds of whom were Mexicans. Of the three, the most important was the Detroit Copper Company, owned by the giant Phelps Dodge & Company, a leading Wall Street corporation. Until 1915 the Western Federation of Miners did little to organize the Mexican-American copper miners, but that year it changed its policy. A strike took place in four months early in 1916 in the eastern Arizona towns of Clifton, Morenci, and Metcalf. Of the five thousands miners on strike, over two-thirds were Mexican-Americans. After four months, without a serious break in the strikers' ranks, the companies were forced to surrender. (For a discussion of the strike, see Foner, *History of the Labor Movement in the United States*, 6: 13–24.)

32. *New York Call*, May 25, 1916.

33. Ibid., Gompers Papers, State Historical Society of Wisconsin.

34. *New York Call*, May 25, 1916.

35. Memorandum, Florence C. Thorne, June 16, 1916, Gompers Papers, State Historical Society of Wisconsin.

36. R. Lee Guard to Lansing, May 25, 1916, Gompers Papers, State Historical Society of Wisconsin.

37. In a letter to Murray, Frank J. Hayes wrote: "I heartily approve of the idea of President Gompers in calling an international labor conference to meet at El Paso, Texas, to consider the questions that interest the workers of Mexico and the United States. I shall give this proposition my hearty support." (Frank J. Hayes to John Murray, June 6, 1916, John Murray Papers, Bancroft Library, University of California, Berkeley.)

38. Memorandum by Florence C. Thorne, June 16, 1916, State Historical Society of Wisconsin.

39. Mother Jones to John Murray, June 30, 1916, John Murray Papers, Bancroft Library, University of California, Berkeley.

40. See *New York Call*, June 13, 1916.

41. Telegrams to Gompers, June 11, 1916, Gompers Papers, State Historical Society of Wisconsin.

42. AFL to Gompers, June 11, 1916; Gompers to AFL, June 12, 1916, Gompers Papers, State Historical Society of Wisconsin.

43. *New York Call*, June 27, 28, 29, 1916. In a dispatch from El Paso, the reporter for the *Albuquerque Evening-Herald* wrote that Jordan had "received a number of threatening letters from interventionists." At that news, Jordan received an invitation from N.W. Benning, Secretary of Albuquerque's YMCA, inviting him "to hold the conference of the American Union Against Militarism" in its headquarters. He also received a wire from the Mayor of Albuquerque, assuring him "of a hearty welcome at the hands of the people of Albuquerque." Jordan informed the press that had been deluged that very morning "with telegrams from all over the country endorsing his stand against a declaration of war on the Carranza government, receiving so many . . . that he 'could make a living selling them for waste paper.' " He added: "If we must intervene in Mexico, of which I am not so sure, let us intervene with school teachers and educators and doctors, but let us leave our guns and cannons behind." (*Albuquerque Evening-Herald*, June 27–29, 1916.)

44. Gompers to Atl, June 22, 1916, Gompers Papers; Memorandum, Florence C. Thorne, June 22, 1916, Gompers Papers, State Historical Society of Wisconsin.

45. Gompers to Atl, June 22, 1916, Gompers Papers; Memorandum, Florence C. Thorne, June 22, 1916, Gompers Papers, State Historical Society of Wisconsin.

46. Memorandum, Florence C. Thorne, June 23, 1916, Gompers Papers, State Historical Society of Wisconsin.

47. *New York Call*, June 24, 1916.

48. B. E. Russell, Brotherhood of Railway Trainmen to William B. Wilson, Secretary of Labor, June 26, 1916. Records of the Department of Labor, National Archives.

49. *New York Call*, June 26, 29, July 2, 3, 1916; *United Mine Workers' Journal*, June 22, 1916, pp. 4–5.

50. Memorandum, Florence C. Thorne, June 30, 1916, Gompers Papers, State Historical Society of Wisconsin; Gompers to William B. Wison, June 28, 1916, GLB.; *New York Call*, July 1, 1916.

51. Memorandum, Florence C. Thorne, June 30, 1916, Gompers Papers, State Historical Society of Wisconsin.

52. Memorandum, Florence C. Thorne, June 30, 1916, Gompers Papers, State Historical Society of Wisconsin.

53. *Papers Relating to the Foreign Relations of the United States, 1916* (Washington, D.C.: 1925), pp. 597–99; Memorandum, Florence C. Thorne, June 30, 1916, Gompers Papers, State Historical Society of Wisconsin.

54. *New York Times*, July 28, 29, 1916.

55. Christopulos points out: "As Lyndon Johnson would do with the Gulf of Tonkin resolution in 1964, Wilson planned to deceive Congress into granting him broad powers for an undeclared war." ("American Radicals," p. 321.)

56. Gerald Chapfield, *For Peace and Justice: Pacifism in America, 1914–1941* (Knoxville, Tenn.: 1971), pp. 24–30; David Starr Jordan, *The Days of a Man*, vol. 2 (New York: 1922) pp. 690–703; Lillian D. Wald, *Windows on Henry Street* (Boston: 1934), pp. 291–98; Christopulos, "American Radicals," pp. 320–24.

57. Whittaker, *op.cit.*, pp. 564–67. Another is Robert F. Smith, *The United States and Revolutionary Nationalism in Mexico, 1916–1932* (Chicago: 1972), pp. 53–54 On the other hand, Harvey Levenstein is incorrect in cynically dismissing Gompers' contribution with the argument that there was "an undercurrent of deception on both sides." "Samuel Gompers and the Mexican Labor Movement," p. 160.

58. Memorandum, Florence C. Thorne, June 22, 1916, Gompers Papers, State Historical Society of Wisconsin.

59. Duffy's union, the United Brotherhood of Carpenters and Joiners, was trying to organize in Quebec, but met with opposition from Archbishop Francois Closister of Quebec on the ground that the AFL was closely linked to the anti-Catholic forces in Mexico led by Carranza. Frank Duffy to Samuel Gompers, April 10, May 2, 1916, Gompers Papers, State Historical Society of Wisconsin.

60. Frank Duffy to Samuel Gompers, July 13, 1916, Gompers Papers, State Historical Society of Wisconsin.

61. Samuel Gompers to Frank Duffy, July 30, 1916, Gompers Papers, State Historical Society of Wisconsin.

62. *New York Call*, July 1, 2, 3, 5, 1916.

63. John Murray in ibid., July 5, 1916.

Chapter XII

1. *Solidarity*, June 26, 1915.

2. *Defense News Bulletin* (formerly *Solidarity*), June 18, 1918; Peter De Shazo, "The Industrial Workers of the World in Chile, 1917–1927" (M.A. thesis, University of Wisconsin, Madison, 1973), pp. 7–25; Fanny Simon, "Anarchism and Anarcho-syndicalism in South America," *Hispanic American Historical Review* 26(Feb. 1946): 52–53; Peter D. Shazo and Robert J. Halsted, "Los Wobblies del Sur: The Industrial Workers of the World in Chile and Mexico" (copy in Archives of Labor and Urban Affairs, Walter P. Reuther Library, Wayne State Univ., n.d.); and Moises Poblete Troncoso, *Labor Organizations in Chile*, U.S. Bureau of Labor Statistics Bulletin No. 461 (Washington, D.C.: 1928).

3. *Proceedings*, AFL Convention, 1915, pp. 56–60.

4. Gompers to Workers of All Countries, July 8, 1916, Gompers Papers, State Historical Society of Wisconsin; John Murray Papers, Bancroft Library, University of California, Berkeley.

5. Burton I. Kaufman, "United States Trade and Latin America: The Wilson Years," *Journal of American History* 58(1971): 358–60.

6. Pan-American Federation of Labor Conference Committee, Manifesto, Feb. 9, 1917, Wisconsin State Historical Society; John Murray Papers, Bancroft Library, University of California, Berkeley.

7. The Spanish version of this part of the "Manifesto" refers to the capitalists having acquired their possessions *"legal y legalmente"* (legally and illegally). *"Manifesto A Los Trabajadores de la America Latina,"* copy in State Historical Society of Wisconsin, and John Murray Papers, Bancroft Library, University of California, Berkeley.

8. Ibid.

9. Ibid.

10. Ibid.

11. *Los Angeles Citizen*, Feb. 23, 1917.

12. Report of Douglas to Gompers (1918), Gompers Papers, State Historical Society of Wisconsin.

13. Sinclair Snow, "Samuel Gompers and the Pan-American Federation of Labor," pp. 56, 60.

14. Ibid., pp. 61–62.

15. The American Alliance for Labor and Democracy was set up by the AFL to promote the war objectives of the U.S. government, and oppose the influence of pacifists and socialists who opposed the war and organized the People's Council for Democracy and Terms of Peace. The American Alliance was closely linked to and received funds from the U.S. Government through the George Creel's war propaganda agency, the Committee on Public Information. Frank L. Grubbs, Jr., *The Struggle for Labor Loyalty: Gompers, the A.F. of L., and the Pacifists, 1917–1920* (Durham, N.C.), pp. 50–64.

16. Snow, *"Samuel Gompers,"*, pp. 63–67.

17. Ibid., p. 67.

18. Ibid., p. 68.

19. Proceedings, First Convention, Pan-American Federation of Labor, in *Pan-American Labor Press* , Dec. 4, 1918, copy in AFL-CIO Archives, Washington, D.C.

20. Ibid.

21. Ibid.

22. Ibid.

23. Ibid.

24. Ibid.

25. Ibid.

26. Ibid.

27. Ibid.

28. Snow, *"Samuel Gompers,"* pp. 70–71.

29. Santiago Iglesias, "Pan-American Federation of Labor, Creation of A. F. of L.," *International Molders' Journal* 63(July 1927): 390–92.

INDEX